DIGITAL
VERTIGO

ALSO BY ANDREW KEEN

The Cult of the Amateur: How Today's Internet Is Killing Our Culture

DIGITAL VERTIGO

HOW TODAY'S ONLINE SOCIAL REVOLUTION
IS DIVIDING, DIMINISHING, AND DISORIENTING US

ANDREW KEEN

CONSTABLE · LONDON

Constable & Robinson
55–56 Russell Square
London WC1B 4HP
www.constablerobinson.com

First published in the USA by St Martin's Press, 2012

First published in the UK by Constable,
an imprint of Constable & Robinson Ltd., 2012

A copy of the British Library Cataloguing in Publication Data
is available from the British Library.

ISBN 978-1-78033-840-8 (paperback)
ISBN 978-1-78033-841-5 (ebook)

Printed and bound in the UK

1 3 5 7 9 10 8 6 4 2

For MK and HK

CONTENTS

Hello hello/I'm at a place called Vertigo/It's everything I wish I didn't know
—U2, "Vertigo" (2004)

On one occasion she asked if I was a journalist or writer. When I said that neither the one nor the other was quite right, she asked what it was that I was working on, to which I replied that I did not know for certain myself, but had a growing suspicion that it might turn into a crime story . . . [1]   —W. G. Sebald, *Vertigo* (1990)

One final thing I have to do and then I'll be free of the past. . . . One doesn't often get a second chance. I want to stop being haunted. You're my second chance, Judy. You're my second chance.   —Alec Coppel and Samuel A. Taylor, *Vertigo* (1958)

INTRODUCTION

HYPERVISIBILITY

@alexia: We would have lived our lives differently if we had known they would one day be searchable.[1]

A Man Who Is His Own Image

Alfred Hitchcock, who always referred to movies as "pictures," once said that behind every good picture lay a great corpse. Hitchcock, an old master at resurrecting the dead in pictures like *Vertigo*, his creepy 1958 movie about a man's love affair with a corpse, was right. The truth is a great corpse makes such a good *picture* that it can even help bring a nonfiction book like this to life.

Behind this book sits the most visible corpse of the nineteenth century—the body of the utilitarian philosopher, social reformer and prison architect Jeremy Bentham, a cadaver that has been living in public since his death in June 1832.[2] Seeking to immortalize his own reputation as what he called a "benefactor of the human race," Bentham bequeathed both his body and "Dapple," his favorite walking stick, to London's University College and instructed that they should be permanently exhibited inside a glass-fronted wooden coffin he coined an "Auto-Icon"—a neologism meaning "a man who is his own image."[3]

His greed for attention is today on permanent exhibition inside a public coffin whose size, *Brave New World* author Aldous Huxley once estimated, is larger than a telephone booth but smaller than an outdoor toilet.[4] Today, he and Dapple now sit in a corridor in the South Cloisters of University College's main Bloomsbury building on Gower Street, strategically situated so that they can be observed by all passing traffic on this bustling metropolitan campus. Bentham, who believed himself to be "the most effectively benevolent" person who ever lived,[5] is now therefore never alone. He has, so to speak, eliminated his own loneliness.

The idea behind this book first came to life in that London corridor. There I serendipitously found myself one recent drizzly November afternoon, a Research In Motion (RIM) BlackBerry smartphone[6] in one hand and a Canon digital camera[7] in the other, looking at the Auto-Icon. But the longer I stared at the creepy Jeremy Bentham imprisoned inside his fame machine, the more I suspected that our identities had, in fact, merged. You see, like the solitary utilitarian who'd been on public display throughout the industrial age, I'd become little more than a corpse on perpetual display in a transparent box.

Yes, like Jeremy Bentham, I'd gone somewhere else entirely. I was in a place called social media, that permanent self-exhibition zone of our new digital age where, via my BlackBerry Bold and the other more than 5 billion devices now in our hands,[8] we are collectively publishing mankind's group portrait in motion. This place is built upon a network of increasingly intelligent and mobile electronic products that are connecting everyone on the planet through services like Facebook, Twitter, Google+, and LinkedIn. Rather than virtual or second life, social media is actually becoming life itself—the central and increasingly transparent stage of human existence, what Silicon Valley venture capitalists are now calling an "internet of people."[9] As the fictionalized version of Facebook president Sean Parker—played with such panache by Justin Timberlake—predicted in the 2010 Oscar-nominated movie *The Social Network*: "We lived in farms, then we lived in cities, and now we're gonna live on the Internet!" Social media is, thus, like home; it is the architecture in which we now live. There is even a community newspaper called *The Daily Dot* that is the paper of record for the Web.[10]

Crouching in front of the mahogany Auto-Icon, I adjusted the lens of my camera upon Bentham, zooming in so that I could intimately inspect his beady eyes, the wide brimmed tan hat covering his shoulder length gray hair, the white ruffled shirt and black rustic jacket clothing his dissected torso, and Dapple resting in his gloved hand. Shifting my camera toward his waxen face, I looked the dead Englishman as closely in the eye as my prying technology would allow. I was searching for the private man behind the public corpse. What, I wanted to know, had led "The Hermit of Queen's Square Place,"[11] as Bentham liked to call himself, best known for his "greatest happiness principle" that human beings are defined by their desire to maximize their pleasure and minimize their pain,[12] to prefer the eternal glare of public exposure over the everlasting privacy of the grave?

In my other hand I held my BlackBerry Bold, RIM's pocket-sized device that, by broadcasting my location, my observations and my intentions to my electronic network, enabled me to perpetually live in public. My social media obligations nagged at me. As a Silicon Valley based networker, my job— both then and now—is grabbing other people's attention on Twitter and Facebook so that I can become ubiquitous. I am an influencer, a wannabe Jeremy Bentham—what futurists call a "Super Node" —the vanguard of the workforce that, they predict, will increasingly come to dominate the twenty-first-century digital economy.[13] So that afternoon, like every afternoon in my reputation-building life, I really needed to be the picture on everyone's screen.

Not that anyone, either on or off my social network, knew my exact location that November afternoon. I happened to be in central London for a few hours, in transit between one social media conference in Oxford that had just finished and another that would begin the following afternoon in Amsterdam, near the Rijksmuseum, the art museum that houses many of the most timeless pictures of the human condition by Dutch seventeenth-century artists like Johannes Vermeer and Rembrandt van Rijn.

But, in London, my interest lay in the living metropolis, what the Anglo-American writer Jonathan Raban calls the "soft city" of permanent personal reinvention, rather than in pictures by dead artists. It was my day off from the glare of public speaking, my opportunity to briefly escape from society and be left alone in a city where I'd been born and educated but no longer lived. As the nineteenth-century German sociologist Georg Simmel wrote, the city "grants to the individual a kind and an amount of personal freedom which has no analogy whatever under any other conditions."[14] My illegibility that afternoon thus represented my liberty. Freedom meant nobody knowing exactly where I was.

"To live in a city is to live in a community of people who are strangers to each other,"[15] writes Raban about the freedom of living in a large city. And I'd certainly spent that chilly November afternoon as a stranger lost amidst a community of disconnected strangers, zigzagging through London's crooked streets, hopping on and off buses and trains, stopping here and there to re-explore familiar places, reminding myself about how the city had imprinted itself on my personality.

Eventually, as so often one does while wandering through London, I happened to find myself in the Bloomsbury neighborhood where, some thirty years earlier, I had attended university as a student of modern history. There, I strolled through Senate House—the forbiddingly monolithic building which had housed my college and which was the model, it is said, for George Orwell's Ministry of Truth in *Nineteen Eighty-four*[16]—before wandering up Gower Street toward Jeremy Bentham's corpse in University College.

@Quixotic

I had come to London that morning from Oxford, where I'd spent the previous few days at a conference entitled "Silicon Valley Comes to Oxford."

This was an event organized by the university's Said Business School in which Silicon Valley's most influential entrepreneurs had come to the closed, haunted city of Oxford to celebrate the openness and transparency of social life in the twenty-first century.

At Oxford, I'd debated Reid Hoffman, the multibillionaire founder of LinkedIn and Silicon Valley's most prodigious progenitor of online networks, a brilliant social media visionary known as @quixotic to his Twitter followers. "When I graduated from Stanford my plan was to become a professor and public intellectual," Hoffman once confessed. "That is not about quoting Kant. It's about holding up a lens to society and asking 'who are we?' and 'who should we be, as individuals and a society?' But I realised academics write books that 50 or 60 people read and I wanted more impact."[17]

To get more impact, Reid Hoffman dramatically magnified the lens with which we look at society. Instead of writing books for fifty or sixty people, he created a social network for 100 million people that is now growing by a million new members every ten days.[18] Today, a new person joins LinkedIn every second[19]—meaning that in the time it's taken you to read this paragraph, @quixotic has had an *impact* on another 50 or 60 people around the world.

No, a Don Quixote tilting at windmills he certainly isn't. Indeed, if social media—what @quixotic has dubbed "Web 3.0"[20]—has a founding father, it might be Hoffman, the suitably cherubic looking early-stage "angel" investor who *San Francisco Magazine* identified as one of Silicon Valley's most powerful "archangels,"[21] *Forbes* ranked third in their 2011 Midas List[22] of the world's most successful technology investors, *The Wall Street Journal* described as "the most connected person in Silicon Valley"[23] and *The New York Times* crowned, in November 2011, as the "king of connections."[24]

The Oxford- and Stanford-educated entrepreneur, now a partner in the venture capital firm of Greylock Partners and a multibillionaire both in terms of his dollar net worth and his global network of business and political relationships, saw the social future before almost anyone else.[25] "Looking back on my life I've come to realize that what I am most driven by is building, designing and improving human ecosystems," Hoffman confessed in January 2011.[26] And, as an architect of "prime human ecosystem" real estate for the twenty-first century, @quixotic has become one of the wealthiest and most powerful men on earth. Grasping the Internet's shift from a platform for data to one for real people, Hoffman not only started the very first contemporary social media business back in 1997—a dating service called SocialNet—but also was an angel investor in Friendster and Facebook as well as the founder, the original CEO and the current Executive Chairman of LinkedIn, America's second most highly trafficked social network[27] whose May 2011 initial public offering was, at the time, the largest technology IPO since Google's in 2004.[28]

"The future is always sooner and stranger than you think," Hoffman, who became an overnight multibillionaire after LinkedIn's meteoric IPO, once remarked.[29] But even @quixotic, back in 1997 when he founded SocialNet, couldn't have quite imagined how quickly he would come to own that future. You see, six years later, in 2003, Hoffman—in partnership with his friend Mark Pincus, another Silicon Valley based social media pioneer who cofounded Tribe.net and is now the CEO of the multibillion-dollar gaming network Zynga[30]—paid $700,000 in auction for an intellectual patent on social networking, thereby making this plutocratic polymath the co-owner, in a sense, of the future itself.

The formal subject of my Oxford debate with Hoffman had been whether social media communities would replace the nation-state as the source of personal identity in the twenty-first century. But the real heart of our conversation—indeed, the central theme of the whole "Silicon Valley Comes to Oxford" event—had been the question of whether digital man would be more socially connected than his industrial ancestor. In contrast with my own ambivalence about the social benefits of the virtual world, Hoffman dreamt openly about the potential of today's networking revolution to bring us together. The shift from a society built upon atoms to one built upon bytes, the archangel publicly insisted at our Oxford debate, would make us more connected and thus more socially united as human beings.

In private, the affable, and I have to admit, the very likeable Hoffman was equally committed to this social ideal. "But what about people who don't want to be on the network?" I asked him as we ate breakfast together on the morning of our debate.

"Huh?"

"Let's face it, Reid, some people just don't want to be connected."

"Don't *want to be connected*?" the billionaire muttered under his breath. Such was the incredulity clouding his cherubic face that, for a moment, I feared I had ruined his breakfast of grilled kippers and scrambled eggs.

"Yes," I confirmed. "Some people simply want to be let alone."

I have to confess that my point lacked originality. I was simply repeating the concerns of privacy advocates like the legal scholars Samuel Warren and Louis Brandeis who, in 1890, wrote their now timeless "The Right to Privacy" *Harvard Law Review* article which, in reaction to the then nascent mass media technologies of photography and newspapers, had defined privacy as "the right of the individual to be let alone."[31]

It may have been a recycled nineteenth-century remark, but at least I'd expressed it in a recycled nineteenth-century environment. Reid Hoffman and I were eating our kippers and eggs in the basement "Destination Brasserie" of Oxford's Malmaison hotel, once a nineteenth-century prison built by a disciple of Jeremy Bentham's architectural theories about surveillance and now reinvented as a chic twenty-first-century hotel distinguished by its cell-style bedrooms that featured the original caste iron doors and bars of the old house of correction.[32]

"After all, Reid," I added, as I glanced around the prison's former solitary confinement cells that were now dotted with individual diners, "some people prefer solitude to connectivity."

@quixotic finished a mouthful of eggs and fish before countering with some recycled wisdom of his own. But whereas I'd quoted a couple of nineteenth-century American legal scholars, Hoffman—who, as a Marshall Scholar at Oxford during the eighties, had earned a masters degree in philosophy—went back even further in history, back to the ancient Greeks of the fifth century B.C., to Aristotle, the founding father of communitarianism and the most influential philosopher of the medieval period.

"You have to remember," @quixotic said, borrowing some very familiar words from Aristotle's *Politics*, "that man is, by nature, a social animal."[33]

The Future Will Be Social

Reid Hoffman certainly hadn't been alone in recycling this pre-modern faith that the social is hardwired into all of us. All the Silicon Valley grandees who came to Oxford and who, like Hoffman and I, were staying in the reinvented prison—Internet moguls like Twitter co-founder Biz Stone, heavyweight investor Chris Sacca,[34] Second Life founder Philip Rosedale, and the technology journalist Mike Malone, the so-called "Boswell of Silicon Valley"—had embraced this same Aristotelian ideal of our natural sociability. But whereas these architects of our social future seemed to possess all the answers about this connected future, my mind was filled only with questions about where we were going and how we would get there.

"So, Biz, what exactly is the future?"[35] I had asked Stone one evening as, by chance, we found ourselves next to one another in the crowded and noisy old dining hall of Balliol College, the Oxford College founded in 1263 by John Balliol, one of the most visible men of medieval England, a feudal landowner so powerful that he had his own private army of several thousand loyal followers.

This was no idle question. Given his significant ownership stake in Twitter, Biz Stone—who, as @biz, has almost 2 million loyal followers in his network—is one of the most powerful virtual landowners of our age, a veritable John Balliol of the twenty-first century, an information baron who knows everything about all of us.

"Biz not only knows what everyone is thinking," Jerry Sanders, the CEO of San Francisco Scientific said of Stone at Oxford during a Union debate about whether we should trust entrepreneurs with our future, "but also where it is that they are thinking what they are thinking."[36]

I thus valued Stone's opinion. If anybody could see the future, it was this all-knowing Silicon Valley magnate, the co-founder of the ever-expanding short-messaging social network which, with its multibillion valuation[37] and its more than two hundred million registered users sending more than 140 million tweets each day,[38] is revolutionizing the architecture of twenty-first-century communications.

Stone—a lifelong social media evangelist and author[39] who, in addition to his current daytime gig as a venture capitalist,[40] moonlights for his friend Arianna Huffington as AOL's Strategic Advisor for Social Impact[41]—leant toward me so that I could hear him above the conversational chatter on the communal wooden benches. "The future," @biz said, sharing his thought with Twitter-like brevity. "The future will be social."

"The killer app, eh?" I replied, trying—not very effectively, I suspect—to emulate both his terseness and profundity.

Stone, a cheeky-looking chappie with chunky black glasses and a geeky mop of hair, grinned. But even this grin was all-knowingly brief. "That's right," he confirmed. "The social will be the killer app of the twenty-first century."

Biz Stone was correct. At Oxford, I had come to understand that the *social*—which meant the sharing of our personal information, our location, our taste and our identities on Internet networks like Twitter, LinkedIn, Google + and Facebook—was the Internet's newest new thing. Every new *social* platform, *social* service, *social* app, *social* page, I learnt, was becoming a piece of this new *social* media world—from *social* journalism to *social* entrepreneurship to *social* commerce to *social* production to *social* learning to *social* charity to *social* e-mail to *social* gaming to *social* capital to *social* television to *social* consumption to *social* consumers on the "*social* graph," an algorithm that supposedly maps out each of our unique *social* networks. And given that the Internet was becoming the connective tissue of twenty-first-century life, the future—*our* future, yours and mine and everyone else on the ubiquitous network—would, therefore, be, yes you guessed it, *social*.

But as I stood alone in that bustling London corridor gaping at the dead Jeremy Bentham, the truth was that I felt anything but *social*—especially with this nineteenth-century corpse. In my eagerness to inspect the deceased social reformer, I'd gotten so close to the Auto-Icon that I was almost touching its glass front. Yet Bentham's great exhibitionism remained a mystery to me. I just couldn't figure out why he would want to be seen by a never-ending procession of strangers, all peering into his beady eyes to excavate the human being behind the corpse.

I was searching for wisdom from old Jeremy Bentham, some special insight that would illuminate the human condition for me. Yes, the likeness of the Auto-Icon to the real Bentham was genuine—a similarity his friend Lord Brougham described as "so perfect that it seems as if alive."[42] And yet the harder I stared at his corpse, the less I could see of what made him human.

From my days as a student of modern history, I remembered John Stuart Mill's dismissive remarks about the utilitarian philosopher. "Bentham's knowledge of human nature is bounded," wrote Mill, Bentham's legal guardian[43] and greatest acolyte, who later became his most acute critic. "It is wholly empirical, and the empiricism of one who has had little experience."[44]

John Stuart Mill, England's most influential thinker of the nineteenth century, thought of Bentham as a sort of human computer, able to add up our appetites and fears but incapable of grasping anything beyond the strictly empirical about what makes us human. "How much of human nature slumbered in him he knew not, neither can we know," Mill—who popularized the word "utilitarian"[45]—wrote of his former mentor. The problem with Bentham, Mill recognized, was that, as somebody who was deficient in both the imagination and experience required to grasp the human condition, "he was a boy to the last."[46]

So if the boy Bentham couldn't teach me about human nature, I wondered, then who could?

I Update, Therefore I Am

It occurred to me that the corpse might make more human sense after I'd expressed myself about it on Biz Stone's Twitter where, as @ajkeen, I had a following of several thousand followers. Squeezing the rectangular Black-Berry between my fingers, I wondered how to socially produce my confusion about Bentham in under 140 characters. Turning away from the Auto-Icon, I noticed that the University College corridor was thronged with students walking to and from their afternoon classes. As I watched this procession of strangers trooping across the Bloomsbury campus, I saw that some of them were glancing at me queerly, perhaps in a similarly foreign way to how I was peering at Bentham's corpse. What impression, I wondered, did these students have of me—this globally networked yet entirely solitary stranger from another continent, determinedly anonymous in the metropolis, gazing with a detached intimacy at a pre-Victorian corpse.

My confusion about the dead social reformer drifted into a confusion about my own identity. Instead of contemplating Bentham's exhibitionism, I began to consider my own personality in the order of things. How, I wondered, could I prove my own existence to my prized army of followers on Twitter, the vast majority of whom neither knew nor would ever know me?

Rather than using Twitter to broadcast my thoughts about the Auto-Icon or to confess what I'd had for breakfast that day (grilled kippers again—eaten at the chic Oxford prison) or to tell the world about my plans to look at the pictures in Amsterdam's Rijksmuseum the following day, I went all Cartesian on my global audience.

I UPDATE, THEREFORE I AM, I thumbed onto "Tweetie," an application on my BlackBerry Bold that enabled me to send a tweet anytime from anywhere.

These twenty-four characters of digital wisdom blinked back at me from the screen, impatient, it seemed, to be pushed out onto the network for the world to see. But my thumb hovered over the BlackBerry's send button. I wasn't ready to publish this private thought out onto the public network. Not yet anyway. I glanced down at my screen once again.

@ajkeen: I UPDATE, THEREFORE I AM

If these words were really true, I asked myself, then what? Would the entire world, all eight billion human beings, have to migrate—like settlers in a promised social media land—onto this new central nervous system of society? What, I wondered, would be the fate of our identities when we all lived without secrets, fully transparent, completely in public, within the *social* architecture that Reid Hoffman and Biz Stone were building for the rest of humanity? I looked again at the dead Bentham, the utilitarian father of the greatest-happiness principle. Would this electronically networked society result in more happiness? I contemplated. Would it lead to the improvement of the human condition? Would it enrich our personalities? Could it create man in his own image?

Questions, questions, questions. My mind drifted to the unwired, to those unwilling or unable to live in public. The thought triggered a feeling of dizziness, as if the external world had speeded up and was now revolving quicker and quicker around me. If, as the fictional Sean Parker argues in *The Social Network*, our future will be lived online, I thought to myself, then what will be the fate of these dissenters, of those who don't update? What,

I wondered, in a world in which we all exist on the Internet, will become of those who protect their privacy, who pride themselves on their illegibility, who—in the timeless words of Brandeis and Warren—just want to be *let alone*?

Will they be alive, I wondered, or will they be dead?

The Living and the Dead

My tweet still unsent, I continued to gaze into the Auto-Icon for enlightenment. As the picture became clearer and clearer, my dizziness intensified and the room began to spin around me with more and more violence. Yes, I now saw, Bentham's corpse did, after all, have something to teach me. The true picture of the future, I realized, had been staring me straight in the face all along.

In spite of my own feeling of vertigo, this vision—a painful kind of epiphany—grabbed me with an icy clarity. I froze momentarily, my mouth half open, my eyes fixed on the corpse. It suddenly became clear that I'd been peering into a mirror. Reid Hoffman was right: the future is always *sooner* and *stranger* than anyone of us think. I realized that the Auto-Icon, this "man who is his own image," represents this future and Bentham's corpse is actually you, me and everyone else who have imprisoned themselves in today's digital inspection house.

What I glimpsed that late November afternoon in Bloomsbury was the *anti-social* future, the loneliness of the isolated man in the connected crowd. I saw all of us as digital Jeremy Benthams, isolated from one another not only by the growing ubiquity of networked communications, but also by the increasingly individualized and competitive nature of twenty-first-century life. Yes, this was the future. Personal visibility, I recognized, is the new symbol of status and power in our digital age. Like the corpse locked in his transparent tomb, we are now all on permanent exhibition, all just images of ourselves in this brave new transparent world.

Like the immodest nineteenth-century social reformer locked in his eternal wooden and glass box, we twenty-first-century social networkers—especially aspiring super nodes like myself—are becoming addicted to building attention and reputation. But like the solitariness of my own experience in that University College corridor, the truth, the reality of social media, is an architecture of human isolation rather than community. The future will be anything but *social*, I realized. That's the real killer app of the networked age.

We are, I realized, becoming schizophrenic—simultaneously detached from the world and yet jarringly ubiquitous. Cultural critics like Umberto Eco and Jean Baudrillard have used the word "hyperreality" to describe how modern technology blurs the distinction between reality and unreality and grants authenticity to self-evidently fake things like William Randolph Hearst's castle in San Simeon, the gothic building on the Californian coast made famous by Orson Wells's 1941 picture *Citizen Kane*. Eco defines hyperreality as "a philosophy of immortality as duplication" where "the *completely real* becomes identified with the *completely fake*."[47]

"Absolute unreality is offered as real presence," Eco thus explains hyperreality. But as I gazed at the Auto-Icon, an equally absurd neologism came to mind: "hypervisibility." The man who is his own image in the digitally networked world, I realized, is simultaneously everywhere and nowhere, and the more completely visible he appears, the more completely invisible he actually is.

Hypervisibility.

In this fully transparent world where we are simultaneously nowhere and everywhere, absolute unreality is real presence, and the *completely fake* is also the *completely real*. This, I saw, was the most truthfully untruthful picture of networked twenty-first-century life.

Now I was ready to broadcast my tweet. Yet before pressing send, I added a word to the short message still blinking on my BlackBerry. It was a single word, just three characters out of Twitter's 140-character limit, but it transformed the tweet from a hopeful expression of digital cartesianism into a chillingly existential plea.

@ajkeen: I UPDATE, THEREFORE I AM NOT

But the RIM electronic device wasn't called a smartphone for nothing. I had been wrong that nobody knew my location that afternoon. As I was about to send my tweet, an uninvited message from Tweetie popped up on the screen. It was a request to give out my Bloomsbury location, so that the app could broadcast where I was to my thousands of Twitter followers.

TWEETIE WOULD LIKE TO USE YOUR CURRENT LOCATION—
DON'T ALLOW or OK

The BlackBerry device, I realized, wanted to betray me by broadcasting my location to the world. No wonder it was made by *Research in Motion*. Switching off the smartphone and shoving it deep into my trouser pocket, I took a deep breath, then another. The silence was symphonic. As my dizziness retreated, I thought again about my conversations in Oxford the previous day with @quixotic, the co-owner of our collective future. I realized that he had been both right and wrong about the future. Yes, there is no doubt that, for better or worse, nineteenth- and twentieth-century industrial atoms are now being replaced by twenty-first-century networked bytes. But no, rather than uniting us between the digital pillars of an Aristotelian polis, today's social media is actually splintering our identities so that we always exist outside ourselves, unable to concentrate on the here-and-now, too wedded to our own image, perpetually revealing our *current location*, our privacy sacrificed to the utilitarian tyranny of a collective network.

History, I realized, was repeating itself. In 1890, nearly sixty years after Jeremy Bentham's body first made its public appearance in University

College, Samuel Warren and Louis Brandeis argued in their iconic *Harvard Law Review* article that "solitude and privacy have become more essential to the individual." The right to be let alone, Warren and Brandeis wrote in "Defense of Privacy," was a "general right to the immunity of the person . . . the right to one's personality." And today, at the dawn of our increasingly transparent social media age, more than a century after the law review article first appeared, this need for solitude and privacy—the primary ingredients in the mysterious formation of individual personality—has, if anything, become even more essential.

Vertigo, Alfred Hitchcock's creepy picture about a man's love for a corpse, was based upon the French novel *The Living and the Dead*.[48] But there is nothing fictional about today's creeping auto-iconization of life and its tragic consequence—the death of privacy and solitude in our social networking world. It was Hitchcock, I think, who once joked that the corpse he most feared seeing was his own. Yet it's no joke if that corpse also happens to be the corpse of mankind, exiled not only from himself, but also from everyone else, billions of people who are their own images whizzing faster and faster around each other on the transparent network, *hypervisible*, all perpetually on show, imprisoned in an endless loop of great exhibitionism, greedy for attention, building their self-proclaimed reputations as benefactors of the human race.

For Jeremy Bentham and his utilitarian school, happiness is a mathematical equation simply quantifiable by substracting our pain from our pleasures. But this utilitarian philosophy—so savagely satirized by Charles Dickens in the ridiculous form of Mr. Gradgrind in *Hard Times*—fails to grasp what makes us human. As Dickens, John Stuart Mill and many more contemporary critics of utilitarianism have argued, happiness isn't simply an algorithm of our appetites and desires. And central to that happiness is the unquantifiable right to be let alone by society—a right which enables us, as human beings, to remain true to ourselves. "Privacy is not only essential to life and liberty; it's essential to the pursuit of happiness, in the broadest and deepest sense.

We human beings are not just social creatures; we're also private creatures."
Thus argues Nicholas Carr, one of today's most articulate critics of digital
utilitarianism. "What we don't share is as important as what we do share."[49]

Unfortunately, however, sharing has become the new Silicon Valley reli-
gion and, as we shall see in this book, privacy—that condition essential to
our real happiness as human beings—is being dumped into the dustbin
of history. "Fail fast," @quixotic, who believes that privacy is "primarily an
issue for old people,"[50] advises entrepreneurs. "You jump off a cliff and you
assemble an airplane on the way down," is his description for what it's like to
do a start-up.[51] But the problem is that, by so radically socializing today's
digital revolution, we are, as a species, collectively jumping off a cliff. And if
we fail to build a networked society that protects the rights to individual
privacy and autonomy in the face of today's cult of the social, we can't—like
the eternally optimistic Hoffman—launch a new company. Society isn't just
another start-up—which is why we can't entirely trust Silicon Valley entrepreneurs like Hoffman or Stone with our future. Failing to properly assemble the social media airplane after jumping off that cliff and crashing to the
ground means jeopardizing those precious rights to individual privacy, secrecy and, yes, the liberty that individuals have won over the last millennium.

That is the fear, the warning of failure and collective self-destruction in
Digital Vertigo. In 2007 I published *Cult of the Amateur*, my warning about
the impact of Web 2.0's user-generated data revolution upon our culture. But
as we go from the Web 2.0 of Google, YouTube and Wikipedia to the Web
3.0 of Facebook, Twitter, Google+ and LinkedIn, and as the Internet becomes a platform for what @quixotic describes as "real identities generating
massive amounts of data,"[52] the story that you are about to read reveals an
even more disturbing mania: today's creeping tyranny of an ever-increasingly
transparent social network that threatens the individual liberty, the happiness and, yes, perhaps even the very personality of contemporary man.

You have two options about this cult: DON'T ALLOW or OK.

The book you are about to read is a defense of the mystery and secrecy of individual existence. It is a reminder of the right to privacy, autonomy and solitude in a world that, by 2020, will contain around 50 billion intelligent networked devices[53] such as my BlackBerry Bold with its all-too-intelligent apps. In a world in which almost every single human being on the planet is likely to be connected by the middle of the twenty-first century, this book is an argument against the radical sharing, openness, personal transparency, great exhibitionism and the other pious communitarian orthodoxies of our networked age. But this book is more than simply an antisocial manifesto. It's also an investigation into why, as human beings, privacy and solitude makes us happy.

Yes, you've seen this kind of picture before too. It's a challenge to Reid Hoffman's mistaken assumption that we are all, *a priori,* social animals. And to begin our journey into this all-too-familiar future where the unknowable mystery of the individual human condition is being overwritten by transparent man, let's return to Jeremy Bentham, that eternal prisoner of his own Auto-Icon, whose late eighteenth-century "simple idea of architecture" to reform the world is, I'm afraid, an eerily prescient warning of our collectively open twenty-first-century fate.

1

A SIMPLE IDEA OF ARCHITECTURE

"Morals reformed—health preserved—industry invigorated instruction diffused—public
burdens lightened—Economy seated, as it were, upon a rock—the gordian knot of the
Poor-Laws are not cut, but untied—all by a simple idea in Architecture."[1]
—JEREMY BENTHAM

The Inspection-House

If this was a picture, you'd have seen it before. History, you see, is repeating itself. With our new digital century comes a familiar problem from the industrial age. A social tyranny is once again encroaching upon individual liberty. Today, in the early twenty-first century, just as in the nineteenth and twentieth centuries, this social threat comes from a simple idea in architecture.

In 1787, at the dawn of the mass industrial age, Jeremy Bentham designed what he called a "simple idea in architecture" to improve the management of prisons, hospitals, schools and factories. Bentham's idea was, as the architectural historian Robin Evans noted, a "vividly imaginative" synthesis of architectural form with social purpose.[2] Bentham, who amassed great personal wealth as a result of his social vision,[3] wanted to change the world through this new architecture.

Bentham sketched out this vision of what Aldous Huxley described as a "plan for a totalitarian housing project"[4] in a series of "open"[5] letters written from the little Crimean town of Krichev, where he and his brother, Samuel, were instructing the regime of the enlightened Russian despot Catherine the Great about the building of efficient factories for its unruly population.[6] In these public letters, Bentham imagined what he called this "Panopticon" or "Inspection-House" as a physical network, a circular building of small rooms, each transparent and fully connected, in which individuals could be watched over by an all-seeing inspector. This inspector is the utilitarian version of an omniscient god—always-on, all-knowing, with the serendipitous ability to look around corners and see through walls. As the French historian Michel Foucault observed, this Inspection House was "like so many cages, so many small theaters, in which each actor is alone, perfectly individualized and constantly visible."[7]

The Panopticon's connective technology would bring us together by separating us, Bentham calculated. Transforming us into fully transparent exhibits would be good for both society and the individual, he adduced, because the more we imagined we were being watched, the more efficient and disciplined we would each become. Both the individual and the community would, therefore, benefit from this network of Auto-Icons. "Ideal perfection," the utilitarian figured, taking this supposedly social idea to its most chillingly anti-social conclusion, would require that everyone—from connected prisoners to connected workers to connected school children to connected citizens—could be inspected "every instant of time."[8]

Rather than the abstract fantasy of an eccentric Englishman whose experience of life, you'll remember, was no more than that of a boy, Bentham's radically transparent Inspection-House had an enormous impact on new prison architecture in the late eighteenth and early nineteenth centuries. The original Oxford jail where I had breakfasted with Reid Hoffman, for example, had been built by the prolific prison architect William Blackburn, "the father of the radial plan for prisons,"[9] who built more than a dozen semicircular jails on Benthamite principles. In Oxford, Blackburn had replaced the medieval "gaol" in the city's castle with a building designed to supervise prisoners' every movement and control their time down to the very minute.

But Bentham's simple idea of architecture "reformed" more than just prisons. It represented an augury of an industrial society intricately connected by an all-too-concrete network of railroads and telegraph lines. The mechanical age of the stream train, the large-scale factory, the industrial city, the nation-state, the motion picture camera and the mass market newspaper did indeed create the physical architecture to transform us into efficient individual exhibits—always, in theory, observable by government, employers, media and public opinion. In the industrial era of mass connectivity, factories, schools, prisons and, most ominously, entire political systems were built upon this crystalline technology of collective surveillance. The last two hundred years have indeed been the age of the great exhibition.

Yet nobody in the industrial era, apart from the odd exhibitionist like Bentham himself, actually wanted to become individual pictures in this collective exhibition. Indeed, the struggle to be let alone is the story of industrial man. As Georg Simmel, the turn-of-the-twentieth-century German sociologist and scholar of secrecy, recognized, "the deepest problems of modern life derive from the claim of the individual to preserve the autonomy and individuality of his existence in the face of overwhelming social forces, of historical heritage, of external culture, and of the technique of life."[10] Thus the great critics of mass society—John Stuart Mill and Alexis de Tocqueville in the nineteenth and George Orwell, Franz Kafka and Michel Foucault in the twentieth century—have all tried to shield individual liberty from the omniscient gaze of the Inspection-House.

"Visibility," Foucault warned, "is a trap."[11] Thus, from J. S. Mill's solitary free thinker in *On Liberty* to Joseph K in *The Castle* and *The Trial* to Winston Smith in *Nineteen Eighty-four*, the hero of the mass industrial age for these critics is the individual who tries to protect his invisibility, who takes pleasure in his own opacity, who turns his back on the camera, who—in the timeless words of Samuel Warren and Louis Brandeis—just wants to be *let alone* by the technologies of the mass industrial age.

Our Age of Great Exhibitionism

Yet now, at the dusk of the industrial and the dawn of the digital epoch, Bentham's simple idea of architecture has returned. But history never repeats itself, not identically, at least. Today, as the Web evolves from a platform for impersonal data into an Internet of people, Bentham's industrial Inspection-House has reappeared with a chilling digital twist. What we once saw as a prison is now considered as a playground; what was considered pain is today viewed as pleasure.

The analog age of the great exhibition is now being replaced by the digital age of great exhibitionism.

Today's simple architecture is the Internet—that ever-expanding network of networks combining the worldwide Web of personal computers, the wireless world of handheld networked devices like my BlackBerry Bold and other "smart" social products such as connected televisions,[12] gaming consoles[13] and the "connected car"[14]—in which around a quarter of the globe's population have already taken up residency. In contrast with the original brick and mortar Inspection-House, this rapidly expanding global network, with its two billion digitally interconnected souls and its more than five billion connected devices, can house an infinite number of rooms. This is a global Auto-Icon that, more than two centuries after Jeremy Bentham sketched out his Inspection-House,[15] is finally realizing his utilitarian dream of allowing us to be perpetually observed.

This digital architecture—described by New York University social media scholar Clay Shirky as the "connective tissue of society"[16] and by U.S.

Secretary of State Hillary Clinton as the new "nervous system of the planet"[17]—has been designed to transform us into exhibitionists, forever on show in our networked crystal palaces. And, today, in an age of radically transparent online communities like Twitter and Facebook, the social has become, in Shirky's words, the "default" setting on the Internet,[18] transforming digital technology from being a tool of second life into an increasingly central part of real life.

But this is a version of real life that could have been choreographed by Jeremy Bentham. As WikiLeaks founder and self-appointed transparency tsar Julian Assange said, today's Internet is "the greatest spying machine the world has ever seen,"[19] with Facebook, he added, being "the world's most comprehensive database about people, their relationships, their names, their addresses, their locations, their communications with each other, and their relatives, all sitting within the United States, all accessible to US Intelligence."[20]

But it's not just Facebook that is establishing this master database of the human race. As Clay Shirky notes, popular[21] geo-location services such as foursquare, Facebook places, Google Latitude, Plancast and the Hotlist, which enable us to "effectively see through walls" and know the exact location of all our friends, are making society more "legible," thus allowing all of us to be read, in good Inspection-House fashion, "like a book."[22] No wonder, then, that Katie Rolphe, a New York University colleague of Shirky, has observed that "Facebook is the novel we are all writing."[23]

Social media is the confessional novel that we are not only all writing but also collectively publishing for everyone else to read. We are all becoming Wiki-leakers, less notorious but no less subversive versions of Julian Assange, of not only our own lives but other people's now. The old mass industrial celebrity culture has been so turned upside down by social networks like Facebook, LinkedIn and Twitter that celebrity has been democratized and we are reinventing ourselves as self-styled celebrities, even going as far as to deploy online services like YouCeleb that enable us to dress like twentieth-century mass media stars.[24]

There has, consequently, been a massive increase in what Shirky calls "self-produced" legibility, thereby making society as easy to read as an open book.[25] As a society, we are, to borrow some words from Jeremy Bentham, becoming our own collective image. This contemporary mania with our own self-expression is what two leading American psychologists, Dr. Jean Twenge and Dr. Keith Campbell, have described as "the narcissism epidemic"[26]—a self-promotional madness driven, these two psychologists say, by our need to continually manufacture our own fame to the world. The Silicon Valley–based psychiatrist, Dr. Elias Aboujaoude, whose 2011 book, *Virtually You,* charts the rise of what he calls "the self-absorbed online Narcissus," shares Twenge and Campbell's pessimism. The Internet, Dr. Aboujaoude notes, gives narcissists the opportunity to "fall in love with themselves all over again," thereby creating a online world of infinite "self-promotion" and "shallow web relationships."[27]

Many other writers share Aboujaoude's concerns. The cultural historian Neal Gabler says that we have all become "information narcissists" utterly disinterested in anything "outside ourselves."[28] Social network culture medicates our "need for self-esteem," adds best-selling author Neil Strauss, by "pandering to win followers."[29] The acclaimed novelist Jonathan Franzen concurs, arguing that products like his and my BlackBerry Bold are "great allies and enablers of narcissism." These kind of gadgets, Franzen explains, have been designed to conform to our fantasy of wanting to be "liked" and to "reflect well on us." Their technology, therefore, is simply an "extension of our narcissistic selves. When we stare at screens in the Web 2.0 age, we are gazing at ourselves. It's all one big endless loop. We like the mirror and the mirror likes us."[30] Franzen says, "To friend a person is merely to include the person in our private hall of flattering mirrors."[31]

We broadcast ourselves and therefore we are (not).

Twenge, Campbell, Aboujaoude, Strauss and Franzen are all correct about this endless loop of great exhibitionism—an attention economy that, not uncoincidentally, combines a libertarian insistence on unrestrained individual freedom with the cult of the social. It's a public exhibition of self-love displayed in an online looking glass that *New Atlantis* senior editor Christine Rosen identifies as the "new narcissism"[32] and *New York Times* columnist Ross Douthat calls a "desperate adolescent narcissism."[33] Everything—from communications, commerce and culture to gaming, government and gambling—is going social. As David Brooks, Douthat's colleague at *The Times*, adds, "achievement is redefined as the ability to attract attention."[34] All we, as individuals, want to do on the network, it seems, is share our reputations, our travel itineraries, our war plans, our professional credentials, our illnesses, our confessions, photographs of our latest meal, our sexual habits of course, even our exact whereabouts with our thousands of online friends. Network society has become a transparent love-in, an orgy of oversharing, an endless digital Summer of Love.

Like the network itself, our mass public confessional is global. People from all around the world are revealing their most private thoughts on a transparent network that anyone and everyone can access. In May 2011, when one of China's richest men, a billionaire investor called Wang Gongquan, left his wife for his mistress, he wrote on the Chinese version of Twitter, Sina Weiba, a service that has 140 million users: "I am giving up everything and eloping with Wang Qin. I feel ashamed and so am leaving without saying good-bye. I kneel down and beg forgiveness!"[35] Gongquan's confession exploded virally. Within twenty-four hours, his post was republished 60,000 times with some of the billionaire's closest and most powerful friends publicly pleading with him to go back to his wife.

This love-in—what the author Steven Johnson, an oversharing advocate who, as @stevenberlinjohnson, has 1.5 million Twitter followers of his own, praised as "a networked version of *The Truman Show,* where we are all playing Truman,"[36] is quite a public spectacle. Rather than *The Truman Show,* however, this epidemic of oversharing, in its preoccupation with immortality, could be subtitled *The Living and the Dead.*

What If There Are No Secrets?

More and more of us are indeed playing Truman in a networked version of our own intimately personalized show. "What if there are no secrets?" imagined Jeff Jarvis in July 2010.[37] A transparency evangelist at the City University of New York, Jarvis popularized the neologism "publicness" in a speech that same year entitled "Privacy, Publicness & Penises."[38] By very publicly announcing his own prostate cancer in April 2009 and turning his life into "an open blog,"[39] Jarvis[40]—the author of the 2011 transparency manifesto *Public Parts,*[41] written in "homage" to shockjock Howard Stern's *Private Parts* biography[42]—certainly promoted his own Benthamite thesis that "publicness grants immortality."[43] Another apostle of publicness, the veteran social theorist Howard Rheingold, who, back in 1993 as a member of the pioneering Whole Earth 'Lectronic Link (the WELL), fathered the term "virtual community,"[44] revealed his own struggle with colon cancer online in early 2010. A third advocate of openness, the British technology writer Guy Kewney, who was afflicted with colorectal cancer, even used social media to chronicle his own impending death in April 2010.

While social media, for all its superhuman ability to see through walls, might not quite guarantee immortality, its impact is certainly of immense historical significance, what Jeff Jarvis describes as an "emblem of epochal change[45]—as profound a technological development, in its own way, as anything invented in the last fifty years. You'll remember that Reid Hoffman defined this explosion of personal data as "Web 3.0." But John Doerr,[46] the wealthiest venture capitalist in the world whom Amazon CEO Jeff Bezos once described as "the center of gravity on the Internet," goes even further than @quixotic in his historical analysis.

Doerr argues that "social" represents "the great third wave" of technological innovation, following directly in the wake of the invention of the personal computer and the Internet.[47] The advent of social, local, and mobile technology now heralds what Doerr calls a "perfect storm" to disrupt traditional businesses.[48] Such, indeed, is Doerr and his venture capitalist firm of Kleiner Perkin's confidence in this social revolution that, in October 2010, in partnership with Facebook and Mark Pincus's Zynga, Kleiner launched a quarter-billion-dollar sFund dedicated to exclusively putting money into social businesses. While on Valentine's Day 2011, the firm made what the *Wall Street Journal* described as a "small" $38 million investment in Facebook,[49] buying the Silicon Valley venture capitalists no more than an affectionately symbolic 0.073% stake in the social media company.[50] "We're making a blue ocean bet that social is just beginning," Bing Gordon, another Kleiner partner thus explains the firm's thinking behind its sFund. "Usage habits will change dramatically over the next 4–5 years."[51]

Mark Zuckerberg, the beneficary of Kleiner's generous Valentine's Day present, *Time Magazine*'s 2010 Person of the Year and the semi-fictionalized "Accidental Billionaire" subject of David Fincher's hit 2010 movie *The Social Network*,[52] agrees with Gordon that we are at the beginning of a social revolution that will change not only the online user experience but also our entire economy and society. Zuckerberg who, as the English novelist Zadie Smith notes, "uses the word *connect* as believers use the word *Jesus*,"[53] is the Jeremy Bentham 2.0 of our digitally networked age, the social engineer who claims to be "rewiring the world."[54] And, like Bentham too, the Facebook co-founder and CEO is a "boy to the last" who lacks any experience or knowledge of human nature and who wants to build a digital Inspection-House in which none of us are ever let alone again.

Zuckerberg's excitement about the five-year horizon is certainly boyish. "If you look five years out, every industry is going to be rethought in a social way. You can remake whole industries. That's the big thing,"[55] Zuckerberg gushed in December 2010. "And no matter where you go," he told Robert Scoble, Silicon Valley's uber-evangelist of social media, "we want to ensure that every experience you have will be social."[56]

Zuckerberg's five-year plan is to eliminate loneliness. He wants to create a world in which we will never have to be alone again because we will always be connected to our online friends in everything we do, spewing huge amounts of our own personal data as we do it. "Facebook wants to populate the wilderness, tame the howling mob and turn the lonely, antisocial world of random chance into a friendly world, a serendipitous world," Time's Lev Grossman explained why his magazine made Zuckerberg their Person of the Year in 2010. "You'll be working and living inside a network of people, and you'll never have to be alone again. The Internet, and the whole world, will feel more like a family, or a college dorm, or an office where your co-workers are also your best friends."[57]

But even today, in the early stages of Zuckerberg's five-year plan to rewire the world, Facebook is becoming mankind's own image. Attracting a trillion page views a month,[58] and now hosting more active users than the entire population of Europe and Russia,[59] Facebook is where we go to reveal everything about ourselves. It's not surprising, therefore, that the satirical website The Onion, confirming Julian Assange's remark about Facebook as history's "most appalling spying machine," presents Mark Zuckerberg's creation as a CIA conspiracy. "After years of secretly monitoring the public, we were astounded so many people would willingly publicize where they live, their religious and political views, an alphabetized list of all their friends, personal e-mail addresses, phone numbers, hundreds of photos of themselves, and even status updates about what they were doing moment to moment," a mock

CIA deputy director reports to Congress in the Onion skit. "It is truly a dream come true for the CIA."[60]

But perhaps the most disturbing thing of all is that Facebook isn't a CIA plant and Mark Zuckerberg isn't an Agency operative. Ironically, Zuckerberg five-year plan might make the CIA redundant or transform it into a start-up business division, what Silicon Valley people would call a "skunk-works" project, within Facebook. After all, professional spooks have little value if we all live in a universal dorm room where anyone can know what everyone else is doing and thinking.

Everyone can become a secret policeman in a world without personal secrets—which is why the CIA really has set up an Open Source Center at its Virginia headquarters where a team of so-called "vengeful librarians" stalk thousands of Twitter and Facebook accounts for information.[61] That may be scary for the traditional powers that be at the CIA, with their industrial-age assumptions about the top-down, exclusively professional nature of intelligence work, but it's even scarier for the rest of us who cannot escape the transparent lighting of a global electronic village in which anyone can become a vengeful librarian.

The Dial Tone for the 21st Century

So for who, exactly, is today's social media a "dream come true"?

Architects of digital transparency, technologists of openness, venture capitalists and, of course, entrepreneurs like Reid Hoffman, Biz Stone and Mark Pincus who are all massively profiting from all these real identities generating enormous amounts of their own personal data. That's who are transforming this "dream" of the ubiquitous social network into a reality.

No, Mark Zuckerberg is far from being the only young social media billionaire gazing, with a mix of communitarian aura and financial greed, onto that five-year horizon when the whole world will have become a twenty-first-century version of Bentham's Inspection-House. Speaking at the launch of the sFund, Zynga CEO Mark Pincus—the co-owner, you'll remember, with his friend Reid Hoffman, of the future itself—concurred with Zuckerberg's vision of a world radically reinvented by social technology. "In five years, everybody will always be connected to each other instead of the web," Pincus predicted.[62] Social companies like Zygna, Facebook, LinkedIn and Twitter, he explained, are becoming the central plumbing for what he called "the dial tones" for the ubiquitous social experience of tomorrow, connecting people through increasingly invisible mobile technology that will always be with them. Connectivity, Pincus predicts, will become the electricity of the social epoch—so ubiquitous that it will be invisible and so powerful that it threatens to become the operating system for the entire twenty-first century.

But even today, it's increasingly difficult to avoid the relentlessly invasive beep of Mark Pincus's social dial tone. The digital networking of the world, this arrival of *The Truman Show* on all of our screens, is both relentless and inevitable.[63] By mid-2011, the Pew Research Center found that 65 percent of American adults were using social-networking sites—up from just 5 percent in 2005.[64] In June 2010, Americans spent almost 23 percent of their online time in social media networking—up a staggering 43 percent from June 2009,[65] with use among older adults (50–64 year olds) almost doubling in this period and the 65+ demographic being the fastest growing age group on Facebook in 2010 with a 124 percent increase in sign-ups over 2009. And by the summer of 2011, the Pew Research Center found that this number has risen dramatically again, with 32 percent of fifty- to sixty-four-year-olds in America accessing networks like Twitter, LinkedIn and Facebook on a daily basis.[66]

Yet, for all Facebook's meteoric growth among the senior digital citizens, it's teens and high school kids who have most fully embraced social media, with Facebook and Twitter replacing blogging as their dominant mode of online self-expression.[67] As Mark Zuckerberg said, in November 2010, when he introduced Facebook's social messaging platform, "high school kids don't use e-mail." Unfortunately, Zuckerberg is correct. In 2010, e-mail—private one-to-one electronic communication that is the digital version of letter writing—was, according to ComScore, down 59 percent among teenagers, replaced, of course, with public social-messaging platforms like Twitter and Facebook.[68]

Facebook, with its members investing over 700 billion minutes of their time per month on the network,[69] was the world's most visited Web site in 2010 making up 9 percent of all online traffic.[70] By early 2011, 57 percent of all online Americans were logging onto Facebook at least once a day, with 51 percent of all Americans over twelve years old having an account on the social network[71] and 38 percent of all the Internet's sharing referral traffic emanating from Zuckerberg's creation.[72] By September 2011, more than 500 million people were logging onto Facebook each day[73] with its then almost 800 million active users being larger than the entire Internet was in 2004.[74] Facebook is becoming mankind's own image. It's where our Auto-Icons now sit.

Not to be outdone, Biz Stone's Twitter, Facebook's most muscular competitor in real-time social networking, added 100 million new members in 2010 who contributed to the 25 billion tweets sent that year[75] and, by October 2011, were authoring a quarter-billion tweets per day (that's more than 10,000 messages authored per second) with more than 50 million users logging onto the site every day.[76] Then there's the social ecommerce start-up Groupon, whose 35-million subscriber base and annual revenue of around $2 billion makes it the fastest growing company in American history. In December 2010, Groupon turned down a $6 billion acquisition offer from Google and instead raised almost a billion dollars of its own from private investors before launching its own oversubscribed November 2011 IPO in which the company was valued at $16.5 billion.[77] Groupon's most direct competitor, LivingSocial, with its rumored $6 billion valuation and expected $1 billion revenue in 2011, is also experiencing meteoric growth.[78]

Meanwhile, Pincus's social gaming start-up Zynga continues its own quest for global domination: Founded in July 2007, the Silicon Valley–based company, which includes Facebook's most popular apps CitiVille and Farm-ville[79] in its network, is now delivering an astonishing 1 petabyte of daily data, adding 1,000 new servers a week and has had its social games played together by 215 million people, which corresponds to about 10 percent of the world's entire online population.[80] No wonder, then, that Pincus's still private three-and-a-half-year-old company raised a $500 million round of investment from a number of venture capitalists—including, of course, Kleiner—at a $10 billion valuation,[81] before launching its own IPO in De-cember 2011.

The rate of growth for younger social media companies is equally jaw drop-ping. Foursquare, one of Silicon Valley's hottest social start-ups, grew by 3400 percent in 2010 and, by August 2011, the then year-old geo-location service was getting 3 million check-ins per day from its 10 million members,[82] with its users growing to 15 million by December 2011.[83] A second, the blogging platform Tumblr, was growing by a quarter billion impression every week in early 2011,[84] and, by September 2011, had raised $85 million in fresh financ-ing and was attracting 13 billion average monthly page views from its 30 mil-lion blogs.[85] Another, the social knowledge network Quora, founded by former Facebook technologists Adam D'Angelo and Charlie Cheever,[86] was valued at $86 million by investors before the advertising free service had even established a business model for making money[87] and was rumored to have "scoffed" at a $1 billion acquisition offer.[88] Not to be outdone, the social pho-tography app Instagram reached 2 million users in only four months since its late 2010 launch—making its phenomenal rate of growth three times faster than that of foursquare and six times more viral than Twitter.

Once just a medium for the distribution of impersonal data, the Internet is now a network of companies and technologies designed around social products, platforms and services—transforming it from an impersonal database into a global digital brain publicly broadcasting our relationships, our intentionality and our personal taste. The integration of our personal data—renamed by social media marketers as our "social graph"—into online content is now the central driver of Internet innovation in Reid Hoffman's Web 3.0 age. By enabling our thousands of "friends" to know exactly what we are doing, thinking, reading, watching and buying, today's Web products and services are powering our hypervisible age of great exhibitionism. No wonder, then, that the World Economic Forum describes personal data as a "New Asset Class"[89] in the global economy.

In early 2011, Sergey Brin, Google co-founder, acknowledged that Google had only "touched" 1 percent of social search's potential.[90] But even today, with social realizing only a few percentage points of what it will eventually become, this revolution is dramatically reshaping not just the Internet but also our identities and personalities. Whether we like it or not, twenty-first-century life is increasingly being lived in public. Four out of five college admissions offices, for example, are looking up applicants' Facebook profiles before making a decision on whether to accept them.[91] A February 2011 human resources survey suggested that almost half of HR managers believed it was likely that our social network profiles are replacing our resumes as the core way for potential employers to evaluate us.[92] *The New York Times* reports that some firms have even begun using surveillance services like Social Intelligence, which can legally store data for up to seven years, to collect social media information about prospective employees before giving them jobs.[93] "In today's executive search market, if you're not on LinkedIn, you don't exist," one job search expert told *The Wall Street Journal* in June 2011.[94] LinkedIn now even enables its users to submit their profiles as resumes, thus inspiring one "personal branding guru" to announce that the 100 million member professional network is "about to put Job Boards (and Resumes) out of business."[95]

Mark Zuckerberg once said "movies are naturally social things."[96] What he forgot to add is that in this brave new world of shared information, re-sumes, pictures, books, travel, music, business, politics, education, shopping, location, finance and knowledge are, it seems, also *naturally* social things.

So my question for Zuckerberg—who already has 51 percent of all Ameri-cans over twelve years old on his network and who believes that kids under thirteen should be allowed to have Facebook accounts[97]—is very simple: Mark, in your vision of the future, please tell me something that *isn't* a social thing?

Nothing. That, of course, would be his answer. Everything is going social, he would say. Social is, to borrow a much overused metaphor, the tsunami that is altering our entire social, educational, personal and business land-scape. And, I'm afraid, Mark Zuckerberg isn't alone in seeing social as that tidal wave that, for better or worse, is flattening everything in its path.

The Emerald Sea

On the wall of an otherwise nondescript fourth-floor Silicon Valley office is a picture of a great wave crashing against the beach. In its foamy, tumescent wake lies the corpse of a small fishing boat. This picture is a copy of "Emer-ald Sea," an 1878 landscape of the Californian coastline by the romantic American artist Albert Bierstadt, and it hangs in the Mountain View office of Google, the dominant Web 2.0 company that is now aggressively trying to transform itself into a Web 3.0 social media player.

No, it's not just me that is using the metaphor of a great wave to describe the social revolution. In the second half of 2010, acknowledging the failure of Buzz and Wave, its first generation social media products, and realizing that social media threatens to turn this Web 2.0 leader into a Web 3.0 laggard, Google established an elite army of engineers and business executives led by its SVP of Social Business, Vic Gundotra and Bradley Horowitz, its VP of product and incorporating eighteen Google products and thirty traditional product teams. What Gundotra described to me as a "project" was called

Emerald Sea and it referred directly to Bierstadt's idealized nineteenth-century landscape, with its enormous wave crashing down against the coastline. "We needed a code name that captured the fact that either there was a great opportunity to sail to new horizons and new things, or that we were going to drown by this wave," Gundotra explained the project that, a year later, conceived the Google + social network. [98]

Bradley Horowitz described Emerald Sea's 100-day ambition of transforming Google into a social company as a "wild-ass crazy, get-to-the-moon" goal. But it was, in fact, a wise move by the once dominant search company that has been forced to play social catch-up to Facebook, Zynga, Groupon, LivingSocial, Twitter, and the rest of the Web 3.0 tidal wave. You see, on today's Internet, it seems, everything—and I mean absolutely *everything*—is going social. The Internet's core logic, its dominant algorithm, has been reinvented to operate on social principles—which is why some technology pundits are already predicting that Facebook will soon surpass Google in advertising revenues. [99]

The result is a flood of new online social businesses, technologies and networks with collaborative names like GroupMe, Socialcast, LivingSocial, SocialVibe, PeekYou, BeKnown, Togetherville, Socialcam, SocialFlow, SproutSocial, SocialEyes and, most appropriately for our hypervisible age, Hyperpublic. And it's not just Kleiner Perkins that is pouring billions of dollars of investment into this social economy. The smartest investors in the Valley are all going social. In the first half of 2011, for example, the Silicon Valley-based VC firm of Andreessen Horowitz, managed by Netscape founder Mark Andreessen, the technologist who sparked the original Web 1.0 boom in August 1995 with his company's historic IPO, invested hundreds of millions of dollars in Facebook, Twitter, Groupon, Zynga and Skype. [100] Then there's Mike Moritz, the legendary Silicon Valley venture capitalist who invested in Google, Yahoo!, Apple and YouTube, who is now a board member at @quixotic's LinkedIn. [101] While Chris Sacca, who *The Wall Street Journal* described as "possibly the most influential businessman in America, is now managing a J.P. Morgan funded billion dollar investment fund which, in early 2011, invested several hundred million dollars in Twitter.[102]

Doerr, Andreessen, Moritz, Sacca and, of course, my old sparring partner @quixotic all recognize the profound changes that are transforming the Web 2.0 into the Web 3.0 economy. The old link Internet market, dominated by Google's artificial search algorithm, is being replaced with the "like" economy, symbolized by the first working product that came out of the Emerald Sea project, Google's "+1" social search. Described by Techcrunch's MG Siegler as a "massive"[103] technological initiative, the prolifically viral +1—which was launched in June 2011[104] and within three months could be found on a million Web sites generating more than 4 billion daily views[105]—adds a social layer of public recommendations from friends not only on top of the dominant search engine's nonhuman artificial algorithm but also above its advertising platform. "Whether they admit it or not," Siegler says of +1, "Google is at war with Facebook for control of the web."

That's because +1 allows us to publicly recommend search results and Web sites, thus replacing Google's artificial algorithm as the engine of the new social economy. In the +1 world, we all will eventually become personalized versions of the old Google search engine—directing Web traffic around our transparent tastes, opinions and preferences. Siegler is correct. The stakes in this new war between Google and Facebook really are about control of the Internet. No wonder, then, that Larry Page, the new Google CEO, tied 25 percent of all Google employee bonuses in 2011 to the success of the company's social strategy.[106]

Gundotra and Horowitz acknowledged the centrality of the company's social strategy when they appeared on my TechcrunchTV show in July 2011[107] to discuss the informal launch of their second product, a social network called Google + that, while still in beta, amassed 20 million unique visitors in just three weeks[108] and, in the seven days after its June 2011 release, increased the company's market cap by $20 billion.[109] Marginalizing the importance of the company's artificial algorithm, Horowitz boasted that Google + puts "people first," while Gundotra presented Google + as "the glue" that unites all of Google's products—from its algorithmic search to YouTube to Gmail to its myriad of advertising products and services.

So is Google now a "social company"? I asked Gundotra.

"Yes," Google's VP of Social replied about the Google + community, which, in the 100 days after its beta launch in June 2011, had grown to 40 million members.[110] and which is predicted to include 200 million members by the end of 2012.[111]

As a social company, it's hardly surprising, therefore, that Google followed up the launch its Google + network with the January 2012 introduction of "Search, plus Your World" (SPYW)—a Web 3.0 product that Steven Levy, the author of *In The Plex* and the world's leading authority on Google, describes as a "startling transformation" of the company's search engine.[112] With SPYW, the content on the Google + social network replaces the company's artificial algorithm as the brain of its search engine; with SPYW, the old Google search engine, once the very heart and soul of the Web 2.0 world, becomes merely what Levy calls an "amplifier of social content."

In George Orwell's *Nineteen Eighty-four*, 2 + 2 was said to equal 5. But in today's social information age, when we are all publicly broadcasting our personal tastes, habits and locations on networks like Google +, what might +1 plus +1 equal?

+1 + +1 + +1 + +1 + +1 + +1 + +1 + 1

It will not quite compute into a googol—10,000,000,000,000,000,000, 000,000,000,000,000,000,000,000,000,000,000,000,000,000,000,000, 000,000,000,000,000,000,000,000,000,000,000 to be exact—but the +1 social economy has already spawned into thousands of new Web sites, billions of dollars of investment and revenue, and countless new apps incorporating all the personal data of the hundreds of millions of people on the social web.

This personal data, what Google's Bradley Horowitz euphemistically calls putting "people first," is the core ingredient, the revolutionary fuel, powering the Web 3.0 economy. But the Internet is radically changing too, its architecture reflecting the new social dial tone for the twenty-first century. Everything on the Web—from its infrastructure to its navigation to its entertainment to its commerce to its communications—is going social. John Doerr is right. Today's Web 3.0 revolution, this Internet of people, is indeed the third great wave of technological innovation, as profound as the invention of both the personal computer and the Worldwide Web itself.

The Internet's business infrastructure, its core architecture, is getting a major social overhaul—so that every technology platform and service is shifting from a Web 2.0 to the Web 3.0 model. Internet browsers, search engines and email services—the trinity of technologies that shape our daily Internet use—are becoming social. Everyone in Silicon Valley, it seems, is going into the business of eliminating loneliness. To compete with Google's SPYW, there are now Facebook-powered "liked results" from Microsoft's Bing search engine,[113] as well as the Greplin and Blekko search engines and a "people" search engine from PeekYou that has already indexed the records of over 250 million people. There are social Internet browsers from Rockmelt and Firefox, and social updating from Meebo's increasingly ubiquitous MiniBar messenger. There is social email from Gmail's People Widget, Microsoft Outlook's Social Connector and from start-ups like Xobni and Rapportive for old fogies like myself who are still relying on archaic email.[114]

It's not just email. All online communications—from video to audio to text messaging to microblogging—is going social. There are real-time social video platforms from Socialcam, Showyou, SocialEyes, Tout and from Airtime, a start-up founded by the real Sean Parker and Shawn Fanning, the co-founder of Napster, which is quite literally focused, according to Parker, on "eliminating loneliness."[115] There are social texting and messaging apps from the Skype acquisition GroupMe,[116] as well as from Facebook's Beluga, Yobongo, Kik and many other equally unpronounceable start-ups. There is social blogging on Tumblr, social "curation" from Pinterest, social "conversation" from Glow,[117] small group social networking on Path that has amassed almost a million users in under a year[118] and workplace social communications from Yammer and Chatter that each have around 100,000 companies using their platforms.[119] Then there is Rypple, a social tool for "internal employee management," which enables everybody in a company to rate everyone else, thereby transforming work into a kind of never-ending real-time show trial.[120]

Entertainment is going social, too. In December 2011, YouTube's homepage went social, emphasizing the Google + and Facebook networks in what the video leviathan called "the biggest redesign in its history."[121] There is social music and social sound from Pandora, the iTunes Ping network, Soundcloud and Soundtracking.[122] There are social reality television shows on *American Idol* and *The X-Factor*,[123] social information about what movies we are watching on GetGlue, social TV networks like Into.Now and Philo, which reveal to the world our viewing habits, and Facebook integration on Hulu which enables us to share our remarks with all our friends. Social TV means everyone will know what everyone else is viewing. "Miso now knows what you're watching, no check-in required," thus warns a headline in *The New York Times* about Miso, a social TV app that can already automatically recognize the viewing habits of DirecTV satellite subscribers.[124]

Most ominously of all, the online movie jugernaut Netflix—already estimated to be the origin of 30 percent of all Internet traffic[125]—is so committed to deeply integrating its service with Facebook that its CEO, Reed Hastings, gazing like Mark Zuckerberg onto the five-year horizon, acknowledged in June 2011 that he has a "five-year investment path" for making social central to his company's product development.[126]

The news industry, another core pillar of twentieth-century media, is trying to transform itself with social technology. There are, for example, socially produced news stories from the *New York Times'* News.me[127] and from Flipboard, the 2010 start-up behind the social magazine app for mobile devices that is already valued at $200 million and includes Kleiner-Perkins and Ashton Kutcher as investors and Oprah Winfrey's OWN cable network as a content distribution partner.[128]

Of all twentieth-century media, it is the once mostly private art of photography that is being most radically socialized by the Web 3.0 revolution. Hundreds of millions of dollars are being poured into social photography so that we can share all our intimate pictures with the world. There are social photos from the social self-portrait network Dailybooth, from the sensationally popular Instagram app, from the $15 million photo and gaming start-up ImageSocial,[129] and from Color, a "proximity based" photo sharing service "with no privacy settings" that raised $41 million in March 2011 before its product had even been launched.[130]

But it's our contemporary mania for revealing our location which is the most chilling aspect of the Web's new collective architecture. There are social geo-location services not only from foursquare, Loopt, Buzzd, Facebook Places and the Reid Hoffman investment Gowalla (which was acquired by Facebook in December 2011), but also from the MeMap app that enables us to track all the check-ins of our Internet friends on a single networked map[131] and from Sonar, which identifies other friends in our vicinity.[132] There is social mapping on Google Maps, social travel recommendations on Wanderfly, social seating on aircrafts from KLM and Malaysia Airlines's MHBuddy,[133] social travel information on TripIt, social driving on the Kleiner-funded Waze app[134] and on the social license plate network Bump.com[135] and, most bizarrely of all, social bicycling from the iPhone app Cyclometer, which enables our friends to track, hear and share exactly where we are and what we are doing on our bicycles.

Even time itself, both the past and the future, is becoming social. Proust, a social network designed to store our memories, is trying—presumably in an attempt to emulate the eponymous French novelist—to socialize the past.[136] There are "social discovery" engines like The Hotlist and Plancast that have aggregated information from over 100 million Web users that enables us to not only see where our friends have been and currently are located but also to predict where they will be in the future. There is even a social "intentionality" app from Ditto that enables you to share what you *will* and *should* do with everyone on your network,[137] while the WhereBerry social networking service enables us to tell our friends what movies we want to see and restaurants that we'd like to try.

But the social media revolution isn't just about obscurely named start-ups— many of which, in today's Darwinian struggle for digital domination, will inevitably fail. Take, for example, Microsoft, the former technology leader that is now trying to buy its way into the social economy. Microsoft's intended $8.5 billion acquisition of Skype, announced in May 2011—the company's largest acquisition in its history—is an attempt to socialize its Internet business. This acquisition seeks to leverage Skype's active 145 million users into a Microsoft centric social network that will maintain the company's relevance in the social media age.[138]

Like Microsoft, every presocial technology company is now trying to surf the Emerald wave. Indeed, there are now so many social business products from large enterprises like IBM (Connections Social Software), Monster. com (the Facebook app Beknown), and Salesforce (Yammer) that one analyst told the *Wall Street Journal* "it's hard to think of a company that isn't selling enterprise social software now."[139] And the corporate world is embracing Web 3.0 technology, too, with "enlightened companies" such as Gatorade, Farmer's Insurance, Domino's Pizza, and Ford investing massively in social media marketing campaigns. "If you want to reach a millennium," wrote one of Ford's social media evangelists in a justification of why they sent a tweeting car across America, "you have to go where they live, and that means on-line."[140]

Yes, the fictional Sean Parker from *The Social Network* got it right: First we lived in villages, then in cities and now we are increasingly living online. And the truth is that today it's hard to actually think of an Internet start-up whose products or services aren't embracing the web's new social architecture. This revolution in sharing our personal data extends to every imaginable nook and crevice of both the online and offline world. Even a partial list makes one's head spin. So the next few paragraph are best read sitting down.

Given that social media advertising's annual revenue is expected to grow from its 2011 total of $5.5 billion to $10 billion by 2013,[141] the online advertising business is now going social, with the meteoric growth of platforms like RadiumOne that serve up ads based on what our friends *like*[142] and SocialVibe, the branding marketing engine that is fuelling the Zynga network.[143] There are now hundreds of collaborative commerce start-ups with communitarian names like BuyWithMe and ShopSocially attempting to emulate Groupon and LivingSocial. For the socially conscious, there are social networks for social entrepreneurs at Like Minded and Craig Connect, social investment from CapLinked,[144] socially generated charity from Jumo and social fund-raising from Fundly. There are social networks for foodies like My Fav Food, Cheapism[145] and Grubwithus[146] and, as an antidote, social dieting apps[147] like Daily Burn, Gain Fitness, LoseIt, Social Workout and Fibit—a social gadget that broadcasts to the world its users' sex lives.[148]

There are social networks like Yatown,[149] Hey, Neighbor!, Nextdoor.com, and Zenergo[150] that have been designed to connect local neighbors and real world activities. There is the bizarre Google+ and Twitter clone Chime.in, which allows you to follow "part of a person.[151] There is social discovery from ShoutFlow, which describes itself as a "magical" app for finding "relevant" people nearby.[152] There is social education from OpenStudy that "wants to turn the world into one big study group."[153] There are social productivity tools from Manymoon and Asana,[154] professional social networking from Be-Known, social event networking from MingleBird, social media analytics from Social Bakers, social investing from AngelList, and social consumer information on SocialSmack and something called a "marketplace for social transactions" from Jig.[155] There is social local data from Hyperpublic, social cardio training from Endomondo[156] and a growing infestation of social networks for children like Club Penguin, giantHello and the creepily named Togetherville—a kids' network that Disney acquired in February 2011.[157] Perhaps most eerily of all, there is even a so-called social "serendipity engine" from Shaker—a well backed and much hyped Israeli start-up that won Techcrunch's 2011 Disrupt championship—which turns Facebook into a virtual bar for meeting strangers.[158]

Phew! And if this vertiginous wave of social networks isn't enough, then there is social reading—offering a giant collective hello to book lovers everywhere. Yes, reading, that most intensely private and illicit of all modern individual experiences, is being transformed into a disturbingly social spectacle. Some of you may even be reading this book socially—meaning that instead of sitting alone with this book, you'll be *sharing* your hitherto intimate reading experience in real time with thousands of your closest Facebook or Twitter friends via your e-readers through social services like Amazon's Kindle profiles.[159] Indeed, in January 2011 Scribd, a social reading company with a mission to "liberate the written word, to connect people with the information and ideas that matter most to them,"[160] raised $13 million in order to add more "social features" to every mobile networked device.[161] Meanwhile, Rethink Books, a collaborative reading company, launched the Bible as a socialized product, perhaps with the intention of creating a "direct social channel" between the book's "Author" and its readers.[162]

Maybe Rethink Books should acquire the social cardio training network Endomondo and rename itself. You see, social reading really does, in a sense, represent *the end of the world*. It means the end of the isolated reader, the end of solitary thought, the end of purely individual literary reflection, the end of those long afternoons spent entirely alone with just a book.

Nervous about the coming social dictatorship? Need a cigarette break with fellow smokers? Don't worry, there is even a social networking device for smokers, introduced by a company called Blu in June 2011, which sells electronically enhanced e-cigarettes ($80 for a five pack) that enable their owners to download their contact information onto personal computers and connect with other smokers.[163]

Endomondo, indeed.

SocialEyes Is Creepy

MingleBird, PeekYou, Hotlist, Rypple, Scribd, Sonar, Quora, Togetherville and the thousands of Web 3.0 companies are creating, social brick by social brick, a global networked electronic Inspection-House, a twenty-first-century home in which we can all watch each other all of the time. Take, for example, SocialEyes (pronounced *socialize*), the social video start-up founded by Rob Glaser, the former Microsoft executive and CEO of RealNetworks, and backed by a number of blue chip West Coast venture capital firms. Launched in beta form in March 2011, SocialEyes unintentionally captures the matrix for our age of great exhibitionism, making it a metaphorical picture of our collective future.

"It looks like there is a wall of video cubes, like the set of *Hollywood Squares*," Glaser explained the SocialEyes interface. "You can see yourself in one of these squares and then start initiating phone calls to anyone in your network."[164] This is the true picture of the social web. When we socialize on SocialEyes, the world becomes a gigantically transparent set of *Hollywood Squares* and we all become cubes inside its wall.

You'll remember that @quixotic once said that his goal was to provide society with a lens to who are we and who should we be, as individuals and as members of society. And that, I'm afraid, is all too literally what new networks like SocialEyes are doing. The emergence of this socialized economy, with its powerful lens directed upon society and its tens of billions of dollars of investment appears now, for better or worse, unstoppable.

So what, exactly, are we telling the world when we use networks like Rob Glaser's SocialEyes, the "social serendipity engine" Shaker or Sean Parker's Airtime—the social network, you'll remember, designed, in Parker's words, to "eliminate loneliness."

"Snoop on me" we are saying. *Snoop on me* we are all saying, each time we use SocialEyes, Airtime, Shaker, foursquare, Into.now or the hundreds of other Orwellian services and platforms that reveal what we are doing and thinking to the world. And *snooping on me* has, indeed, become so central to the Internet's architecture that there is even a Web site called SnoopOn.me which, quite literally, enables our online followers to watch everything we do on our personal computers. Equally chilling is an app called Breakup Notifier which tracks people's relationship status on Facebook and then alerts everyone when our love life changes and we become divorced or single. When launched in early 2011, Breakup Notifier attracted 100,000 users in a few hours before, thankfully, being blocked by Facebook.[165]

But even creepier than Breakup Notifier or SnoopOn.me is Creepy, an app that enables us to track the exact location of our Twitter or Facebook friends on a map.[166] With Creepy, we all know where everybody else is all the time.

The simple architecture of the digital Inspection-House is now all around us. Has *Nineteen Eighty-four* finally arrived on all of our screens?

2

LET'S GET NAKED

@ericgrant A friend is waiting for a friend while she gets an abortion and he's texting me about it. Why does that make me uncomfortable?![1]

Ownlife

Yes, it all seems so chillingly *Orwellian*. George Orwell would have probably agreed with @quixotic that the future is always sooner and stranger than we think. Within 1948. Orwell imagined a future in which SnoopOn.me and the Creepy app had become the law. "In principle a Party member had no spare time, and was never alone except in bed," Orwell wrote in *Nineteen-Eighty-four*. "It was assumed that when he was not working, eating, or sleeping he would be taking part in some kind of communal recreation: to do anything that suggested a taste for solitude, even to go for a walk by yourself, was always slightly dangerous. There was a neologism for it in Newspeak: *Ownlife*, it was called, meaning individualism and eccentricity."[2]

And there was another neologism in Newspeak: "facecrime," Orwell coined it. "It was terribly dangerous to let your thoughts wander when you were in any public place or within range of a telescreen," he wrote. "The smallest thing could give you away. A nervous tic, an unconscious look of anxiety, a habit of muttering to yourself—anything that carried with it the suggestion of abnormality, of having something to hide. In any case, to wear an improper expression on your face (to look incredulous when a victory was announced, for example) was itself a punishable offence. There was even a word for it in Newspeak: facecrime, it was called."

Yes, as Christopher Hitchens reminds us, Orwell still "matters."[3] On January 22, 1984, to celebrate the introduction of the Apple Macintosh, the world's first real personal computer, Ridley Scott's iconic Super Bowl XVIII commercial told us "why 1984 won't be 1984."[4] But that may have been because "1984" got delayed a quarter of a century. Unfortunately, today, in the midst of the contemporary social media revolution, *Ownlife* is once again in trouble. But Newspeak's "facecrime" has been turned on its head in our world of endless tweets, check-ins and status updates. In *Nineteen Eighty-four*, it was a crime to express yourself; today, it is becoming unfashionable, perhaps even socially unacceptable not to express oneself on the network.

Instead of Big Brother, what exists in today's age of great exhibitionism is what the American novelist Walter Kirn calls, a "vast cohort of prankish Little Brothers equipped with devices that Orwell, writing 60 years ago, never dreamed of and who are loyal to no organized authority."[5] Kirn's "Little Brothers" are all of us, the people—the *peeps,* in both form and function— whose smartphones, tablets and billions of other so-called "post-PC" devices put as much surveillance technology in each of our hands as Orwell gave Big Brother's entire regime in *Nineteen Eighty-four.*

We—you and I—are the loci of twenty-first-century power. Our personal expressions and feelings are, in the words of British filmmaker Adam Curtis, the "driving belief of our time." Personalized social networks are thus, according to Curtis, the "natural center of the world" and tweets and Facebook updates "reinforce the feeling that this is the natural way to be."[6]

Early twenty-first-century networks like SocialEyes, Shaker and Airtime reverse Big Brother's telescreen, so that everyone becomes a cube in the wall both watching and being watched by every other cube. "The invasion of privacy—of others' privacy but also our own, as we turn our lenses on ourselves in the quest for attention by any means—has been democratized,"

Walter Kirn argues.[7] He is right. In the industrial age, the ideal of privacy was taken for granted as the dominant cultural norm, but today, as we-the-peeps turn the telescreen on ourselves so that everyone can watch us, it is Jeff Jarvis's cacophonic ideal of publicness that's becoming the default mode of existence.

"Privacy is taking a back seat to the notion that our every thought, act or desire should be publicized," confirms University of Southern California's social media research scientist Dr. Julie Albright. "Our social lives are becoming more transparent and public, and a lot of people don't really consider the fact that once it's out there, it's out there." [8]

The Age of Networked Intelligence

Yet for the wired intelligentsia seeking to "reboot" the human condition, this increasingly transparent network—@quixotic's Web 3.0 and John Doerr's third wave of technological innovation, represents an unambiguously positive development in the evolution of mankind. As one digital engineer of the human soul, social media evangelist Umair Haque, argued in the *Harvard Business Review*, the "promise of the Internet . . . was to fundamentally rewire people, communities, civil society, business and the state—through thicker, stronger, more meaningful relationships. That's where the future of media lies."[9]

But even the clownlike Haque, who describes himself to his over 100,000 Twitter follows as an "advisor to revolutionaries"[10] and was ranked by the *London Independent* newspaper the fifth most influential member of the United Kingdom's Twitter "elite" (sandwiched, appropriately enough, between the two comedians Russell Brand and Stephen Fry),[11] doesn't quite grasp the epochal significance of today's revolution of invasive social networks like Plancast, Airtime, Hitlist, SocialEyes and foursquare. Rather than just the future of media, the twenty-first-century electronic network might actually represent the post-industrial future of everything.

As best-selling digital evangelists Don Tapscott[12] and Anthony D. Williams argue in their 2010 book *MacroWikinomics*,[13] today's Internet represents "a turning point in history." We are entering what they call "the age of networked intelligence," a "titanic" historic shift, they pronounce, equivalent to the "birth of the modern nation-state" or the Renaissance.[14] Mark Pincus's always-on social dial tone, Tapscott and Williams argue, represents a "platform for the networking human minds" that will enable us "to collaborate and to learn collectively." Echoing Mark Zuckerberg's five-year vision of social media's revolutionary impact on the broader economy, Tapscott and Williams predict that politics, education, energy, banking, healthcare and corporate life will all be transformed by what these social utopians embrace as the "openness" and "sharing" of the networked intelligence age.

Silicon Valley's king of connections, Reid Hoffman, shares Tapscott and William's faith in this new social economy. At our Oxford breakfast, he insisted that network transparency rewarded integrity. When everything is discoverable, the former Marshall Scholar in moral philosophy explained to me, a trust economy will emerge in which our reputations will be determined by what others think of us. Networks like his own LinkedIn, @quixotic predicts, will help create a truer meritocracy by exposing disreputable individuals and by rewarding those with proven integrity. Rather than becoming the "global village" predicted by the twentieth-century communications guru Marshall McLuhan, then, the world will shrink into a version of a premodern village a universal digital dorm room in which everyone will know everything about our slightest, most hidden or, I'm afraid, our most imaginary actions.

This universal dorm room already exists. On today's Internet, anonymity—for better or worse—is dead. "These Days the Web Unmasks Everyone," screamed a June 2011 headline in *The New York Times*. "The collective intelligence of the Internet's 2 billion users, and the digital fingerprints that so many users leave on Web sites, combine to make it more and more likely that every embarrassing video, every intimate photo, and every indelicate e-mail is attributed to its source, whether that source wants it to be or not. This intelligence makes the public sphere more public than ever before and sometimes forces personal lives into public view," explains *The Times* social media guru Brian Stelter.[15]

At the heart of this increasingly transparent and networked world will be what the social ideologists call "reputation banks." "Now with the web we leave a reputation trail," Rachel Botsford and Roo Rogers recognize in their collaborative consumption manifesto *What's Mine Is Yours: How Collaborative Consumption Is Changing the Way We Live.* "With every seller we rate; spammer we flag; comment we leave; idea, comment, video or photo we post; peer we review, we leave a cumulative record of how well we collaborate and if we can be trusted."[16]

But Botsford, Rogers, Tapscott, Williams and the rest of the social media quixotics are wrong that the Internet is resulting in a new age of "networked intelligence." In fact, the reverse may well be true. From Zuckerberg's Facebook, Hoffman's LinkedIn and Stone's Twitter to SocialEyes, SocialCam, foursquare, ImageSocial, Instagram, Living Social and the myriad of other digital drivers of John Doerr's third great wave, the network is creating more social conformity and herd behavior. "Men aren't sheep," argued John Stuart Mill, the nineteenth century's greatest critic of Benthamite utilitarianism, in his 1859 defense of individual freedom *On Liberty.*[17] Yet on the social network, we seem to be thinking and behaving more and more like sheep, making what cultural critic Neil Strauss describes as "the need to belong,"[18] rather than genuine nonconformity, the rule.

"While the Web has enabled new forms of collective action, it has also enabled new kinds of collective stupidity," argues Jonas Lehrer, a contributing editor to *Wired* magazine and a best-selling writer on both neuroscience and psychology. "Groupthink is now more more widespread, as we cope with the excess of available information by outsourcing our beliefs to celebrities, pundits and Facebook friends. Instead of thinking for ourselves, we simply cite what's already been cited."[19]

The degeneration of "the smart group" into what Lehrer calls "the dumb herd" can be increasingly seen in Web 3.0 networks. Take, for example, the Silicon Valley network, AngelList, designed to build what it calls "social proof" for technology entrepreneurs and angel investors. Yet, as Bryce Roberts, the co-founder of O'Reilly AlphaTech Ventures argues, in a controversial explanation of why he deleted his AngelList account,[20] " 'social proof' is turning into a form of peer pressure where angels feel compelled to invest for fear of missing the boat everyone else is getting on." Roberts isn't alone in his skepticism about the value of social proof. Another AngelList sceptic, GRP Partners venture capitalist Mark Suster agreed, adding "my biggest fear is that people confuse the 'social proof' of other prominent investors on AngelList for real insight."[21]

But Jonas Lehrer reminds us that *real insight* means "thinking for oneself"—something that, in spite of the messianic promise that we are on the verge of an age of networked intelligence, is increasingly in short supply on today's social Web.

Yes, in a social media world dominated by Lehrer's Groupthink, "thinking for oneself" is increasingly scarce. "The crowd was at the heart of some of the most memorable events of 2011, demonstrating the power of the group driven by common identity and capacity for decision-making," thus noted the *Financial Times* about a year defined by the collective actions of the Arab Spring, the London riots and the Occupy Wall Street movement. "They are classic examples of the herd mentality—the shared and self-regulated thinking of individuals in a group."[22]

Or as David Carr (@carr2n), *The New York Times* media critic, tweeted (thereby truly uniting the collective medium with its message): "Twitter = a convention of charming exhibitionists w/a lot on their minds. Mass externalization of thought creates hive mind."

Let's Get Naked

At the March 2011 South By Southwest conference, in a speech entitled "Let's Get Naked: Benefits of Publicness versus Privacy," Jeff Jarvis argued that the social media revolution is returning us to a preindustrial "oral culture" in which we will all share more and more information about our real selves. This "publicness," for Jarvis, will result in a more tolerant society because everything will be known about everyone and thus traditional social taboos, such as homosexuality, will supposedly be undermined. Jarvis argues that by openly revealing their sexual preferences in the social media age, the homosexual is saying "too bad, I'm public just like you."[23] Thus, in a blog post published just before his speech, Jarvis wrote that "the best solution is to be yourself." Our reputations, he said, depend on us sharing more and more of our identity with the world. "An act of transparency," Jarvis quoted Harvard University Berkman Center philosopher David Weinberger, "must be an act of forgiveness."[24]

Borrowing liberally from the communitarian theories of German social thinker Jurgen Habermas, Jeff Jarvis argues that social media offers us the opportunity to rebuild the so-called "public sphere" of the eighteenth-century coffee house. But rather than plowing through the dense Habermas, a more instructive author to read on the so-called "public" sphere of preindustrial life is the nineteenth-century American writer Nathaniel Hawthorne whose chilling novel about life in Puritan New England, *The Scarlet Letter,* deals with the prudery of small-town society in which individuals who just want to be themselves have little, if any privacy from the gaze of the intolerant collective.

One doesn't need to go back to seventeenth-century Boston to excavate the Scarlet Letter. Today, it can be found on the Internet, on social forums like Topix, where the lynch mob has publicly demonized individuals who have yet to be proven guilty of any crime. *The New York Times* notes that rural America's use of social media is often characterized by "hubs of unsubstantiated gossip, stirring widespread resentment in communities where ties run deep, memories run long and anonymity is something of a novel concept."[25] In the small town of Mountain Grove, Missouri, for example, one mother of two was accused on Topix of being a "freak" and "a methed-out, doped out whore with AIDS."[26] And the problem with rural America and the Internet is both have very long memories. "In a small town," one Mountain Grove victim of online gossip explains, "rumors stay forever."[27]

Or take, for example, what *Time* magazine calls "the social media trial of the century"—the trial in Orlando, Florida, of young mother Casey Anthony, accused of murdering her two-year-old daughter Caylee. *Time* describes the legal case as being "astonishingly weak," but that didn't stop the online mob transforming social media into "arenas for mass, lip-licking bloodlust" dominated by Facebook comments like: "think im gonna puke in my mouth over them trying to get an acquittal shes GAULITY GAULITY GAULITY!!! Justice for Cayce."[28]

Tragically, the ideal of the universal dorm room and Jarvis's advice to "get naked" are more than just silly metaphors about life on the digital network. In the Web 3.0 world, transparency doesn't always reward integrity. The truth is that social media's open architecture often encourages those completely lacking in integrity to wreck the reputations of innocent people. Indeed, in our hypervisible age, all it takes is a camcorder and a Skype account to actually destroy somebody's life.

On September 19, 2010, a Rutgers student called Dharan Ravi tweeted about his eighteen-year-old dorm roommate Tyler Clementi: "Roommate asked for the room till midnight. I went into Molly's room and turned on my webcam. I saw him making out with a dude. Yay." A few days later, after Ravi had Skyped a live video feed of Clementi "making out with a dude," the young man posted on his Facebook page: "Jumping off the gw bridge sorry."

The body of the accomplished violinist, a victim of what Walter Kirn calls "Little Brother in the form of a prying roommate with a camera,"[29] was found in the Hudson River underneath the George Washington Bridge by police on September 29.

Therein lies Umair Haque's "thicker, stronger, more meaningful relationships" of our hypervisible age. Social utopians like Haque, Tapscott and Jarvis are, of course, wrong. The age of networked intelligence isn't very intelligent. The tragic truth is that getting naked, *being yourself* in the full public gaze of today's digital network, doesn't always result in the breaking down of ancient taboos. There is little evidence that networks like Facebook, Skype and Twitter are making us any more forgiving or tolerant. Indeed, if anything, these viral tools of mass exposure seem to be making society not only more prurient and voyeuristic, but also fuelling a mob culture of intolerance, schadenfreude and revengefulness.

Inevitably, much of this prurience focuses on the physical act of getting naked. One hypervisible American politican, Anthony Weiner, the Democratic congressman from New York, published pornographic photos of himself on Twitter and engaged in erotic conversations with women he met on Facebook and Twitter (some of whom were fake identities created by his Republican enemies),[30] a story that even the normally circumspect *New York Times* greeted with the headline "Naked Hubris."[31] Another, New York Republican congressman Christopher Lee, sent suggestive photographs of himself to a woman he met on Craigslist. After these photographs were published on the Internet, the social media hysteria over this inappropriate but not illegal behavior resulted in the destruction of both politicians' reputations and a collective stench of vindictive self-congratulation. Then there is the case of Ryan Giggs, a prominent Welsh soccer player, who supposedly had an extramarital affair with *Big Brother* reality television star Imogen Thomas. In spite of a British High Court super injunction against broadcasting this information, 75,000 people tweeted Gigg's identity—an electronic mob clearly intent on humiliating a gifted sportsman who had done none of them any personal harm nor broken any law.

The problem is more cultural than technological. As National Public Radio's executive editor Dick Meyer argues in his perceptive 2008 book *Why We Hate Us*, we live in "an age of self-loathing" in which "everyone is part of a counterculture."[32] Today's zeitgeist is a corrosive hostility toward all forms of authority—from politicians like Christopher Lee and Anthony Weiner to sporting superstars like Ryan Giggs and Lebron James[33] to reality television icons like Imogen Thomas. Thus, the supposedly tolerant social networks of Jeff Jarvis's dream are, in fact, fuelling the corrosive belligerence that has infected much of the snarky, gotcha public discourse in contemporary society.

This belligerent cynicism is not only ugly, but can also be self-destructive. In a WikiLeaks culture where we all now have Twitter and Facebook accounts, many of us are tempted to become mini Julian Assanges and publicly inform on our bosses, our companies and sometimes even our clients or our pupils. But the problem is that none of us actually are Assange, with the resources to skip international justice and avoid the consequences of our actions.

"Twitter is a danger zone," warns *Time* columnist James Poniewozik, "especially for its most adept users."[34] Thus, from a couple of Canadian car workers dismissed in August 2010 for writing critical comments on Facebook about the safety records of their dealerships[35] to the British teenagers sacked in February 2009 for describing her boss on Facebook as "boring"[36] to the New York City math schoolteacher who was fired in February 2010 for saying on Facebook that she hated her students' guts and wished they would drown,[37] to the voice of the Aflac duck fired for tweeting jokes about the 2011 Japanese tsunami,[38] to the British plumber on trial for tweeting about his wife's alleged extramarital affair,[39] to the eleven-year-old girl in southern England who posted sexually derogatory messages on a ten-year-old friend's Facebook account,[40] to the 11,000 menacing tweets posted about a Maryland Buddhist leader by a fellow Buddhist,[41] we are finding that Jeff Jarvis's call to "get naked" and broadcast our honest opinions on the network results not in forgiveness or more personal integrity, but instead in unemployment, criminal charges and public humiliation.

In 1940, eight years before he wrote *Nineteen Eighty-four,* George Orwell wrote an essay entitled "Inside the Whale" in which, noting that "the ordinary man" is "passive," he argued that professional writers should be actively engaged in the social issues of their day. "The whale's belly is simply a womb big enough for an adult," Orwell wrote. "There you are, in the dark, cushioned space that exactly fits you, with yards of blubber between yourself and reality, able to keep up an attitude of the completest indifference, no matter *what* happens."[42]

But just as a networked mob of twenty-first-century small brothers have replaced Orwell's solitary twentieth-century Big Brother, so the passivity of being inside the whale has been replaced in our social media age by the crude mindlessness of much so-called public discourse. Orwell was right, in 1940, to critique people who retreat inside the whale; but if he was around today, with 75,000 people on Twitter illegally broadcasting the intimate details of a stranger's sex life and the tens of thousands of people baying for the blood of a young woman who hasn't been proven guilty of any crime, one wonders if Orwell would have been so critical of those "yards of blubber," that "dark, cushioned space" that separates us from what he called "reality."

Zuckerberg's Law

In January 2011, four months after Tyler Clementi jumped off the George Washington Bridge, a couple of Silicon Valley entrepreneurs released a geolocation app called WhereTheLadies.at which enables men to aggregate foursquare data to track local bars or clubs popular with women. And a couple of months after that, some other entrepreneurs started up Whoworks. at, an app that—deploying LinkedIn data—reveals where we work.

Yet, instead of WhereTheLadies.at or Whoworks.at, what really lies on the five-year horizon is *WhereI'm.at*. That's the Orwellian future of the Internet. *WhereI'm.at*—however chilling for those of us who still cherish our illegibility—is being embraced in Silicon Valley where *Ownlife* has already been dumped into the dustbin of history. @quixotic is far from alone in declaring privacy to be dead. "The progression toward a more public society is apparent and inevitable," predicts the gleefully deterministic Jeff Jarvis about our hypervisible age.[43] And technology titans like Google executive chairman Eric Schmidt, Oracle CEO Larry Ellison, ex–Sun Microsystems CEO Scott McNealy, Techcrunch founder Mike Arrington and social media uber-evangelist Robert Scoble all concur, declaring privacy to be little more than a corpse. While Sean Parker, Facebook's first president whose new company, you'll remember, is planning to eliminate loneliness, says simply that privacy "isn't an issue."[44] In the twenty-first century, they agree, all information will be shared. Individual privacy is a relic, they say. It has a past, but no future.

For many of these supposed visionaries, the death of privacy is no different, in principle, from the retirement of the horse and cart or the disappearance of gaslights from city streets. "Today's creepy is tomorrow's necessity," Sean Parker thus argues. The disappearance of privacy is a casualty of progress, Parker and his fellow entrepreneurs promise us, just another consequence of technological change. Yet these entrepreneurs and futurists are blinkered by their ability to only look forward, onto that five-, ten-, or fifty-year horizon. They have no interest or knowledge in the history of privacy, in the intimate connection between individual liberty and individual autonomy, in the consequences on *Ownlife* of today's universal digital dormroom.

"Expressing our authentic identity will become even more pervasive in the coming year," thus projects Facebook's Chief Operating Officer, Sheryl Sandberg, about the continued demise of individual privacy in 2012—a development from which, of course she and her company will radically profit.

"Profiles will no longer be outlines, but detailed self-portraits of who we really are, including the books we read, the music we listen to, the distances we run, the places we travel, the causes we support, the video of cats we laugh at, our likes and our links. And yes, this shift to authenticity will take getting used to and will elicit cries of lost privacy."[45]

This banal unsentimentality about privacy's corpse is encapsulated by Scott McNealy who, as early as 1999, said, "you have zero privacy anyway—get over it." Eric Schmidt, the ex–Google CEO who confessed to "screwing up" the company's social networking strategy,[46] even had the audacity to say, in response to a question about his company's right to retain our personal data, that anyone concerned with online privacy had "something to hide." "If you don't want anyone to know," the willfully empirical Schmidt said, with classic Benthamite ignorance about the complexity of the human condition, "don't do it."[47] In August 2010 the former Google CEO even told the *Wall Street Journal* that the young people of the future should be "entitled to automatically be able to change his or her name on reaching adulthood" because of all the incriminating online information about them.[48]

Most ominously of all, the social media revolution's chief-rewiring-officer, Facebook co-founder and CEO Mark Zuckerberg—whose company is developing the utilitarian Gross Happiness Index to quantify global sentiment[49]—has not only declared the age of privacy to be over[50] but has also invented his own historical law to explain this dramatic change in social life. "I would expect that next year, people will share twice as much information as they share this year, and next year, they will be sharing twice as much as they did the year before," thus, he mapped out his own eponymous law.[51]

"Zuckerberg's Law" is one which its young author wants, in every sense, to own. At the Facebook f8 Conference in April 2010, he laid out his vision of transforming the Web into a series of "instantly social experiences" tied together by the company's Open-Graph and Social Plugins technology.

Zuckerberg told the conference that "we are building a web where the default is social."[52]

A year later, at the September 2011 f8 conference, Mark Zuckerberg gave his eponymous law what Liz Gannes, AllThingsD's social media expert, described as "a big push."[53] Adding something called "Frictionless Sharing" to his Open Graph integration, Zuckerberg is, in the ominous words of serial Silicon Valley entrepreneur Ben Elowitz, "boldly annexing the web" by establishing a "social operating system" which will turn Facebook into "the hub for every user's action—watching a video, reviewing a recipe, reading an article, and much more."[54]

Facebook's new social operating system, introduced at the 2011 f8, is designed, according to the scrupulously impartial journalism site Poynter, to turn "sharing into a thoughtless process in which everything we read, watch or listen to is shared with our friends automatically."[55] Zuckerberg's goal with Frictionless Sharing on the Open Graph is to encourage its hundreds of millions of members to automatically share what they are reading on the *London Guardian* and *Wall Street Journal*, what they are listening to on Spotify and Rhapsody, what they are watching on YouTube and Hulu, and where exactly they happen to be driving, flying, eating, or sleeping.

"If you read articles in *The New York Times*, for instance, Facebook will begin to know your interests, your views, your reading habits, your diversity of views, your passions and pursuits, as well as the friends you are sharing the material with. It will know what you encounter—and also what you want to encounter," warns Ben Elowitz. "This is a massive change from the status quo."[56]

No wonder that the headline in the *Financial Times* about the Open Graph advises us to "take care how you share"[57] or that the parallel headline on AllThingsD warns us to "prepare for the oversharing explosion."[58] No wonder, either, that Poynter worries about the "chilling effect" of this oversharing on "online privacy"[59] or that Ben Werd, CTO of the video streaming start-up Latakoo describes it as "undeniably creepy, to a level we've been hitherto unprepared for in human society."[60]

Equally creepy, is Facebook's introduction in December 2011 of "Timeline," a feature that, according the *New York Times*'s Jenna Wortham, "makes a user's entire history of photos, links and other things on Facebook accessible with a single click." As Wortham notes, Timeline will "make it harder to shed past identities," to reinvent oneself and thus to forget the past. "All the mouse droppings that appear as we migrate around the Web will be saved," warns Harvard law professor Jonathan Zittrain about a product that grants Mark Zuckerberg possession of our most precious thing— the story of our lives.[61] Perhaps it's no wonder then that in 2011 *Forbes* magazine ranked Zuckerberg, the owner of all our life histories, the ninth most powerful person in the world, more powerful than either the British Prime Minister, the Presidents of Brazil, France and India or the Pope.[62]

Facebook's Open Graph integration and Timeline feature what is known, in Silicon Valley, as a "platform play." By sticking Facebook Connect plug-ins and buttons on every Web site and mobile app, by automating the broadcast of our online media consumption through frictionless sharing, and by accessing our lives with a single click, Facebook is trying to own the social web. And owning this social web means owning all of us, too. "By knowing us intimately—who we are, what we do, and what our interests are—Facebook is in the position to answer our every desire," explains Ben Elowitz about this new social operating system.[63] And that's why Mark Zuckerberg's private company was valued by Goldman Sachs in January 2011 at over $50 billion,[64] which is more than the annual GDP of 80 percent of African countries[65]—a price the financial writer William D. Cohan described as "vertigo-inducing,"[66] yet one that authoritative business journalists in both *The Financial Times* and *The Wall Street Journal* believe could turn out to be a "bargain" because of the increasingly ubiquity of social media.[67] These Facebook bulls may well be right. By late March 2011, Facebook's value had surged to $85 billion[68] with some even predicting that the Mark Zuckerberg production will eventually top $100 billion after its 2012 IPO.

As Facebook historian David Kirkpatrick argues, "Facebook is founded on a radical social premise—that an inevitable enveloping transparency will overtake modern life."[69] In this zeal for radical transparency, Zuckerberg, Sandberg, and the other Silicon Valley social media moguls and evangelists are today's utilitarian social reformers. Like Jeremy Bentham, these enlightened pied pipers of great exhibitionism promise that by separating us as individual nodes on the collective network, digital technology can bring us together for the benefit both of society and of the individual. Like Bentham's Inspection-House, this is presented as a virtuous circle—a magical staircase elevating us up to a future world in which individual freedom and social harmony are both abundant. More individual transparency on the network through technologies like Open Graph and Timeline, social media ideologues promise, leads to a "healthier society";[70] more truth leads to more togetherness, they say; and more togetherness, their logic spirals, leads to a better society.

But like Bentham's creepy greatest happiness principle, which reduces human beings to simple abacuses of pleasure and pain, Zuckerberg's creepy conception of individual identity fails to grasp the complexity of the human condition. Rather than the mysterious thing at the heart of every human being, identity for the young multi billionaire is as quantifiable as a line of computer code. Like Bentham, Zuckerberg is a "cost-benefit expert on a grand-scale"[71] who views human identity in the strictly empirical terms of a perpetual child.

"You have one identity. Having two identities for yourself is an example of a lack of integrity," was thus how Zuckerberg—who, of course, wants to own and profit from that single identity—calculated in 2009.[72] But Zuckerberg's utilitarian notion of identity, like Sheryl Sandberg's idea of "authentic identity" squeezes all the ambiguity and subtlety—the unquantifiable humanness—out of the human condition.

Take, for example, MingleBird, the event networking start-up launched in February 2011,[73] that is designed to make conference networking less awkward. MingleBird provides something called "MingleWords" that automatically provides users with the language to meet strangers at events. On MingleBird life is turned into a childish game, a quantifiably Huxleyan world in which social awkwardness—that most human of qualities—is replaced with a networking tool that not only automatically introduces people to strangers but also awards them points if they then have their photos taken together.

Worse still, today's digital network is commodifying friendship so that it becomes, quite literally, the currency of the new social economy. Online services like Klout, PeerIndex, Kred, and Hashable value us by quantifying our social influence.[74] Kleiner's first sFund investment Cafebot, Flavor.me and the AOL-acquired About.me[75] provide online platforms for super nodes to manage their assets. There is even a "social media exchange" called Empire Avenue that has established a stock market in the buying and selling of individual reputations.

Wealth equals connectivity in the Web 3.0 world. The more "friends" you have on Twitter or Facebook, therefore, the more potentially valuable you become in terms of getting your friends to buy or do things. We "manage" our friends in the social networking world in the same way as we "manage" our assets in the financial marketplace. "There is something Orwellian about the management speak on social networking sites," notes the ever perceptive Christine Rosen, who adds that such terminology encourages "the bureaucratization of friendship."[76]

Yes, George Orwell still matters. "Most people who bother with the matter at all would admit that the English language is in a bad way," Orwell worried about the political and economic corruption of language in his great 1946 essay "Politics and the English Language."[77] But even the author of Newspeak and the Ministry of Truth never imagined the new language of Facebook—a development *The Atlantic's* Ben Zimmer describes as "the rise of the Zuckerverb." At the 2011 f8 conference, the event you'll remember when Mark Zuckerberg introduced the doublethink of "frictionless sharing," he also launched a new language that included *verbs*. "When we started, the vocabulary was really limited. You could only express a small number of things, like who you were friends with. Then last year, when we introduced the Open Graph, we added nouns, so you could like anything that you wanted. This year we're adding verbs. We're going to make it so you can connect to anything in any way you want," Zuckerberg announced, without any self-evident irony, at f8.[78]

One wonders what new social language Zuckerberg will introduce at f8 2012 to improve our connectivity. The Zuckerconjunction, perhaps.

In his critique of Zuckerberg's choice of words, *The Atlantic's* Ben Zimmer notes that "language is being recast in a more profound way, turned into a utilitarian tool for "expressing" relationships to objects in the world in a remarkably unexpressive fashion."[79] And this Orwellian corruption of language is, of course, a reflection of a deeper and more troubling political and economic malaise. As Jeremiah Owyang, a social media analyst at the Altimeter Group notes the problem with the Zuckerverb and with utilitarian networks like Klout and Kred is that they "lack sentimental analysis."[80] In this economy friendship is transformed from a private pleasure without monetary value into a profit center. Take, for example, eEvent, a start-up social platform that financially rewards people who encourage their friends to attend an event.[81] But do any of us really want "friends" who profit financially if we attend an event, buy an airline ticket or eat at a restaurant?

As the twentieth-century American philosopher John Dewey recognized, our personalities are neither as rationally self-interested, quantifiable or fixed as Zuckerberg or the other evangelists of social media believe. Rather than "something complete, perfect, finished, an organized whole of parts united by the impress of a comprehensive form," our individual identity, Dewey argued, is actually "something moving, changing, discrete, and above all initiating instead of final."[82] And this may be why Dewey believed that "of all affairs, communication is the most wonderful."[83]

And this also explains why, as *Wall Street Journal* columnist and former Reagan speechwriter Peggy Noonan reminds us, America is a place of "second chances" in which the essence of our liberty is rooted in our right to shed a previous identity and reinvent ourselves as different individuals. "Gamblers, bounders, ne'er-do-wells, third sons in primogeniture cultures—most of us came here to escape something!" Noonan says about the cultural complexity of the American experience. "Our people came here not only for a new chance but to disappear, hide out, tend their wounds, and summon the energy, in turn, to impress the dopes back home."[84]

Indeed, if we are to believe Aaron Sorkin's screenplay of *The Social Network*, even Mark Zuckerberg himself is an example of a young American who went west—fleeing from Cambridge, Massachusetts to Palo Alto, California—to escape a broken relationship with his original Facebook cofounder and begin all over again. Yet, for Zuckerberg, it seems, there is nothing problematic about the unforgiving nature of individual transparency and network openness.

"To get people to this point where there's more openness—that's a big challenge," Zuckerberg thus confessed with the straight-faced understatement of a spokesman from the Ministry of Truth about his grand historical project to reengineer the human condition. "But I think we'll do it. I just think it will take time. The concept that the world will be better if you share more is something that's pretty foreign to a lot of people and it runs into all these privacy concerns."[85]

Privacy concerns, eh, Mark? Yes, I have one or two.

3

VISIBILITY IS A TRAP

Brock Anton: Maced in the face, hit with a Batton, tear gassed twice, 6 broken fingers,
blood everywhere, punched a fucken pig in head with riot gear on knocked him to the
ground, through the jersey on a burning cop car flipped some cars, burnt some smart
cars, burnt some cop cars, I'm on the news . . . . One word . . . History ☺☺☺

Ashley Pehota: brockkkk! Take this down!!! Its evidence![1]

Privacy Concerns

Let's start with three of my deepest concerns about individual privacy and
autonomy in the age of networked intelligence. Firstly, what exactly will be
the fate of privacy when you and I and everyone else are trapped, for better
or worse, in a radically transparent network of "frictionless sharing" that
has done away with secrecy and solitariness? Secondly, what happens in just
eight years' time, in 2020, when everything—from our intelligent cars to our
intelligent televisions to our intelligent telephones to our other 50 billion
networked devices—are connected? And thirdly, what are the *human* implications of this great rewiring, this cult of the social which, according
to Don Tapscott and Doug Williams, represents a grand historical *turning
point* equal to the Renaissance in the history of mankind?

We've already described Mark Zuckerberg's first five-year plan of transforming the world into a social experience. But there's a second five-year plan,
too, and it's even more chilling than the first. In ten years' time, according to
Zuckerberg, "a thousand times more information about each individual will
flow through Facebook." That's Zuckerberg's Law. And what it means, he

predicts, is that "people are going to have a device with them at all times that's [automatically] sharing" this cornucopia of personal information.[2]

What it means is that everyone—via transparent online networks like SocialEyes, Hotlist, Facebook's Open Graph and Timeline, SocialCam, Waze, TripIt, Plancast and Into.now—will know everything we are doing, watching, reading, buying, eating and, most ominously, thinking. What it means is that, in ten years' time, we'll have eliminated loneliness and the only place you'll be able to find privacy is in museums, where its corpse will, no doubt, be hung next to pictures of the human condition by old masters like Johannes Vermeer and Rembrandt Van Rijn.

But, like Jeremy Bentham, Mark Zuckerberg is wrong—radically wrong that this *shared* future makes us more human, wrong that this "automatic sharing" of information necessarily makes the world a *better* place, wrong that Zuckerberg's Law benefits either society or the self. Rather than a virtuous cycle, this social media revolution may well represent a descent—perhaps even a dizzying fall—into a vicious cycle of less and less individual freedom, weaker and weaker communal ties, and more and more unhappiness.

Rather than the next Renaissance, the age of networked intelligence could well represent a new Dark Ages, a nonfictional remix of the feudal world of John Balliol, with its radical economic and cultural inequalities, its myriad of fragmented worlds and its hierarchical networks of international elites. Instead of making us happier and more connected, social media's siren song—the incessant calls to digitally connect, the cultural obsession with transparency and openness, the never-ending demand to share everything about ourselves with everyone else—is, in fact, both a significant cause and effect of the increasingly vertiginous nature of twenty-first-century life.

The inconvenient truth is that social media, for all its communitarian promises, is dividing rather than bringing us together, creating what Walter Kirn describes as a "fragmentarian society."[3] In our digital age, we are, ironically, becoming more divided than united, more unequal than equal, more anxious than happy, lonelier rather than more socially connected. A November 2009 Pew Research report about "Social Isolation and New Technology,"[4] for example, found that members of networks like Facebook, Twitter, MySpace and LinkedIn are 26 percent less likely to spend time with their neighbors (thus, ironically, creating the need for social networks like Nextdoor.com and Yatown that connect local communities). A 2007 Brigham Young University research study, which analysed 184 social media users, concluded that the heaviest networkers "feel less socially involved with the community around them."[5] While a meta-analysis of seventy-two separate studies conducted between 1979 and 2009 by the University of Michigan's Institute for Social Research showed that contemporary American college students are 40 percent less empathetic than their counterparts in the 1980s and 1990s.[6] Even our tweets are becoming sadder, with a study made by scientists from the University of Vermont of 63 million Twitter users between 2009 and 2011 proving that "happiness is going downhill."[7]

Most troubling of all, a fifteen-year study of 300 social media subjects by Professor Sherry Turkle,[8] the director of MIT's Initiative on Technology and the Self, showed that perpetual networking activity is actually undermining many parents' relationship with their children.[9] "Technology proposes itself as the architect of our intimacies," Turkle says about the digital architecture in which we are now all living. But the truth, her decade and a half of research reveals, is quite the reverse. Technology, she finds, has become our "phantom limb,"[10] particularly for young people who, Turkle finds, are sending up to 6,000 social media announcements a day and who have never either written nor received a handwritten letter. No wonder, then, that teens have not only stopped using email, but also no longer use the telephone—both are too intimate, too private for a digital generation that uses texting as a "protection" for their "feelings."[11]

Turkle's conclusion on what she calls today's always online "post-familial family" is disturbing, particularly when imagined in terms of the Internet as architecture comprising many small theaters in which we are entirely alone. "Their members are alone-together each in their own rooms, each on a networked computer or mobile device," she concludes her depressing study of our Internet habits. "We go online because we are busy but end up spending more time with technology and less with each other."[12] Perhaps it's not surprising, therefore, that, according to one American law firm, 20 percent of new divorce cases reference inappropriate sexual conversations on Facebook as a factor in the marriage breakup.[13] Here, Turkle's notion of technology proposing itself as "the architect of our intimacies" is sadly prescient. The problem with flirting on Facebook is that Mark Zuckerberg's creation has been architected as a public dorm room rather than as a private bedroom. That's why so many extra-marital Facebook intimacies are ending up in the divorce court.

It's not just veteran academics like Sherry Turkle who worry about the solitariness of hypervisible life in the social media age. Jean Meyer, the twenty-eight-year-old founder of DateMySchool.com, an Internet matchmaking service for college students that prioritizes privacy over social transparency, concurs with Turkle about the failure of the wired generation to establish emotion connections with each other. "People in the 21st century are alone," Meyer told *The New York Times* in February 2011. "We have so many new ways of communicating, yet we are so alone."[14]

Not only is networking technology dividing us from others, but it is also splintering the self. "You have one identity," Mark Zuckerberg infamously said. But just as social is remaking every industry, so it is also splintering traditional notions of individual personality and thus breaching Zuckerberg's childish and self-serving notion of identity. In describing what she calls the "practice of the protean self,"[15] MIT's Turkle argues that "we have moved from multitasking to multi-lifing."[16] But while we are forever cultivating our collaborative self, she argues, what is being lost is our experience of being alone and privately reflecting on our emotions. The end result, Turkle explains, is a perpetual juvenile, somebody she calls a "tethered child,"[17] the type of person who, like one of Turkle's subjects in her study, believes that "if Facebook were deleted, I'd be deleted too."[18]

Dalton Conley, New York University's professor of Social Sciences, offers a similar critique to Turkle of today's networked protean self. He describes the people of our digital age as "intraviduals"—fragmented souls always caught *between* identities, possessing "multiple selves competing for attention within his/her own mind, just as externally, she or he is bombarded by multiple stimuli simultaneously."[19] Rather than the coherent and centered individual identity of analog man, therefore, the intradividual's plastic "self" reflects the perpetual flux of social media's myriad streams of information. As Guy Debord, a twentieth-century critic of electronic society, noted in his Situationalist manifesto *Society of the Spectacle,* the "society which eliminates geographical distance reproduces distance internally as spectacular separation."[20]

Turkle and Conley's sociological observations about the perpetually divided and ungrounded self are also supported by scientists like Oxford University neuroscientist Baroness Susan Greenfield. Greenfield—who debated Second Life founder Philip Rosedale at the "Silicon Valley Comes to Oxford" event about the reality of virtual reality—claims that social media networks like Facebook and the 140-character Twitter shorten our attention spans and fragment our brains with their incessant updates and continual need to reiterate our online existence.

"We know how small babies need constant reassurance that they exist," Professor Greenfield explains, perhaps also offering a scientific explanation for the thinking of Jeremy Bentham, that "boy to the last," behind his Auto-Icon. "My fear is that these technologies are infantilizing the brain into the state of small children who are attracted by buzzing noises and bright lights, who have a small attention span and who live for the moment."[21]

The Digital Aristocrazia

No, social media isn't very social. "The ties that we form through the Internet are not, in the end, the ties that bind," Sherry Turkle reminds us. And as best-selling author Malcolm Gladwell argues in a *New Yorker* critique of Clay Shirky's communitarian politics, "the platforms of social media are built around weak ties,"[22] thus turning us into perpetual joiners rather than the active participants that political theorists like Alexis de Tocqueville saw as the essential ingredients of a successful democracy. So social media networks connect people that mostly haven't and will never meet, thereby transforming these "communities" into libertarian aggregations of autonomous intravriduals in constant motion who reinvent their identities at will, and who join, unjoin then rejoin these groups with the click of a mouse.

We caught a glimpse of this dystopian future during the English riots of August 2011, where the utopian ideal of "networked intelligence" was transformed into a distributed, viral version of *A Clockwork Orange*. Utilizing Twitter, Facebook and the private BBM messaging system on RIM's Black-Berry network, individual rioters were able to use "social" media to keep one step ahead of the police, forming and reforming in real-time as they systematically destroyed neighborhoods and looted stores. Arguing that the use of social media in the riots was a "mirror" to society, Google chairman Eric Schmidt insists that we shouldn't "blame the internet" for this civic disorder.[23] In one sense, Schmidt is right and, like him, I strongly disagree with calls by English politicians for either Twitter and Facebook "blackouts"[24] during emergencies or for the "banning"[25] of suspected rioters from social media. But Schmidt misses the real meaning of the riots. Rather than a one-way mirror, the Internet is, as the fictional Sean Parker said, where we now live. So when we look at the Internet, we are gazing at something that reflects not only ourselves but also the dominant values of society. The highly individualized 2011 riots are, in many ways, therefore indistinguishable from social media—they are the mirror of a networked world in which we are living alone together. This is a world inhabited by Conley's "intradividuals" who collectively make up Walter Kirn's "fragmentarian society." It's a world that Joshua Cooper Ramo, a former editor at *Time*, dubs our "Age of the Unthinkable"—an epoch characterized by endless viral disorder and real-time social pandemics.[26]

The BlackBerry fuelled, nihilistic riots of 2011 are, however, only one reflection of our social media age. The other, politically more positive side are today's popular demonstrations against economic injustice such as Occupy Wall Street (OWS) driven, in part, by networks like Facebook and Twitter. As a mirror of the Internet, OWS is a loosely organized, hyper-democratic movement which encourages everyone to tell their own unique stories on networks like the protean WeArethe99Percent Tumblr blog. Thus, the 10,000 to 15,000 tweets an hour, the 900 OWS events set up on Meetup.com and the thousands of Facebook groups dedicated to the national protests[27] are all a reflection of our fragmentarian society in which we, as intravividuals with multiple selves, are using social media as our personalized and often narcissistic broadcast platforms. And so, as the politically progressive *Guardian* columnist Simon Jenkins notes, "with no leaders, no policies, no programme beyond opposition to status quo," the OWS protests are, like Facebook or Twitter themselves, just background noise, a never-ending conversation, "mere scenery."[28]

Of course, not all political protest organized via social media is purely scenic. I happened to be in Moscow in December 2011, on the weekend of the election that triggered the very real protests against Vladimir Putin's regime and, as I acknowledged in a CNN dispatch,[29] there is no doubt that Russian social media networks like LiveJournal and Vkontakte, as well as Twitter and Facebook, were critical in organizing these popular demonstrations. Indeed, from Moscow's Lubyanka Square to Wall Street's Zuccotti Park to Cairo's Tahrir Square, 2011 was the year that social media became an important organizational tool in challenging economic and political injustice. *Time* magazine even made "The Protestor" its 2011 Person of the Year and, as Kurt Andersen, who wrote *Time*'s cover story for this issue,[30] told me on my TechcrunchTV show, the initial Arab Spring rebellions could never have happened without social media.[31]

But even in the contemporary Middle East, it still remains unclear how central a role social media will play in the formation of democratic governments. Judging by the speed with which the political optimism of the Arab Spring has evaporated, the auguries for Twitter or Facebook helping build the architecture of democracy in Egypt, Palestine or Tunisia are not particularly encouraging. The problem is that political democracy is more than just the so-called "people power" of fanciful Facebook users committed to the same vague political cause. For example, one member of the Palestinian social media "March 15 movement" described it as a leaderless association of "bubbles" that has yet to congeal.[32] While another Palestinian activist, sounding like an OWS protestor dreamily described the goal of the movement as to "liberate the minds of our people." But, for democracy to *congeal* in organizations like March 15, for 2011 to avoid becoming a repeat of 1848, another year of failed revolutions against authoritarian states, leaders have to emerge and translate social media's undoubted potential into properly financed, structured movements with accountable leadership and a viable political agenda that goes beyond the vague promise of liberating people's minds.

Besides, in spite of Kurt Anderson's faith in The Protestor, it's not really clear how central the role of social networks have been in the overthrow of repressive regimes in the Middle East—especially since even in the relatively advanced Egypt only 5 percent of the citizens use Facebook and 1 percent are on Twitter.[33] "We've had a lot of revolutions before Twitter," George Friedman, the geo-strategic futurist and best-selling author of 2011's *The Next Decade: Where We've Been . . . And Where We're Going,*[34] reminded me when he appeared on my TechcrunchTV show in April 2011. In the Egypt of early 2011, Friedman explained, the vast majority of Egyptian citizens viewed what he regards as the staged uprising against the Mubarak regime with suspicion. The "ignorance" of the Western media is "breathtaking," Friedman told me, when it comes to exaggerating the role of social media in contemporary political upheaval. And that's because, he explained, extensive use of social media in authoritarian societies seems to confirm western liberal values. "If they tweet," Friedman dryly commented on the western media's self-centered obsession with Twitter or Facebook, "they must be like us."

And sometimes, I'm afraid, if *they* tweet, they actually are *us*. Take, for example, the case of the imprisoned Syrian lesbian blogger, Amina Araf, during the 2011 revolution against the Baathite regime in Syria. Fourteen thousand Facebook users loaned their names to a campaign to release Araf from jail. The only problem was that Araf turned out to be a fake. "She" was really Tom MacMaster, a failed American writer living in Scotland with as much experience of life inside a Syrian jail as you or I.[35]

So what is the real value of social media in repressive regimes? "Twitter is a wonderful tool for secret policeman to find revolutionaries," Friedman told me. His analysis reflects the so-called "Morozov Principle"[36] of Stanford University scholar Evgeny Morozov, whose 2010 book, *The Net Delusion: The Dark Side of Internet Freedom*[37] argues that social media tools are being used by secret policemen in undemocratic states like Iran, Syria, and China to spy on dissidents. As Morozov told me when he appeared on my TechcrunchTV show in January 2011,[38] these authoritarian governments are using the Internet in classic Benthamite fashion—relying on social networks to monitor the behavior, activities and thoughts of their own citizens. In China, Thailand, and Iran, therefore, the use of Facebook can literally be a facecrime and the Internet's architecture has become a vast Inspection-House, *a wonderful tool for secret policemen* who no longer even need to leave their desks to persecute their own people. In November 2011, for example, the Thai government warned Facebook users who "liked" antimonarchy groups that they would be liable for prosecution.[39] A month later, the Chinese government announced tough new laws that required people to register with their real names on indigenous social networks like Sina and Tencent.[40] Then in

January 2012, Iran imposed equally "draconian" restrictions on the country's cybercafés designed to spy on Iranian social media users.[41]

Visibility can often be the bloodiest, most tragic kind of trap. The Morozov Principle extends to criminal gangs who are intimidating and even executing social media users as a warning against online whistle-blowing. In Mexico, for example, where some particularly reactionary local politicians want to make the use of Twitter illegal,[42] gangs have taken revenge on citizens who use social media to denounce drug cartel activity. "A woman was hogtied and disemboweled, her intestines protruding from three deep cuts on her abdomen. Attackers left her topless, dangling by her feet and hands from a bridge in the border city of Nuevo Laredo. A bloodied man next to her was hanging by his hands, his right shoulder severed so deeply the bone was visible," reports CNN on the killings in Mexico. "This is going to happen to all of those posting funny things on the Internet," a sign, left near the bodies, said. "You better (expletive) pay attention. I'm about to get you."[43]

The New Numerati

Not only is social media being used by repressive regimes or oganizations to strengthen their hold on power, but it is also compounding the ever-widening inequalities between the influencers and the new digital masses. If identity is the new currency and reputation the new wealth of the social media age, then today's hypervisible digital elite is becoming a tinier and tinier proportion of the population. Reid Hoffman believes that the Internet's empowerment of the individual increases what he calls "the liquidity of the individual."[44] But for all the egalitarian rhetoric of super-nodes like Robert Scoble (@scobleizer) with over 200,000 Twitter followers and Jeff Jarvis (@JeffJarvis) with nearly 100,000, some people—*liquid people* like Scoble and Jarvis—are, to borrow another of Orwell's chilling phrases, much "more equal than others"[45] on today's network. On Twitter, for example, only 0.05 percent of people have more than 10,000 followers with 22.5 percent of users accounting for 90 percent of activity,[46] thus reflecting the increasingly unequal power structure of an attention economy in which the most valuable currency is being heard above the noise.

"Monopolies are actually even more likely in highly networked markets like the online world," wrote *Wired* editor-in-chief Chris Anderson. "The dark side of network effects is that rich nodes get richer."[47] This dark side is compounded by reputation networks like Klout, Kred and Peer Index, which may be creating what one analyst calls a "social media caste system" in which supernodes receive preferential treatment over those with low reputation scores.[48]

The inequalities between rich and poor nodes is even more exaggerated in the wake of 2009's Great Recession. "The people who use these [social media] tools are the ones with higher education, not the tens of millions whose position in today's world has eroded so sharply," notes *Time* magazine business columnist Zachary Karabell.[49] Social media contribute to economic bifurcation. . . . The irony is that social media widen the social divide, making it even harder for the have-nots to navigate. They allow those with jobs to do them more effectively and companies that are profiting to profit more. But so far, they have done little to aid those who are being left behind. They are, in short, business as usual."

Karabell's observations are accurate. But this "business as usual" reflects a deeper historical truth about the unpalatable reality of political and economic power. "Except during short intervals of time, people are always governed by an elite. I use the word elite [Italian: *aristocrazia*] in its etymological sense, meaning the strongest, the most energetic, and most capable—for good as well as evil," wrote the early twentieth-century Italian sociologist Vilfredo Pareto in *The Rise and Fall of Elites*.[50] This argument, which later became known as Pareto's "80–20 principle" or "the law of the vital few" is as true today, in the digital age, as it was during the industrial revolution of the nineteenth century, when a new elite of factory owners, replaced the old landowning aristocracy and vindicated their new wealth and power in the language of the free market and of democracy.

Today, the emerging elite of the twenty-first century, *for good as well as evil*, are the multibillionaire bankers of networked personal information, digital plutocrats like the Oxford and Stanford educated philosopher Reid Hoffman and the Harvard computer scientist Mark Zuckerberg, whose companies are amassing vast amounts of other people's personal information. They, these owners of the private networks, are the new global *aristocrazia* of our social media age, the twenty-first century's ruling numerati,[51] and it is in the gulf between them as the owners and we as the producers of personal information where the greatest inequality of our knowledge economy lies.

Hypervisibility Is a Hypertrap

Michel Foucault was correct. Visibility is, indeed, a trap. Franz Kafka could have invented today's great digital exhibitionism, with its cult of the social and its bizarre fetish with sharing. Just as Joseph K unwittingly *shared* all his known and unknown information with the authorities in *The Trial*, so we are now all *sharing* our most intimate spiritual, economic and medical information with all the myriad of "free" social media services, products and platforms on the network like @quixotic's LinkedIn. And, given that the dominant and perhaps only business model of all this social media economy is adverting sales, it is inevitable that all this *shared* personal information will end up, one Kafkaesque way or another, in the hands of our corporate advertising "friends" like Facebook and Twitter.

As Meglena Kuneva, the European Consumer comissioner, said in March 2009, "personal data is the new oil of the Internet and the new currency of the digital world."[52] Yes, it's the fuel, but everything else too. "Information is what our world runs on," adds the historian of information, James Gleick, "the blood and the fuel, the vital principle."[53]

Yes, social information is becoming the *vital principle* of the global knowledge economy. And it is this contemporary revolution in the generation of personal data that explains the vertiginous valuations of today's social media companies. If the twentieth-century's industrial economy was shaped by bloody wars over oil, today's digital economy is increasingly characterized by conflict over its vital principle—personal information. From all the outrage over Facebook's Open Graph initiative to Google's exploitation of its voyeuristic Streetview technology, rarely a week goes by without another story of a sensational leak of our information by one of the Internet's private information superpowers. In today's advertising driven social media economy, you see, it's data about us that has the most financial value. As one technology CEO told the *Wall Street Journal*, "advertisers want to buy access to people, not web pages."[54] Which explains why, as the newspaper confirms, "one of the fastest-growing businesses on the Internet is the business of spying on Internet users."[55]

If visibility is a trap, then hypervisibility is a hypertrap.

The problem is that our ubiquitous online culture of "free" means that every social media company—from Facebook to Twitter to geolocation services like foursquare, Hitlist, and Plancast—relies exclusively on advertising for its revenue. And it's information about us—James Gleick's "vital principle"[56]—that is driving this advertising economy. As MoveOn.org president Eli Pariser, another sceptic concerned about the real "cost" of all these free services, argues in his 2011 book *The Filter Bubble*, "the race to know as much as possible about you has become the central battle of the era for Internet giants like Google, Facebook, Apple and Microsoft."[57]

"It is fundamentally impossible for a digital advertising business to care deeply about privacy, because the user is the only asset it has to sell. Even if the founders and executives want to care about privacy, at the end of the day, they can't: the economic incentives going the other direction are just too powerful," Michael Fertik, the Silicon Valley–based CEO of Reputation. com, a company dedicated to protecting our online privacy, told me. Fertik's argument is reiterated by the media theorist and CNN columnist Douglas Rushkoff who explains that rather than being Facebook's customers, "we are the product."[58]

Sharon Zukin, a sociology professor at the City University of New York, goes even further than Fertik or Rushkoff in her critique of social media's allure. "Our entire bodies and histories are being opened up and colonized and stored by the very people who want to sell us things," she says. "Online shopping is becoming a master of these technologies of simultaneous coercion and seduction."[59]

Yes, we—you and I and the other 800 million people on the "free" Facebook—are, indeed, the product that is being simultaneously coerced and seduced. We are the personalized data that Facebook and many other social companies are selling to their advertisers. And the problem is that the more these Web 3.0 companies track us, the more effective and thus valuable their advertisements. Indeed, research by Catherine Tucker, a professor at the M.I.T Sloan School of Management has discovered that the effectiveness of online marketing drops by 65% when the tracking of online users is regulated. Web tracking, Professor Tucker testified to Congress, enables companies "to deliver online advertising in an extraordinarily precise fashion"—a precision that seems to consumers, she added, to be "creepy."[60]

The economic incentives of the $26 billion annual online advertising market have become so powerful that there is now a massive Silicon Valley investment boom in those tracking companies that target our online personal data. Between 2007 and early 2011 venture capitalists have, according to Dow Jones VentureSource, invested $4.7 billion into 356 creepy online tracking firms such as eXelate, Media6Degrees, 33Across and MediaMath. These tracking firm are all "trying to find better slices of data on individuals," one venture capitalist explained the current investment boom to the *Wall Street Journal*. "Advertisers want to buy individuals. They don't want to buy Web pages."[61]

Orwell's enemy of *Ownlife*, Big Brother, has arrived on all of our screens. Today he goes under the name of tracking firms like eXelate, Media6Degrees, 33Across and MediaMath. He wants to buy us. And he won't let us alone.

This chasm—between ourselves, Rushkoff's "product," and the advertisers who want to know everything about us, between the producers of personal knowledge and those that seek to profit from this information—is well captured by the English novelist Zadie Smith. "To ourselves, we are special people, documented in wonderful photos, and it also happens that we buy things.... To the advertisers, we are our capacity to buy, attached to a few personal, relevant photos," she wrote in *The New York Review of Books*.[62]

Things have become so creepy on the Internet that the *Wall Street Journal* dedicated a five-part series of 2010 investigative reports, suitably entitled "What They Know,"[63] to the Orwellian business of spying on us. But neither Kafka nor Orwell, at their most surreal, could have dreamed up the story of the real-time mobile app that is always watching us. Yet that "eternal child" Jeremy Bentham dreamed up such a scenario while he was consulting with the Russian enlightened despot Catherine the Great. And he called it the Inspection-House.

The *Wall Street Journal* reported in December 2010 that "apps" from popular services like TextPlus, Pandora and Grindr on our iPhones and Android phones are passing on our information to third-party organizations. And as the managing director of the Mobile Marketing Association told the *Journal*, "in the world of mobile, there is no anonymity. A cell phone is always with us. It's always on."[64] This is why Apple—the sponsor of that original television commercial explaining why 1984 won't really be like *Nineteen Eighty-four*—is now facing a class-action lawsuit which alleges that "nonpersonal information" collected by Web sites like Pandora and the Weather Channel is being used to identify us and our behavior on the Internet.

It's not just apps that are watching us. In an online economy driven by "likes" rather than "links," even social widgets such as Facebook's "Like," Google's "+1" and Twitter's "Tweet" buttons are watching us. As *The Wall Street Journal* reported in May 2011,[65] these "prolific" widgets, which have been added to 20–25 percent of the top 1,000 Web sites, enable networks like Facebook, Google and Twitter to track the browsing habits of users. To be followed by one of these buttons, all a user needs to have done is log onto a social network once in the past month. Then, irrespective of whether or not we actually click on any buttons, the widgets notify Facebook, Google and Twitter about all the Web sites that we visit, thereby transforming these social networks into omniscient inspection-houses of our online behavior.

"We are seeing a race to the privacy bottom," Reputation.com's Fertik explained to me. "The 'older-school' companies that don't feel comfortable selling as much detailed information about you are being forced to do so because the 'young turk' companies don't feel that ethical or business constraint and are therefore commanding higher CPMs."

Facebook is the most visible and aggressive of these young Turk companies. As *The Wall Street Journal*'s Julia Angwin argues, Facebook is making friending "obsolete" by enabling us to know as much about the intimate business of our distant acquaintances as we do about our closest friends. In June 2011, the company even introduced a "super creepy" face-tagging system that automatically scans our photos and identifies our friends.[66] "Just as Facebook turned friends into a commodity," Angwin explains, "it has likewise gathered our personal data—our updates, our baby photos, our endless chirping birthday notes—and readied it to be bundled and sold."[67]

Facial recognition technology is, of course, really creepy. Researchers at Carnegie Mellon University have even discovered that this technology can now be used to accurately predict our social security numbers.[68] Meanwhile, in early 2011, *The New York Times* alerted us to something even creepier than either snooping apps or all-knowing facial recognition technology: "Computers That See You and Keep Watch Over You."[69] The resemblance to Bentham's Inspection-House is uncanny—or, as a social media metaphysician like Steven Johnson might say, "serendipitous."[70] As the *Times* reported, these computers—which contain artificially intelligent software designed to recognize facial gestures and group action—started off in prisons, but are now also being used in hospitals, shopping malls, schools and offices. This all adds up, of course, to Bentham's simple idea of architecture with which we are already very familiar. "At work or school, the technology opens the door to a computerized supervisor that is always watching," *The New York Times* warns us about our hypervisible age. "Are you paying attention, goofing off or daydreaming? In stores and shopping malls, smart surveillance could bring behavioral tracking into the physical world."[71]

That computerized supervisor may already be in your pocket, making WhereI'm.at the default setting of anyone who owns an Apple or Google smartphone. That's because our gadgets, to borrow the chilling title of a 2011 book by electronic security expert Robert Vamosi, are already *betraying* us. Two data scientists have discovered that all our Apple iPhones have been recording their locations and then saving all the details to secret files on the "intelligent" device, which then gets copied onto our computers when we synchronize it with our iPhone. "Apple has made it possible for almost anybody—a jealous spouse, a private detective—with access to your phone or computer to get detailed information about where you've been," one of the researchers told the appropriately named "Where 2.0" conference in April 2011.[72]

That intelligent device in their pocket should equally worry owners of Google's Android smartphones. In late April 2011, *The Wall Street Journal* reported research showing that Android phones "collected its location every few seconds and transmitted the data to Google at least several times an hour."[73] Google might, as Nicholas Carr argued,[74] be making us stupid, but the company itself is anything but stupid. As Steve Lee, a Google product manager, revealed in a publicly disclosed 2010 email, location data is "extremely valuable" to the search engine. "I cannot stress how important Google's Wi-Fi location database is to our Android and mobile-product strategy," Lee added in this email to Larry Page, Google's co-founder and current CEO.[75]

But it's not just smartphone owners who should be paranoid about their all-knowing devices. In December 2011, Amazon—which make the popular

Kindle tablet—were granted a patent that not only uses mobile devices to learn where we've been and our current location, but also is able to determine where we will go next. Like Apple and Google, of course, Amazon wants to own us. And this "Big Brother patent, by knowing where we've been and where we will go, promises to be a particularly intrusive algorithm of digital coercion and seduction."[76] Indeed, Amazon is racing Apple and Google for control of the rapidly growing location-based services economy, a $2.9 billion market (in April 2011) that research firm Gartner predicts will almost triple to $8.3 billion by 2014. Yes, Reid Hoffman's Web 3.0 revolution, that avalanche of "real identities generating massive amounts of data," is now a reality and it's why Amazon, Google and Apple are now scrambling to gather location information that will enable them to build huge databases that can automatically identify our exact locations via our smartphones.

It is a particularly chilling irony that the all-knowing devices at the very heart of what one social media guru describes as our "trust economy,"[77] are fundamentally untrustworthy. Indeed, as *We the Media* author Dan Gillmor notes, even *The Wall Street Journal,* the newspaper which has done such a fine job exposing the crisis of online privacy, is itself connecting "personally identifiable information with Web browsing data without user consent.[78] Yes, our gadgets, and even some of our newspapers, are *betraying* us.[79] So who, exactly, *can* we trust in our so-called "trust economy"?

Nobody, it seems. *New Scientist* magazine reports that Chinese and American academics have developed software that, whether we like it or not, will be able to determine our location to a few hundred meters by simply looking at our Internet connection. This new technology, jointly developed by computer scientists at Northwestern University and the University of Electronic Science and Technology of China in Chengdu, will enable advertisers, criminals, security agencies and even friends or family to stalk anyone who happens to be using a network device.[80]

Big Data

"Big Oil, Big Food, Big Pharma. To the catalog of corporate bigs that worry a lot of us little people, add this: Big Data," wrote *The New York Times*' Natasha Singer at the end of April 2011, the week after the Apple and Google smartphone allegations went public.[81]

Are you worried yet?

Many of us are—one in four Americans, to be exact. A January 2011 survey revealed that more Americans worry about the violation of their online privacy than becoming unemployed or having to declare bankruptcy. This research, conducted by market research company YouGov and published on "Data Privacy Day," found that 25 percent of Americans are fearful of being watched online and having their privacy breached, more than either the 23 percent who worry about bankruptcy or the 22 percent who fear losing their job.[82] But, rather than Big Brother, what we fear most of all is Big Data, with a June 2011 survey from the University of Southern California showing that nearly half of American adult Internet users fear snooping companies versus only 38 percent worrying about snooping government.[83]

So how has this remixed Dark Age—with its 0.05 percent liquid numerati of super nodes like @scobleizer and @quixotic, its underclass of anxious and lonely intradividuals, and its ideological orthodoxy of openness and transparency that makes it increasingly impossible for anyone to be let alone—crept up on us? What are the intellectual, technological and economic origins of this twenty-first-century networked intelligence era—a time when, in the words of MIT professor Sherry Turkle, we are all *alone together*? How has the age of the great exhibition metastasized into our age of great exhibitionism?

The next chapters offer a vertiginous history of social media that connects Jeremy Bentham's industrial Inspection-House with Mark Zuckerberg's Open Graph. And to begin this story, let me show you another picture that you've probably seen before—a picture so creepy that it has not one, but three corpses lying behind it.

4

DIGITAL VERTIGO

"As in the case with all great films, truly great films, no matter how much has been said and written about them, the dialogue about it will always continue. Because any film as great as Vertigo *demands more than a sense of admiration—it demands a personal response."*[1]
—MARTIN SCORSESE.

Three Lies and Three Corpses

The picture is entitled SAN FRANCISCO IN JULY 1849. It's a landscape of some windswept farmhouses sheltering beside the Bay painted in the romantic nineteenth-century style of Albert Bierstadt's "Emerald Wave." There is a single horse with two riders in the foreground of the picture and a clump of barren hills looming in the far distance. This arrestingly pastoral nineteenth-century scene has been painted with a northerly perspective—the artist imagining San Francisco from its southern peninsula, from the perspective of the valley between the Diablo and Santa Cruz mountain ranges, a thirty-square-mile area known for most of the twentieth century as the Santa Clara Valley, but more widely known today as Silicon Valley.

Now fast-forward a hundred years. It's the middle of the twentieth century in San Francisco and the little windswept village beside the Bay has grown into a thriving technological and industrial metropolis, a manufacturing center for the shipbuilding, defense and electronics industries. Two old college friends, both graduates of Stanford, the university from down on the peninsula founded by the nineteenth-century railway baron Leland Stanford, are looking at this picture. One, a graying, faintly shabby former

San Francisco detective named John "Scottie" Ferguson, is standing near the painting, while the other, Gavin Elster, a dapper shipbuilding magnate with a trim moustache, is commenting upon it from behind the desk in his office.

There is a vivid contrast between the simple painting and Elster's ornate San Francisco office. The middle-aged industrialist—who runs the shipyard on behalf of his young wife's family—is seated behind a grand mahogany desk in a sumptuously furnished office. The wood-paneled walls of the office are lined with rare prints and exotic maritime memorabilia. Behind Elster's desk is a cavernous window with such a panoramic view over his industrial domain that it could be a working model of Jeremy Bentham's Inspection-House. From this window, the magnate is able to survey the entire shipyard—from the whirling cranes and half-finished hulls to the small army of shipworkers employed in this large-scale, labor-intensive industrial enterprise.

The two men are comparing rural mid-nineteenth-century with industrial mid-twentieth-century San Francisco. "Well, San Francisco's changed," Elster says in a voice as meticulously tailored as his dark business suit. "The things that spell San Francisco to me are disappearing fast."

"Like all this?" Scottie replies, spreading his arms as he walks closer to the painting of San Francisco in July 1849.

"Yes, I should have liked to have lived there then," Elster confesses, his clubby voice competing with the hum of the cranes from the shipyard outside. He sinks back into his leather chair, raises his eyes toward the ceiling and adds, "Color, excitement, power, freedom."

At first glance, this conversation between the wealthy industrialist and the everyman ex-cop appears to be a private social interaction between two old college friends to whom fate had dealt very different hands. But its reality is the reverse. Everything about this entirely public conversation is actually a lie. It doesn't contain a single word of truth.

The first lie is that we are watching fiction rather than real life. This meeting between Gavin Elster and Scottie Ferguson is actually part of Alfred Hitchcock's 1958 motion picture *Vertigo*—a lavishly produced and meticulously staged piece of mid-twentieth-century Hollywood drama in which we, the mass audience, paid to watch professional actors playing the private lives of fictional characters. Everything in the scene from this Paramount Studio–financed production is invented—from the fake painting in the fake office[2] to the fake conversation[3] between the two men to the fake Scottie Ferguson played by Jimmy Stewart and the fake Gavin Elster played by Tom Helmore. There are no obvious truths in this scene from *Vertigo*. It is a spiral[4] of lies.

The painting itself, with its bucolic landscape, is also a lie. Instead of rural heaven, the San Francisco of July 1849 was more actually like a protoindustrial urban hell. Eighteen months earlier, at the beginning of 1848, that fateful year of failed European revolutions, there were only 12,000 settlers in California—making it more like the idyllic state of nature represented in the picture on Elster's wall. But on January 24, 1848, an eccentric carpenter named James Marshall discovered gold on the American River at Sutters Mill, a sawmill in the foothills of the Sierra mountains some fifty miles to the northeast of San Francisco Bay. By December 1848, President Polk, having confirmed the rumors in his outgoing message to Congress, triggered the most dizzying gold rush in history, a mania so dramatic that, in 1849, the population of the increasingly industrial and urban San Francisco sometimes doubled every ten days—a meteoric rate of social growth that even rivals that of the Facebook community more than 150 years later. In 1849 alone, over 500 vessels left eastern ports bound for the San Francisco Bay, packed with tens of thousands of dreamers—Peggy Noonan's "gamblers, bounders, ne'er-do-wells, third sons in primogeniture cultures"—all seeking to escape their pasts and pull the curtain on the second act of their lives.

But even the "color, excitement, power and freedom" that Elster romanticizes about the San Francisco of 1849 is a lie. As F. Scott Fitzgerald, the chronicler of a later collective bout of irrational exuberance, once said, in vivid contrast with Peggy Noonan's reading of history, "there are no second acts in American lives."[5] And, unfortunately, this was true for the vast majority of the "Forty-niners" as it has been for the participants in every other mania in American history—from the Wall Street stock market boom of the 1920s that Fitzgerald himself chronicled in *The Great Gatsby*, to the irrational social exuberance of the sixties counterculture, to the dot.com hysteria of the late nineties.

"This was the Gold Rush as Iliad, as a disastrous expedition to foreign shores."[6] So Kevin Starr, the author of a much-acclaimed multivolume history of California, describes the San Francisco of 1849. The truth is that these nineteenth-century fortune seekers had, like Gavin Elster, fallen in love with something that, for the most part, didn't exist. As Gray Brechin, another chronicler of San Francisco's vertiginous history, noted, "most left the 'diggings' bitterly disappointed."[7] By the summer of 1849 San Francisco had become a high-tech mining camp teeming with vagabondage, alcoholism, sickness, suicide and murder—an antisocial graveyard of broken dreams rather than Elster's idyllic community of "color, excitement, power, freedom."

But it's the third lie that is the deadliest of them all. In Hitchcock's *Vertigo*, Scottie is being set up by Elster to fall in love with a corpse. The shipbuilding magnate has invited the ex-cop to his office knowing that he suffers from vertigo, a pathological fear of heights with which he'd been afflicted after failing to prevent a police colleague from falling to his death from a San Francisco rooftop. His vertigo is such a debilitating affliction that even standing on a chair triggers an overpowering feeling of dizziness in Scottie as the world whirls faster and faster around him. It has disabled the former San Francisco detective. He no longer can function in society.

So, after spinning his disingenuous nostalgia about the San Francisco of July 1848, Elster invents a story about his wife Madeleine's obsession with a suicidal nineteenth-century ancestor and hires Scottie to shadow the beautiful young woman as she drives around the city. And thus begins Scottie Ferguson's disastrous expedition to foreign shores. You see, the blonde whom Scottie follows around and around the twisted streets of San Francisco is a trap. Madeleine Elster is anything but her own image. She is a fake, who, not unlike today's technologies of social shopping, has been designed to seduce and coerce him.

Contrary to Mark Zuckerberg's dictum that we all only have one identity, Madeleine the ethereal blonde is also Judy the earthy brunette. She has taken Eric Schmidt's advice and reinvented herself. Rather than Madeleine Elster, she is actually Elster's young mistress, a dark-haired store assistant from Kansas called Judy Barton,[8] who, by dying her hair and wearing exquisitely designed outfits,[9] is only playing the role of the shipping heiress.

At first, the plan works perfectly. Scottie is transformed into Jeremy Bentham's voyeuristic fantasy—the eye of the ubiquitous camera, Madeleine's shadow, the inspector of all her movements. First he follows her to San Francisco's little Mission Dolores Church where, from behind a gravestone, he watches her put flowers on her nineteenth-century ancestor's grave. He then follows Madeleine to the city's Palace of the Legion of Honor Museum where he watches from behind a door as the mesmerized young woman gazes at a painting of her ancestor—a beautiful, bejeweled figure who so resembles Madeleine that she might have been narcissistically gazing at herself in a mirror.

The ex-detective not only suffers from vertigo, but from a compulsive voyeurism—a condition we might dub "social eyes." All he can do is watch Madeleine. As Francois Truffaut remarked about Jimmy Stewart's role as Scottie Ferguson, he "isn't required to emote: he simply looks—three or four hundred times."[10] Indeed, Scottie becomes so completely transfixed by Judy's reinvented identity as a San Francisco heiress that, having fished the blonde out of the Bay from underneath the Golden Gate Bridge after she dreamily stumbles into the water, he falls in love with her. The murderous crime then unfolds. Elster kills his real wife and hurls her corpse from the top of a church tower at the same moment that the fake Madeleine stages a suicidal leap from this same building. Meanwhile, the vertigo-afflicted Scottie, doubly traumatized by his inability to follow Madeleine up the twisting staircase of the tower and by her seemingly tragic death, suffers a nervous breakdown and is institutionalized in a San Francisco mental asylum.

Among the many reason critics see *Vertigo* as Hitchcock's creepiest investigation of the human condition[11] lies in the haunting sequence of scenes that follow the fake suicide. After Scottie's release from the asylum, he, by chance, bumps into Judy Barton—who has, in the meantime, been abandoned by Elster—on a San Francisco street. Glimpsing his original lover in Judy (but not having access to facial recognition technology so he can recognize her real identity), he picks her up and then forces the brunette to dye her hair and to dress herself in Madeleine's clothes. And so the store assistant from Kansas once again transforms herself into the shipbuilding heiress, thereby enabling Scottie, who sees his beloved Madeleine in everyone and everything, to first resurrect and then make love to a corpse.

The savage truth is finally revealed to Scottie in *Vertigo*'s penultimate scene. Just as Judy slips back into playing Madeleine, she gives herself away by putting on a bloodred necklace that had also been worn by the original Madeleine. It is the most haunting few seconds in the movie. Finally, he sees the woman's real image—as a fake and an accomplice to murder. The camera freezes momentarily on Scottie's half opened mouth and unblinking blue eyes as he silently grasps the crime to which he's been exposed, both as an innocent accomplice and victim.[12] At first it seems that his epiphany—the realization that everything he had believed in was a lie—would have a cathartic impact on Scottie. But, Hitchcock being Hitchcock, even this catharsis turns out to be a delusion.

"One final thing I have to do and then I'll be free of the past," Scottie tells Judy in the movie's final scene as they drive south from San Francisco down toward the eighteenth-century mission settlement of San Juan Bautista, the site of the original crime.

"One doesn't often get a second chance—you are my second chance," Scottie then breathlessly tells her as, overcoming his dizzying fear of heights, he drags Judy back up the twisted staircase of the church tower where the murdered body of Madeleine Elster was hurled to the ground. But it's not really a second chance—as F. Scott Fitzgerald reminds us, they are mostly illusionary in the lottery of American life.

So instead of completely freeing himself of his past, *Vertigo* ends with a second corpse, Judy's frightened leap from the tower and the death of all Scottie's dreams. Thus behind Hitchcock's *Vertigo* lies two great corpses, or perhaps three, if you include Scottie Ferguson, the deluded and solitary soul who fell in love with a chimera—something that didn't and couldn't exist.

Color, Excitement, Power, Freedom

Not quite everything in *Vertigo* is invented. While the scene in Elster's office was filmed in a Hollywood studio, some of the movie really was made on location in the San Francisco Bay Area. Judy Barton's fake suicidal jump into the Bay, for example, was filmed in early October 1957 under the Golden Gate Bridge, while her suicidal leap from the church tower really did get shot a couple of weeks later in San Juan Bautista—the little town southeast of San Jose, the Bay Area city that today is the epicenter of Silicon Valley.

"Yes, I should have liked to have lived there then—color, excitement, power, freedom," you'll remember Gavin Elster saying, with disingenuous nostalgia, about "San Francisco in July 1849." But would it be equally disingenuous to borrow these words as a description of mid-twentieth-century San Francisco Bay Area? Was there *color, excitement, power, freedom* in the place where Hitchcock made his timeless picture?

To borrow another of Elster's words, the Bay Area certainly has *changed* over the last half century, particularly its economy. Back in October 1957, power—or at least economic power—was held by large scale, hierarchical organizations along the lines of Elster's fictional shipbuilding company—firms[13] with the logistic and organizational power to mass manufacture mechanical products for the industrial networked economy. This local economy was, therefore, dominated by companies such as the peninsula's largest employer, the defense and aircraft manufacturer Lockheed and electronics manufacturers like Westinghouse, General Electric, IBM and Sylvania. Many of these firms still operated on the scientific management principles of the late-nineteenth-century mechanical engineer Frederick Winslow Taylor—a thinker deeply indebted to Jeremy Bentham's surveillant utilitarianism—which prioritized quantifiable workplace efficiency and productivity over more human or creative goals.

This large organizational arrangement is what social media evangelists John Hagel and John Seely Brown describe as a "push" economy. "In a push system there is a hierarchy, with those in charge offering rewards (or punishments) to those lower down the ladder," Hagel and Seely Brown describe the top-down power structure of the firm in mid-twentieth-century life. "The people participating in push programs are generally treated as instruments to ensure that activities are performed as dictated. Their own individual needs and interests are purely secondary, if relevant at all."[14]

It was large hierarchical industrial firms like Lockheed, GE and Westinghouse which employed the "Organization Man," a term popularized by *Fortune* magazine business journalist William H. Whyte in his 1956 best-selling critique of the conformity of this push economy. According to Whyte, these Organization Men were neither the industrial laborers nor the white-collar workers of traditional industrial society. "These people work for The Organization," he observed. "They are the ones of our middle class who have left home, spiritually as well as physically, to take the vows of organizational life." But what most concerned Whyte was the replacement of the individual with the group as a supposed "creative vehicle" for business innovation. In his concern for the rights of the individual, Whyte echoed earlier critics of collective thinking like John Stuart Mill and George Orwell. "The most misguided attempt at false collectivization is the current attempt to see the group as a creative vehicle. Can it be?" he asked rhetorically. "People very rarely think in groups; they talk together, they exchange information, they adjudicate, they make compromises. But they do not think; they do not create."[15]

As David Halberstam notes in his history of the fifties, the "conformity of American life" had, by the middle of the decade, become "a major intellectual debate" attracting not only social critics like Whyte, John Kenneth Galbraith and C. Wright Mills, but also novelists like Sloan Wilson.[16] Wilson confronted the problem of group-think and spiritual impoverishment in his 1955 best-selling *The Man in the Gray Flannel Suit*, a novel that was turned into a 1956 movie featuring the music of Bernard Herrmann, the composer who also wrote the score for *Vertigo*. But whereas Herrmann's romantically garish music in Hitchcock's movie provided a suitably exaggerated soundtrack to this apotheosis of cinematic voyeurism, his work in *The Man in the Gray Flannel Suit* is more muted and private. That's because the picture reflected both the fragmented social reality of the fifties as well as the growing disenchantment with the human costs of its impersonal economic system, its industrial technology, and its work culture. This is a movie about marketing executives at large media companies who, ironically, can't communicate and whose public and private lives have become so disconnected that they are alienated from their colleagues, their friends, their families and themselves. It was a society, many believed, of too much private affluence and not enough public good—a world that sixties activist and chronicler Todd Gitlin described as "cornucopia and its discontents."

But alongside this monochromic industrial culture, the region, especially the Santa Clara Valley, also possessed a less discontented cornucopia—a colorful and thriving agricultural economy. Indeed, had Alfred Hitchcock and his *Vertigo* production crew chosen to take Interstate 101 on their journey from the Golden Gate Bridge down to San Juan Bautista they would have driven through a pastoral landscape so redolent with the color and aroma of its cherry and apricot orchards that it was still known locally as the "valley of heart's delight." Back in the fall of 1957, you see, Silicon Valley didn't exist.[17] There was no fifty-mile sprawl of high-tech office parks merging San Francisco with San Jose, no collective congestion on 101, no smart posses of entrepreneurs in their Toyota Prius hybrids and Bentley convertibles chasing the next big social thing, no roadside electronic billboards every mile flashing advertisements for the hottest new network. Back then, the Bay Area's future—a social future that is now spinning faster and faster around all of us—had only just been invented.

The Arrival of the Future

That future was the digital computer. The analogue computer, as a mechanical calculating machine, had existed, in theory at least, since the year after Jeremy Bentham's death, having been conceived by the English polymath Charles Babbage as the "Difference Engine" in 1833, just a year after Bentham's corpse first appeared in public, and then tinkered with until Babbage's own death in 1871. Over the next century, the technology of analogue computers matured considerably, but—to cram a hundred years of remarkably complex scientific, mathematic and technical development into a single sentence[18]—its functionality was always compromised by the prodigious amount of electricity required to power these machines and, as a consequence, by their unwieldy size and heat. What solved these hitherto intractable problems and transformed the mechanical computer from a technological curiosity into the central reality of contemporary social life was the invention of the transistor, a silicon-based semiconductor device that enabled solid-state amplification of power and the seemingly limitless miniaturization of electric circuits.

Like James Watt's eighteenth-century invention of the steam engine or Thomas Edison's nineteenth-century invention of the electric lightbulb, its invention is one of those once-in-a-century technological transformations that turned the conventional world upside down. *Newsweek* senior editor and Silicon Valley chronicler David Kaplan described this transistor as the "substructure of the future" and "elemental to the digital age."[19] Without this little transistor, there would be no personal computer or Internet, no smartphones or smart televisions, no Tweetie, foursquare or Facebook Open Graph, no central digital tissue of society, and no age of networked intelligence. Without the little transistor, the future—our social future—still wouldn't exist.

This future had actually been discovered ten years before Hitchcock came to the Bay Area to film *Vertigo*. Three Nobel prize–winning physicists—William Shockley, John Bardeen, and Walter Brattain—invented the transistor at the Bell Labs in New Jersey in 1947. But it was Shockley, one of the twentieth century's most prescient scientists and, in the words of Mike Malone, "the first citizen of Silicon Valley," who exported the transistor to the San Francisco Bay Area. Shockley, a native of Palo Alto, had thought deeply about what he called the "electric brain" and he understood that the transistor would provide the "ideal nerve cell" for computing machines.[20] Returning to the Bay Area in 1956 and assembling a team of some of the most gifted young scientists in America—including Gordon Moore, a twenty-seven-year-old Caltech graduate who grew up in Pescadero, a Pacific coast fishing village on the other side of the Santa Cruz mountains—he set up Shockley Semiconductor Laboratory, a start-up dedicated to the commercial development of the transistor.

But there was a problem with this plan. In addition to being a scientific

genius, Silicon Valley's first citizen was, perhaps not entirely uncoincidentally, a shameless narcissist, whose antisocial behavior made him uniquely
unsuited to leading this all-star technology team. So in September 1957, a
couple of weeks before Hitchcock filmed a false Madeleine Elster faking
her suicide underneath the Golden Gate Bridge, the so-called "Traitorous
Eight"—a group of America's most brilliant young physicists and electrical
engineers including Gordon Moore and Robert Noyce, his later co-founder
of Intel[21]—left Shockley Semiconductor Laboratory to found what David
Kaplan calls "Silicon Valley's greatest hardware company."

It was called Fairchild Semiconductor and it was based in Mountain
View, the peninsula town near Stanford University where the Googleplex,
Google's global headquarters, is now located. Not only was Fairchild Semiconductor the mother of Silicon Valley start-ups, later spawning companies
like Intel and Advanced Micro Devices (AMD), but it was also the first.
Founded in October 1957 and funded by Arthur Rock, the first Californian venture capitalist, Fairchild Semiconductor was the first company that
discovered the rich vein of gold in the transistor. It was, as Mike Malone
explains, a dizzying moment, equivalent in historical vertigo to James Marshall's discovery of gold at Sutter's Mill in January 1848.

It was as if a door had been flung open, Malone explains. "The scientists at
Fairchild suddenly looked down into a bottomless abyss microscoping from
the visible world into that of atoms—an abyss that promised blinding speed
and power, the ultimate calculating machine. When they let their minds
wander they realized that not just one transistor could be put on a chip, but
even ten, maybe a hundred. . . . For Christ's sake, millions. It was dizzying."[22]

It was so dizzying, in fact, that in 1965 Gordon Moore coined his own
law to explain the transformational power of the transistor. Moore's Law, as
it has come to be universally known, correctly predicted that the number
of transistors that could be placed on a computer chip would double—yes,
double—every two years. This biannual doubling in computational power

has not only enabled faster and faster and tinier and tinier personal computers, but also in the pervasive Internet and our contemporary mania with social media.

Moore's Law—the model for Zuckerberg's Law about the annual doubling of networked personal information—has become the single constant of our vertiginous digital age. It is both the engine of perpetual economic and technological innovation as well as the cause of what Austrian economist Joseph Schumpeter, in a more aphoristic law, described as the "creative destruction" inevitably wrought by the capitalist free market.[23] Moore's and Schumpeter's laws explain why there are no longer any cherry or apricot orchards in the valley of heart's delight. And they are also the reasons why, in the words of veteran *New York Times* technology writer John Markoff, "perhaps more than any region, Silicon Valley has transformed the world in the last half century."[24]

But like one of Hitchcock's great corpses, the history of Silicon Valley isn't quite as straightforward as it first appears. Just as *Vertigo* is more than just a kinky fifties picture about necrophilia on the twisted streets of San Francisco, so the real history of Silicon Valley isn't simply a cheerful Whiggish narrative about the progressive impact of ever shrinking electric circuit boards upon an increasingly networked humanity. No, the contemporary digital revolution—like the nineteenth-century industrial revolution—is too epochal an event in human history, too great a journey to foreign shores, to be seen deterministically, purely as a consequence of technological innovation.

The idea of technology as the first mover, as the-thing-in-itself that triggers all consequent social, economic and cultural change, is a trap into which both smart techno-skeptics and techno-utopians alike—from Kevin Kelly to Nicholas Carr[25]—have fallen. Thus, as Richard Florida argues, "the deep and enduring changes of our age are not technological but social and cultural."[26] Florida is correct to present social and cultural change—as well, of course, as economic—as at least equal to technology in terms of shaping our digital age. In parallel, therefore, with the innovation of technologists like the Traitorous Eight, the history of Silicon Valley must also be understood in terms of its social values, moral judgments and economic ideas—in the context of what some sociologists would call its "ideology." And it's in the complex architecture of these collective ideas, rather than that the simpler architecture of an electric circuit, where the origins of today's digital cult of the social can be most effectively excavated.

But to get to this excavation, we need to return to the earlier question about the mid-twentieth-century Bay Area. The truth is that, in spite of its technicolored orchards, the San Francisco Bay Area—with its monochrome industrial infrastructure of large electronics, defense and energy companies managed by supposedly repressed and repressive Organizational Men—was neither a strikingly exciting nor a colorful place in the fall of 1957. Yet this would change dramatically over the next decade. Between 1957 and 1967 the Bay Area experienced such a powerful explosion of social color and excitement that the region—and, indeed, the world—has never been quite the same since.

The Love-In

By 1967, the people of San Francisco had replaced their gray flannel suits with rainbow-colored clothes and psychedelic scarves. By 1967, love had usurped scientific management as the metric of human value. By 1967, the cornucopia of hidden discontent had been substituted by a cornucopia of transparent desire. And, by 1967, tens of thousands of San Franciscans had, like poor Scottie Ferguson, fallen in love with something that didn't really exist.

"If you're going to San Francisco, be sure to wear some flowers in your hair," sang Scott McKenzie in mid-June 1967 at the Monterey Pop Festival. The song was called "San Francisco (Be Sure to Wear Some Flowers in Your Hair)" and John Philips, the lyricist of the Mamas and Papas and one of the

organizers of the festival, had written it especially for McKenzie to be debuted at Monterey.

Rather than a single song, however, Monterey debuted an entire epoch.
Like Fairchild Semiconductor, the three-day Monterey Pop Festival—with
its social focus of bringing together many different musicians and a large,
diverse audience of strangers—was the first of its kind. Just as the company
founded by the Traitorous Eight would spawn larger chip companies like Intel
and AMD, so Monterey would inspire larger social music festivals like Wood-
stock and Altamont. And just as Fairchild Semiconductor was more than another high-tech company, so the Monterey Pop Festival was more than just
another musical event.

In mid-June 1967, a crowd of at least 50,000—some estimate as many
as 100,000—intimate strangers, had come down the northern Californian
coast to Monterey, a Spanish colonial town not far from the old mission of
San Luis Bautista where Hitchcock filmed the suicide scenes in *Vertigo*.
They came, some with flowers in their hair, for the festival, not only to hear
Scott McKenzie, Jimmy Hendrix and Janis Joplin, the Who, the Mamas
and the Papas, and the Grateful Dead, but also to celebrate a fresh flowering
of togetherness that appeared to signify a new beginning, a second chance
for America and the world to unite together as friends.

*"If you're going to San Francisco, you're gonna meet some gentle people
there,"* Scott McKenzie sang at Monterey. "San Francisco (Be Sure to Wear
Some Flowers in Your Hair)" both created and reflected the zeitgeist of the
age. It became an instant number one hit around the world, selling more
than 7 million copies and emerging as the anthem of social togetherness for
the sixties' counterculture.

It was indeed the promise of *meeting people* that drew so many thousands
of people to Monterey in June 1967. As much as a music concert, the three-
day event was a social experiment in sharing, in bringing people together
through music, in transforming strangers into friends. At Monterey, there

was a breakdown of the rigid fifties boundaries between public and private life and, as a consequence, the creation of a new transparent public space designed to create intimacy amongst strangers. The children of 1967 even invented language for this kind of social orgy: they called it a "love-in."

"If you come to San Francisco," Scott McKenzie promised the tens of thousands who came to Monterey, *"summertime will be a love-in there."*

"Haven't you ever been to a love-in?" a wide-eyed young woman asks her interviewer at the beginning of D. A. Pennebaker's *Monterey Pop,*[27] the definitive documentary movie about the festival. "It's gonna be like Easter and New Year and Christmas and your birthday all together. . . . The vibrations are just going to be flowing everywhere."

The summer of 1967 certainly began as if every day was Easter, New Year, Christmas and all of our birthdays. *"Love, love, love, love, love, love, love, love, love. There's nothing you can do that can't be done,"* sang the Beatles in "All You Need Is Love," the other big hit that summer. In fact, the Monterey Pop Festival marked the beginning of the Summer of Love, a two-year-long countercultural experiment in friendship, sharing and collaboration.

June 1967 was like a predigital Occupy Wall Street. Globally headquartered in San Francisco's Haight-Ashbury neighborhood, the Summer of Love represented an audacious attempt to unite all the "gentle people" of the world. Behind the lurid headlines of sex, drugs and rock 'n' roll, the people who came to the city in the summer of 1967 were seeking the loving ideal of global social connectivity—what the *San Francisco Oracle*, sounding like Don Tapscott or Umair Haque, described as the "renaissance of compassion, awareness, and love, and the revelation of unity for all mankind."[28]

This ideal of the *unity for all mankind* became a central, if not *the* central theme of the counterculture. As sixties historian Todd Gitlin explains, it represented "hippie as communard: the ideal of a social bond that could bring all hurt, yearning souls into sweet collectivity, beyond the realm of scarcity and the resulting pettiness and aggression."[29] According to Gitlin, between

50,000 and 75,000 people flocked to the 1967 love-in on Haight-Ashbury to openly share their possessions, their minds, their bodies, their good vibrations, their stimulants, their pasts and their futures.

"All across the nation such a strange vibration, people in motion," sang Scott McKenzie at Monterey. *"There's a whole generation with a new explanation."* But what, exactly, was this "new explanation" and who, precisely, was doing the *explaining* during the Summer of Love?

Social Man

The intellectual origins of this cultural rebellion can be traced back to the time when the Traitorous Eight were setting up shop in Mountain View and Hitchcock was filming *Vertigo*. In September 1957, a month before the creation of Fairchild Semiconductor, Jack Kerouac's *On the Road* had been published,[30] and quickly became an *explanation* for an entire generation— including Bob Dylan, who confessed to Beat poet Allen Ginsberg that it "changed my life like it changed everyone else's." Kerouac changed everyone's life by transforming the cornucopia of discontent into literature and, as a peripatetic bohemian, an outsider on the edge of society, sneering at the supposedly inauthentic conventions of contemporary family, school, suburb and workplace. With other libertarian Beat poets like Ginsburg, Timothy Leary and Gary Snyder, Kerouac challenged every form of traditional authority—from mainstream media and big government to The Organization and The Man in the Gray Flannel Suit. This was the new vibration: a colorful eruption of bohemianism against what the Frankfurt School Marxist philosopher Herbert Marcuse called, in his unlikely 1964 best-seller, the *One-Dimensional Man,* conventional industrial society.

But the new explanation went beyond the bohemian rebellion of the Beatniks against traditional authority. This was a communal uprising that, to borrow some language from London School of Economics sociologist

Richard Sennett, had a "collective personality generated by a common fantasy." And that fantasy was centered on what Sennett calls "the intimacy of social relations." In parallel with the radical libertarianism of the bohemian rebel, lay the communitarian idealism of sixties radicals like Marcuse and the writer Paul Goodman, whom historian Theodore Roszak called the "foremost tribune" of the counterculture.[31]

As engineers of the human soul, theorists like Marcuse and Goodman were trying to create a new version of mankind, upgrading the fifties corporate *One-Dimensional Man* with a social version of man, the unifier of all humanity. Their communitarian belief system rested upon a Gavin Elster–style nostalgia for an invented past, a preindustrial world of hearts' delight, a perpetual love-in where a "scaled down" industrialism would serve as a "handmaiden to the ethos of village or neighborhood." Whether it was Paul Goodman's atavistic faith in restoring the communities of precolonial Indians, or Herbert Marcuse's theories of man's spiritual alienation from capitalism and his promise of a postrevolutionary social unity, or the voluntary primitivism of hippie communalist groups like the San Francisco Diggers, the end result was the same embrace of an imaginary collective social past, that same connected oral culture that social utopians like Don Tapscott and Jeff Jarvis now idealize. As Walter Benjamin, another luminary of the Frankfurt School put it, "the utopian images that accompany the emergence of the new always concurrently reach back to the ur-past."[32]

Their faith in the communal purity of the past certainly wasn't new. Two centuries earlier, Jean-Jacques Rousseau had reached back into the ur-past and launched a similar assault on the supposed heartlessness and inequalities of society. In the invaluable five volume *A History of Private Life*, the French historian Jean Marie Goulemont describes Rousseau's obsession with "the idea of a citizenry transparent to itself."[33] As Rousseau himself wrote with characteristic communitarian nostalgia in his 1758 *Letter to*

D'Alembert, "what peoples have better grounds to assemble often, and to form among themselves the sweet bonds of pleasure and joy than those who have so many reasons for loving one another and remaining always united?"[34]

If only we could reach back, the logic of Goodman and Marcuse's Rousseauian nostalgia went, back before Lockheed and IBM, back before The Organization Man and the military-industrial complex, back to when everybody wore flowers in their hair, back to the authentic society of the village or neighborhood—then we would rediscover the real color, the excitement, the power and the freedom of what it supposedly meant to be human.

In "The 18th Brumaire of Louis Bonaparte," his essay about the failed French Revolution of 1848, Herbert Marcuse's muse, Karl Marx, argued that "men make their own history, but they do not make it as they please; they do not make it under circumstances chosen by themselves, but under circumstances directly encountered, given and transmitted from the past."[35] And this was as true in 1848 as in 1967 or, for that matter, as in 2011, the year of the Protestor. You see, for all their obsession with preindustrial community during the Summer of Love, the tens of thousands who flocked to the love-ins on Haight-Ashbury in 1967 were, in Theodore Roszak's words, "technocracy's children"—products of the very leviathan late-industrial world from which they were trying to escape.[36]

This was a generation of increasingly autonomous rebels seeking both individual authenticity[37] and collective togetherness, a lonely crowd of disruptive individuals wanting to build what the LSE's Richard Sennett calls "intimate society."[38] The cult of the social, then, in the Summer of Love was what Harvard sociologist Daniel Bell described as a "cultural contradiction of capitalism" in which people's economic circumstances in society and their cultural thinking about those circumstances were diametrically opposed. The more atomized and lonely people became, the more separated from traditional community, the more they fell in love with the idea of the social. But their definition of the social was so individualized, so much a reflection of their own discrete identities that their cult of social authenticity was simultaneously a cult of the authentic self—thereby creating, in the memorable words of cultural critic Christopher Lasch, a *Culture of Narcissism* in which the narcissist "cannot live without an admiring audience."[39]

This irony—between an increasingly individualized society and an increasing longing for communal identity—was recognized by Alvin Toffler, whose 1970 best-selling book, *Future Shock*, is an uncannily prescient warning about the impermanence of today's Web 3.0 age, with its stock market trading in individual reputations and its fast flowing streams of information. "It is ironic," Toffler observed, "that the people who complain most loudly that people cannot *relate* to one another, or cannot *communicate* with each other, are often the very same people who urge greater individuality."[40] Thus, as Toffler noted, postindustrial man is "modular man," able to create a diversity of "temporary interpersonal relationships" that precludes us—in contrast with our preindustrial ancestors—from a strong sense of communal identity. "For just as things and places flow through our lives at a faster clip," Toffler wrote in *Future Shock*, "so, too, do people."

Unfortunately, most of the kids at the Monterrey Pop Festival were too busy with their *temporary interpersonal relationships* to give much thought to the contradiction between their strong sense of individualism and their longing for community. "This is my generation, this is my generation, baby," sang the Who at Monterey, the words were from "My Generation," another sixties anthem. But this was *My* Generation in the same way as social media is *My* Space—a narcissistic generation of bohemians all constructing their own communities according to their own discrete needs and desires. These bohemians are the early ancestors of Dalton Conley's intraviduals, or Sherry Turkle and Jonathan Franzen's self-absorbed digital youth—the free-floating, fragmented butterflies of today's age of foursquare, Airtime and Plancast, who flit narcissistically from networked community to community and from personalized online experience to experience at will.

Like the impossibly beautiful and rich Madeleine Elster, the Summer of Love was simply too good to be true. On the one hand, the counterculture promoted the new man—a strongly individualistic free thinker liberated from the shackles of traditional community; on the other hand, however, it promised a return to the communitarian womb of the preindustrial village. The chances of successfully synthesizing this bohemian individualism with a primitive collectivism were about as realistic as the plot of a Hitchcock movie. The Summer of Love couldn't work. And, as we all know, it didn't.

This is a picture we've seen before, of course, not only in the movies, but also in real life. The fashionably threadbare youngsters who poured into San Francisco in 1967 with *One-Dimensional Man* and *On the Road* in their rucksacks may have been less impoverished than the threadbare fortune hunters of 1849, but their libertarian dreams about uniting all of mankind in a global love-in were just as chimerical as the forty-niner's faith in discovering gold. And so it was hardly surprising that the revolutionary Summer of Love experiment ended in discord rather than global connectivity.

"Hope I die before I get old," sang the Who at Monterrey, before smashing their instruments on stage in a catharsis of adolescent rage that represented a dress rehearsal of how the sixties itself would die.

Many of the "gentle people" of San Francisco had indeed turned violent and cynical by the late sixties, unhinged in part by their unholy overdose of radical communitarianism and individualism. As the English documentary filmmaker Adam Curtis, argues, "What tore them apart was the very thing that was supposed to have been banished: power. Some people were more free than others—strong personalities dominated the weak, but the rules didn't allow any organized opposition to the suppression because that would be politics."[41] The Manson family, thus, replaced the love-in. Nor was it purely coincidental that, in its homelessness, hunger, drug addiction, crime and sickness, the Haight-Ashbury of 1969 began to look increasingly like the San Francisco of 1849—a graveyard lined with the corpses of broken people and dreams.

But as we know from Hitchcock's *Vertigo*, a corpse is never quite as dead as it looks. Or as Marx memorably put it in his essay on the failed revolutions of 1848: "The tradition of all the dead generations weighs like a nightmare on the brain of the living." The truth is that the Summer of Love generation, *My Generation*, didn't really die in 1969. It just went online. And today, that vibration is all around us.

It is called social media.

5

THE CULT OF THE SOCIAL

"Movies are naturally social things."
—MARK ZUCKERBERG

The Macguffin

In a 1939 lecture at Columbia University, Alfred Hitchcock revealed the narrative trick behind his pictures. "We have a name in the studio and we call it the 'Macguffin.' It is the mechanical element that usually crops up in any story. In crook stories it is almost always the necklace and in spy stories it is most always the papers."

Even though the Macguffin catches the viewers' attention, it never turns out to be central to the real plot of the movie. As Hitchcock's biographer, Patrick McGilligan, notes, by the end of any Hitchcock picture, the Macguffin has "become an absurdity—and deliberately beside the point."[1]

The mechanical element that crops up in any story about the Internet is technology. That's the Macguffin in this book. Of course, today's social media revolution couldn't have happened without major advances in technology. By the early seventies, the electrical engineers of Silicon Valley had made two critical technological breakthroughs—the introduction of standards for packet switching networks, and a first-generation microprocessor developed by Gordon Moore and Robert Noyce's Intel Corporation—that enabled the large scale networking of digital devices. John Hagel and John

Seely Brown describe this as the "Big Shift" from a centralized and hierarchical industrial economy to a flatter and supposedly more social and egalitarian digital economy.[2] This Big Shift empowered personal computers to communicate with one another, thereby not only marking the most significant development in communications technology since Alexander Graham Bell's invention of the telephone in 1876, but also laying down the "connective tissue of society" heralded by contemporary communitarians like Clay Shirky and Don Tapscott.

Yet these technological developments are mostly beside the point—at least in terms of uncovering the real history of social media. You'll remember that the *New York Times* technology journalist John Markoff wrote that "perhaps more than any region, Silicon Valley has transformed the world in the last half century." But Markoff was only half correct. Yes, Silicon Valley has transformed the world with its revolutionary microprocessors and packet switching networks; but that world has also changed Silicon Valley, transforming it from a twentieth-century scientific center for the development of digital technology into the engine room of the twenty-first-century global social, cultural and economic revolution.

"Technology affects character," Ross Douthat, the culturally conservative *New York Times* columnist argues.[3] Perhaps. More important, however, character affects technology. As cultural historians of Silicon Valley, such as Markoff himself,[4] Stanford University's media historian Fred Turner,[5] the *Financial Times'* James Harkin,[6] and Columbia University law scholar Tim Wu[7] have all meticulously documented, the birth and death of the counterculture was intimately interwoven with the origins of the personal computer and the worldwide Web. Many of the leading apostles and architects of digital connectivity and community—such as the eccentric network visionaries J.C.R. Linklider and Douglas Englebart, Whole Earth Catalogue and WELL founder Stewart Brand, *Wired* magazine's founding editor Kevin Kelly, Apple founders Steve Jobs and Steve Wozniak and Grateful Dead lyricist and

Electronic Frontier Foundation co-founder John Perry Barlow—were them-selves bohemian products of the counterculture. These pioneers, whom Fred Turner calls "new communalists," imported the sixties' disruptive libertarian-ism, its rejection of hierarchy and authority, its infatuation with openness, transparency and personal authenticity, and its global communitarianism into the culture of what has become known as "cyberspace." Their vision was to unite all human beings in a global network linked by computers. "This strange idea," Tim Wu writes, "was the basis of what we now call the Internet."[8]

"The web is more a social creation than a technical one," thus confessed Tim Berners-Lee, the original architect of the Worldwide Web, about the Internet's core social purpose. "I designed it for a social effect—to help people work together—and not as a technical toy. The ultimate goal of the Web is to support and improve our weblike existence in the world. We clump into families, associations, and companies. We develop trust across the miles and distrust around the corner."[9]

It wasn't just serendipity, therefore, that the Internet's architecture—what Tim Wu calls its "network design" (which, he correctly observes, "like all design, can be understood as ideology"[10])—happened to mirror the bo-hemian values of its pioneers. Like Kerouac's perennial outsider Dean Mori-arty from *On the Road*, the idea of cyberspace—a global network of human beings connected by computer—developed as all edge and no center, an in-finitely expandable universe that naturally lent itself to the restless individu-alism of the peripatetic bohemian who regarded himself as a global citizen. As such, it became a way of keeping alive the disruptive spirit of the Summer of Love, with its challenge to traditional corporate and cultural hierarchies. "The purpose of personal computing would go hand in glove with the idea of computer network communication," Tim Wu explains. "Both were radi-cal technology; and, fittingly, both grew out a kind of counterculture."[11] The personal computer and the Internet, then, emerged as the natural home of the homeless, to the refugees of the love-in who no longer had any allegiance to a physical community but who had, through networked technology, graduated to membership into a global community of like-minded souls.

"I live at Barlow@eff.org. That is where I live. That is my home," explained John Perry Barlow, sounding suspiciously like Facebook's fictionalized Sean Parker from *The Social Network*. Or, as Ester Dyson, another of the Silicon Valley hipster founding class put it, "Like the Net, my life is decentralized. I live on the Net."[12]

Nor was it coincidental that, as the sixties' countercultural elite entered the American workforce, they reshaped broader economic life with both their rebellious individualism and their romantic communitarianism. As contemporary observers of all political persuasions have noted—from conservative *New York Times* columnist David Brooks to liberal *Wall Street Journal* columnist Thomas Frank—the ideal of the outsider, the disrupter who challenges authority, has become one of the most valuable economic commodities of early twenty-first-century life. The corporate Man in the Gray Flannel Suit has thus metamorphosized into Brooks's contemporary free-floating bourgeois bohemian, the "Bobo,"[13] skilled in the marketing and sales of what Frank described as a "hip consumerism"[14]—a new orthodoxy of nonconformity best summarized by the 1997 Apple Computer marketing edict to "Think Different."[15] As Harvard Business School professor Shoshana Zuboff notes, the post mass-production economy "produced a new human mentality—of a self-determining individual. This mentality was once the unique precinct of the elite: the wealthy, artists, poets, philosophers. And it became the mentality of everyone."[16] Or, to requote NPR executive editor Dick Meyer, "Everyone is part of a counterculture now."

While We Weren't Paying Attention, the Industrial Age Just Ended

Meanwhile, the digital revolution has also been both a central cause and effect of another deep structural shift on the economic landscape—the transition from an industrial economy dominated by corporate monoliths like IBM, Lockheed and General Electric into a much more individualized economy, shaped by what Peter Drucker, the influential twentieth-century management theorist, defined as the "knowledge" or "information" economy. This revolution is of such economic and social historical significance, Drucker believed, that it is equivalent to the great industrial revolutions of the nineteenth century.

"We cannot yet tell with certainty what the next society and the next economy will look like. We are still in the throes of a transition period," Drucker wrote in the spring of 2001. "Contrary to what most everybody believes, however, this transition period is remarkably similar to the two transition periods that preceded it during the 19th century: the one in the 1830s and 1840s, following the invention of railroads, postal services, telegraph, photography, limited-liability business, and investment banking; and the second one, in the 1870s and 1880s, following the invention of steel making; electric light and electric power; synthetic organic chemicals, sewing machines and washing machines; central heating; the subway; the elevator and with it apartment and office buildings and skyscrapers; the telephone and typewriter and with them the modern office; the business corporation and commercial banking."[17]

Drucker is describing the great transformation from a trade-based economy of industrial production to an economy dominated by the exchange of information—what he describes as the shift in the "center of gravity" from the manufacturer or the distributor to the "customer."[18] Tomorrow's "free market," Drucker argues, "means flow of information rather than trade."[19] And the key producers of value in this new, increasingly digital information economy of social networks like Facebook, LinkedIn, Google + and Twitter are what best-selling author Daniel Pink calls the "free agent nation"[20] of self-employed and autonomous knowledge workers. In the most profound socioeconomic change of the early twenty-first century, the Organization

Man of the large-scale industrial firm has changed into what Pink calls a new "species" of knowledge worker such as @scobleizer and @quixotic. Sloan Wilson's Man in the Gray Flannel Suit, therefore, has been transformed into the free-floating self-employed "knowledge" or "information" worker whose creativity and innovation is uncannily suited to a globalized marketplace of incessant individual mobility and creative economic destruction.

"While we weren't paying attention, the industrial age just ended," Seth Godin, one of the knowledge economy's most prescient observers, told me when he appeared on my Techcrunch.tv show in February 2011.[21] The Schumpeterian innovation economy that Godin describes is a Darwinian struggle of survival between ever-increasingly innovative individuals. "Average is over," Godin argues in *Linchpin*, his 2010 self-help book on maintaining our "indispensability" in this competitive reputation economy.[22] Others put it even more bluntly. *Ignore Everybody* is Hugh MacLeod's *Wall Street Journal* best-selling manual on nonconformity.[23] Gary Vaynerchuk, one of social media's most successful self-promoters with over a million followers as @garyvee on Twitter, tells us to *Crush It* if we are to "cash in on our passion" and remain indispensable in the global creative economy.[24]

"We've met the market and it's us," Daniel Pink says about this post-industrial Me-economy—a working environment ideally suited to the bohemian culture of an increasingly individualized and self-promoting digital elite. Schumpeter's organizational "creative destruction" of twentieth-century capitalism has been replaced by an increasingly individualized struggle of self-invention and reinvention. Borrowing the title of Reid Hoffman's 2012 book,[25] *New York Times* columnist Thomas Friedman describes this world as "The Start-up of You," an economy in which we are all entrepreneurs in perpetual start-up mode.[26] The winners in this hypercompetitive twenty-first-century economy are the masters and mistresses of reinvention—globally powerful individuals like AOL's editor-in-chief, Arianna Huffington and blogging superstar Andrew Sullivan (respectively presidents of the

Cambridge and Oxford debating unions)—who have successfully rearchi-
tected their identities to suit every new twist and turn in our global culture
and politics.

And yet, just as in the Summer of Love, the more atomized and competitive society has become, the more the cult of the social has flowered
amongst the faithful. Kevin Kelly, Silicon Valley's most articulate libertarian collectivist, best summarized this in his 1995 book *Out of Control*[27] in
which he presented the Internet as a "post-Fordist economic order" managed by the "hive mind" of a new, digitally connected social order.[28]

John Perry Barlow echoed Kelly's transcendental communitarianism in
his vision of the digital revolution. "As a result of the opening of cyberspace,
humanity is now undergoing the most profound transformation of its history," the Grateful Dead lyricist wrote. "Coming into the Virtual World, we
inhabit Information. Indeed, we become Information. Thought is embod-
ied and the Flesh is made Word. It's weird as hell."[29]

Such social-transcendentalism was as *weird as hell*. Unfortunately,
however, Kelly and Barlow weren't the only peddlers of this messianic romanticism. Through the work of thinkers like MIT mathematician Norbert
Wiener[30] and Canadian new media guru Marshall McLuhan, Silicon Valley's digital version of the cult of the social began to attract a wider currency.
In particular, McLuhan's arguments from books like *Gutenberg Galaxies*
(1962) and *Understanding Media* (1964), about cyberspace uniting all of
mankind in a single "global village," has become one of Silicon Valley's central beliefs among social network entrepreneurs like Mark Zuckerberg. It's
not surprising, therefore, as David Kirkpatrick notes in *The Facebook Effect*,
that the Canadian new media guru is a "favorite" at a company that, with its
close to a billion members, might be on the brink of realizing the McLuhanite vision of a "universal communications platform that would unite the
planet."[31]

What is most striking about McLuhan's embrace of technology is his nostalgic love-in with the imaginary past. *Yes, I should have liked to have lived there then*, McLuhan is saying about ancient society, *color, excitement, power, freedom*. The end of history for McLuhan, like for other digital communitarians is, therefore, a return to the distant past. Therein lies the value of technology for this new media guru. It's an Ur-past time machine—one that travels backward rather than forward.

As James Gleick notes in *The Information*, McLuhan "hailed the new electric age not for its newness but for its return to the roots of human creativity."[32] He sees value of information technology as "winding the tape backwards" and drawing us back into what he called our "tribal mesh" of a premodern oral culture.

The technological futurism of Marshall McLuhan and disciples like Mark Zuckerberg is, thus, in reality, a nostalgia for a paradise lost. Which is why, as Mike Malone so memorably put it, "nostalgia for the future is Silicon Valley's greatest contribution to the age."[33]

The Bowling Alone Syndrome

The corpse of the Summer of Love has, therefore, been resurrected as the Internet with social media emerging as the great hope for romantic communitarians desperate to bring humanity together and rebuild community in the twenty-first century. Think of this nostalgia for the future as the "Bowling Alone syndrome"—a reference to the communitarian theories of Harvard University sociologist Robert Putnam, whose highly influential and best-selling *Bowling Alone* regards the digital network as the solution to what he considers as the crisis of local community.

Writing, in 2000—only a couple of years after @quixotic created the first social media business—Putnam sees electronic media as the twenty-first-century means of reinventing community engagement. "Let us find ways to ensure that by 2010 Americans will spend less leisure time sitting passively alone in front of glowing screens and more time in active connection with our fellow citizens," he argued with communitarian fervor. "Let us foster new forms of electronic entertainment and communication that reinforce community engagement rather than forestalling it."[34]

Ten years later, this Bowling Alone syndrome—a social utilitarianism premised on the idea that community makes us, as individuals, both happier and more prosperous—has become almost as ubiquitous as Facebook, foursquare or Twitter. A recent avalanche of kumbaya books with good-vibration titles like *We-Think*,[35] *The Wealth of Networks*,[36] *Socialnomics*,[37] *Here Comes Everybody*,[38] *Open Leadership*,[39] *Six Pixels of Separation*,[40] *What's Mine Is Yours: How Collaborative Consumption is Changing the Way We Live*, *We First*,[41] *Generation We*,[42] *Connected*,[43] *Reality Is Broken*,[44] *The Mesh: Why the Future of Business Is Sharing*[45] and *The Hyper-Social Organization*[46] all sing from the same transformational song sheet about the miraculous power of community.

This intellectual obsession with the social, an obsession with sharing—what today, "as the arc of information flow bends toward ever greater connectivity,"[47] is fashionably called a "meme" (but is, in many ways, a virus)—can be seen across many different academic disciplines. The concepts of togetherness and sharing have acquired such religious significance that, in stark contrast with the research of Oxford University's Baroness Susan Greenfield, some scientists are now "discovering" its centrality in the genetic makeup of the human condition. One "neuroeconomist," a certain Dr. Paul Zak from the California Institute of Technology, has supposedly found that social networking activates the release of "generosity-trust chemical in our brains."[48] Larry Swanson and Richard Thompson from the University of Southern California are even "discovering" that the brain resembles a interconnected community—thereby triggering the ridiculous headline: "Brain works more like internet than 'top down' company."[49]

Even David Brooks, the normally hardheaded *New York Times* columnist, seems in part to have fallen under the spell of the social, arguing in his

2011 best-selling *The Social Animal: The Hidden Sources of Love, Character and Achievement* that worldly success is a result of sociability and that solitariness or reclusiveness afflict only poorly parented or dysfunctional people.[50] And yet Brooks is much too sober an analyst to have drunk fully from the social media Kool-Aid, particularly in terms of the countercultural narcissism that also characterizes the Facebook and Twitter generation. "It's not all about you," Brooks thus told American graduates in a warning against what he called "the litany of expressive individualism" that, he says, "is still the dominant note in American culture."[51]

Meanwhile Steven Johnson, another hypervisible super-node who, you'll remember approvingly, described our "oversharing cuture" in *Time* magazine as "a networked version of the Truman Show," has gone as far as to argue that the social is somehow written into the natural laws of the universe. In *Where Good Ideas Come From: The Natural History of Innovation*,[52] his 2010 communitarian polemic cleverly disguised as sober intellectual history, Johnson attempts to collapse Charles Darwin's biological theories of life's origins with the eternal value of the digital network. "A good idea is a network,"[53] he writes, claiming that our best ideas, like a biologically successful coral reef, rely on what he calls a social "ecosystem"—presumably the same "human ecosystem" that @quixotic has been building, designing and improving since the late nineties. The short history of the Web, Johnson tells us, citing the examples of social networks like Twitter, foursquare and his own hyperlocal social new platform Outside.In, "started as a desert, and it has been steadily transforming into a coral reef."[54]

From Robert Putnam to Steven Johnson to Clay Shirky to Jeff Jarvis to Kevin Kelly, the message about the core value of the social network remains the same. The network is our salvation as a human race, their meme says. Digital social networks are enabling us to come together as a human race, the faithful explain, a collectivist vision that a skeptical Jaron Lanier, the inventor of virtual reality, has critiqued as "digital Maoism."[55] The network will finally enable us to realize ourselves both as individuals and as social beings, these digital communitarians promise. Business, leadership, media, identity, culture, wealth, freedom, innovation, motivation, the brain, even, perhaps the universe itself—everything, they say, is transformed by the digital revolution. The future, they all echo Biz Stone, will inevitably be social.

The Long March Back into the Future

"This will be a long march," John Hagel and John Seeley Brown argue about the transition to a social knowledge economy, in a presumably unintentional nod to old Chairman Mao. "For the first time ever, we have the real opportunity to become who we are and, more importantly, who were meant to be."[56]

According to Jeff Jarvis, this is a long march into the future that might lead us back to the sixteenth century and what he calls the "idyllic" and "transparent society" of Henry VIII's England. But Jarvis's utopian version of early modern European society is based upon a fatal misunderstanding of a classic dystopian text. "In 1516, Sir Thomas More argued in his novel *Utopia* that the idyllic society is the transparent society," he argues with characteristic communitarian nostalgia in *Public Parts*. "In More's time, everyone worked under the gaze of everyone else. Public business was conducted out of private homes; the cobbler made his shoes there, the alehouse was a house. Privacy in the modern sense was not expected."[57] Yet Jarvis fundamentally misreads Sir Thomas More's *Utopia*—a book that imagines a society of such radical transparency that the entire community dines collectively at long wooden tables. Jarvis fails to understand that, in this classic defense of individual liberty and privacy, More—who was hung, drawn and quartered in 1535 for high treason—was actually offering a dystopian warning about working "under the gaze" of an all-seeing tyrant like his executioner, Henry VIII.

Yet even more than Jarvis or Hagel, this Rousseauian nostalgia for an imaginary preindustrial community in which we can finally "become who we are" and enable our intrinsic human nature is best encapsulated by uber-communitarian Clay Shirky, whose 2010 *Cognitive Surplus*[58] picks up where Putnam's *Bowling Alone* left off ten years earlier.

"The atomization of social life in the 20th century left us so far removed from participatory culture that when it came back, we needed the phrase participatory culture to describe it," Shirky argues, articulating Jean-Jacques Rousseau's ideal of a citizenry transparent to itself. "Before the 20th century, we didn't really have a phrase for participatory culture; in fact, it would have been something of a tautology. A significant chunk of culture was participatory—local gatherings, events and performances—because where else could culture come from but the people.[59]

The digital revolution changes everything, Shirky says, because "participatory culture" does away with the old hierarchies of twentieth century industrial media. We therefore no longer need a well-financed Hollywood studio like Paramount or an authoritarian movie director like Alfred Hitchcock to make *Vertigo*. The twentieth-century Hollywood monopoly of media is replaced with what Shirky calls the Internet's "social production" in which culture is created by all of us rather than by elites. Digital media thus literally becomes the "connective tissue of society," the participatory source of both culture and community. To requote John Perry Barlow, we thus all *become Information*—each of us a participatory node in this collective production of culture.

But Shirky—not for nothing dubbed the Herbert Marcuse of today's Web intelligentsia[60]—is right for all the wrong reasons. In the twentieth century, we went to the theater to be terrorized by Hitchcock's pictures about innocent men like Scottie Ferguson who were dragged into nightmares they neither understood nor controlled. But when the lights came on, the nightmare ended and we were free to leave the movie theater and get on with our regular lives.

Today, however, Hitchcock's *Vertigo* has been radically democratized so that we are all now participants in the drama. That's the truth about Shirky's "participatory culture." You see, social media has been so ubiquitous, so much the connective tissue of society that we've all become like Scottie Ferguson, victims of a creepy story that we neither understand nor control.

Yes, this digital version of *Vertigo* is as weird as hell.

Just as Gavin Elster idealized an invented San Francisco of June 1849 and Scottie Ferguson fell in love with the fake Madeleine Elster, Shirky and his fellow communitarians have fallen in love with a preindustrial participatory culture that probably never really existed and certainly can't be resurrected in our highly competitive and increasingly individualized twenty-first-century world. And just as Elster enticed his own old Stanford University classmate into a dark fantasy of deceit and heartbreak, these romantic communitarians are, for one reason or another, dragging all of us into a future that most of us really don't want—a digital love-in of default publicness, a Darwinian struggle of hypervisibly networked individuals, a "global village" where secrecy and forgetting are disappearing, a "participatory culture" that shines an unwanted transparency upon all of our lives, a Creepy SnoopOn.Me world of incessant foursquare check-ins, computers that know us and Facebook facial scans in which nobody is ever let alone.

While Steven Johnson favorably compares the Internet's "ecosystem" to one of Charles Darwin's biologically teeming coral reef, while Nicholas Christakis and James Fowler promise us that "when you smile, the world smiles with you,"[61] while Jeff Jarvis offers us a return ticket to the "idyllic" transparency of Henry VIII's England," and while Clay Shirky guarantees that "humans intrinsically value a sense of connectedness,"[62] what networked technology has really engineered is the resurrection of Jeremy Bentham's Auto-Icon—a self-glorification machine promising, with all the seductiveness of a coercive Hitchcock heroine, to make us all immortal.

The Internet—with its virtual worlds like Second Life—has transformed the idea of immortality from a religious metaphor into a digital possibility. According to the University of Pennsylvania historian John Tresch, today's social media system encourages all of us to manage what he calls our "fame machine" so that we can transform ourselves into icons. In this life in the crystal palaces of our digital age, "We must all now pass through a mobile, multifaceted, and omnipresent fame machine to enter even the modest arenas of friendship, family, and work." And the goal is to build followers and establish what Tresch calls our "own cloud of glory."[63]

So, like Hitchcock's *Vertigo*, social media—with its claim that technology unites us—is the exact reverse of what it seems. Behind the communitarian optimism of the digital utilitarians lies a vertiginous and socially fragmented twenty-first-century truth. It's a postindustrial truth of increasingly weak community and a rampant individualism of super-nodes and super-connectors. It's the truth of an "attention" economy that uses individual "reputation" as its major currency on networks like Klout. And, most troubling of all, it's the antisocial truth of a socioeconomic world of increasing loneliness, isolation and inequality—a socially dysfunctional condition that Sherry Turkle describes as being "alone together."

Just as in a good Hitchcock picture, everything is illusionary. Those accidental Maoists, John Seely Brown and John Hagel, were right about their "long march." But it's a long march back into the past rather than the future. History repeats itself, first as tragedy, then as farce, Marx wrote in his essay about the failure of the 1848 revolution. Perhaps. But there is no doubt that—as Silicon Valley's technology transforms the twenty-first-century world—the story of the nineteenth-century industrial revolution is, in some ways, being played over again in today's digital revolution. The social tyranny that is encroaching upon individual liberty in today's hypervisible age, for example, is a familiar problem from the mass mechanical epoch. And so is the utopian promise that contemporary technology can overcome the divisions in mankind and unify all of us in a global village of mutual understanding and sympathy.

So let's take that long march into the past and return from our culture of great exhibitionism to the nineteenth-century age of the great exhibition. And we will begin this journey in the haunted old university city of Oxford, where we'll find a series of pictures so faded from the walls of history that, in contrast to Hitchcock's *Vertigo*, none of you will have ever seen any of them before.

6

THE AGE OF THE GREAT EXHIBITION

"The transparency is too good to be true. . . . What lies behind
this falsely transparent world?"
—JEAN BAUDRILLARD[1]

The Holy Grail

The architects of our public future had, in the fading light of an Oxford autumn evening, stepped back into the private architecture of the past. The
lozenge-shaped, decagonal library, built in 1853 by Benjamin Woodward—an
Irish architect described by his friend, the Pre-Raphaelite artist Dante Gabriel Rossetti, as "the silliest creature that ever breathed out of an oyster,"[2]
had become the stage for the architects of our brave new hypervisible world.
Dotted around Woodward's gothic Oxford library, with its infinite book-
shelves and half-invisible murals of scenes from King Arthur's court on
seven of its ten dark walls, were the senior lieutenants, the great knights of
today's global social network.

Silicon Valley, you see, had come to Oxford. The Californian designers
of today's age of transparency had come to the ancient university city of private cloisters and hidden quadrangles, locked doors and wrought-iron gates,
forbidding walls and crooked alleyways, illicit passages and tunneled vaults.
These enablers of twenty-first-century visibility had come to a place that the
great travel writer Jan Morris, noting its fifty acres of graveyard, described as
"the most haunted of cities"—so haunted, in fact, Morris explains, that

Jeremy Bentham, the inventor of the Inspection-House, who, in 1760, came up to Queens College (the same college, as it happens, that Tim Berners-Lee, the inventor of The Worldwide Web, attended two centuries later), was in "perpetual fear of spooks."[3] And Silicon Valley had come to the very haunted heart of Oxford, to the Oxford Student Union, Benjamin Woodward's eccentrically ornate building, a graveyard where the reputations of many aspiring intellects had been buried over the last two centuries.

From Bentham to Berners-Lee, "everyone comes this way, sooner or later,"[4] Jan Morris writes about this shimmering yet half-invisible city sitting, as she notes, in Middle England's "no man's land"[5] between London and Birmingham. So perhaps it was appropriate then that Silicon Valley's *aristocrazia*—the architects of the digital no-man's-land in which we are all spending more and more of our social lives—had now come to this ancient university city to paint their vision of our connected future.

Silicon Valley had come to Oxford both literally and as an idea, a symbol of future innovation. It was there physically, in the persons of Silicon Valley's most innovative figures—Reid Hoffman, Biz Stone, Chris Sacca, Mike Malone and Philip Rosedale. But the Valley had also come to Oxford in the symbolic form of "Silicon Valley Comes to Oxford," a two-day conference of debates and speeches, organized by the university's Saïd Business School and attended by students wanting to see a picture of our collaborative social future.

So there they were, then, these architects of our globally networked digital society. Dressed in tuxedos, with flutes of champagne in one hand and smartphones in their other, Silicon Valley's social media aristocracy was scattered around Woodward's Victorian library, socializing in both analog and in digital form. They were physically networking, mingling in small groups (this crowd of super-connectors had no need, of course, for MingleBird's social introduction app), clinking glasses in dark corners of the library while conspiring over the latest social media merger or acquisition; and simultaneously, in a parallel digital universe, they were using their smartphones to electronically network with their global followers and friends, networking to burnish their already glowing virtual reputations, networking on their own social networks, forever networking.

Or *there we were,* I should say, since I—as an aspiring super-node myself—was also there, networking with Philip Rosedale, the creator of Second Life, the three-dimensional, transparent society designed as a "place to connect"[6] for citizens of the digital world. "We're doing it because we believe increased transparency is the key to a stable economy and economic growth," Rosedale said of Second Life. "Those economies that have the most transparency and the most information are the ones that grow the fastest."[7]

The following day, Rosedale would debate with the Oxford professor of neuroscience, Baroness Susan Greenfield, about "The Universe, The Brain and Second Life," while I would do battle with @quixotic on whether social networks were becoming the nation-states of the twenty first century. But that evening, we were both spectators to another, more pressing debate. We were all about to go downstairs from the library to the Union's debating chamber, the place where some of the most powerful men and women of the last two centuries—from Winston Churchill and Margaret Thatcher to Ronald Reagan, Albert Einstein and Malcolm X—had come to debate the most important issues in modern history.

Over the last hundred and fifty years, the Union has also been the stage on which Oxford undergraduates, Pareto's aspiring *aristocrazia*, have established their intellectual reputations by debating the great questions of the age. Previous student presidents of the Union include British Prime Ministers Edward Heath and Herbert Asquith, the assassinated Pakistani prime minister Benazir Bhutto, the current mayor of London Boris Johnson and that master of reinvention Andrew Sullivan, one of the most hypervisible brands in today's social media world. Even Bertie—Queen Victoria and Prince Albert's eldest son, the longtime Prince of Wales and the future

Edward VII, who came up to Christ Church as an undergraduate in 1859, would visit the Oxford Union every Thursday to listen to the debates. "Compared with the rest of his life there," one historian of the Union commented on the adventures of the unscholarly Bertie at Oxford, "it was a positively thrilling experience."[8]

"This house believes that the problems of tomorrow are bigger than the entrepreneurs of today," the Oxford Union was about to debate. On one side of this debate were the risk takers of today—Biz Stone and Reid Hoffman, entrepreneurs skilled at jumping off cliffs and assembling airplanes on their way down. On the other were skeptics such as World Bank vice-chairman Ian Goldin and the writer Will Hutton, who were doubtful that "failing fast" was a solution to the social problems of the twenty-first century. It was a debate about whether the entrepreneurs of Silicon Valley, the architects shaping today's Web 3.0 revolution, could be trusted with our future in a digitalized world where the boundaries between first and Second Life were quickly dissolving.

As we stood together drinking champagne in the fading light of the Oxford evening, Rosedale—a bronzed Southern Californian whose athletic physique seemed more suited to the well lit utopia of Second Life than to a darkly gothic nineteenth-century Oxford library—and I warmed up for the Union debate with a little intellectual joust of our own. We were comparing the merits of Benjamin Woodward's nineteenth-century physical building with the transparent architecture of the twenty-first-century virtual network.

"So how does being here contrast to being on the Internet?" I asked him, sweeping my half empty champagne flute around the library. "Which experience, do you think, is more memorable?"

Rosedale gazed up at the paintings of King Arthur's court on the library walls. In the artificial light of the Gothic library, the tuxedoed Californian technologist, his bronzed face tilted toward the heavens, emanated an exaggerated presence, as if a brilliant force, some alternative light, was publicly

illuminating him. Bathed in light and color, this twenty-first-century architect of virtual reality seemed superimposed on the gothic library. He appeared as a picture of the future, *hypervisible*, not unlike the way in which
the avatars in his Second Life online network stand out from its three-
dimensional canvas.

I also looked up to the pictures on the walls of the library, pictures
that appeared to be a replacement for windows in Woodward's dark gothic
building. But not only were these windows glassless, they were also opaque.
In contrast, you see, with the hypervisible Rosedale, these seven paintings of
King Arthur's court—frescoes that included King Arthur with his knights
of the Round Table, the heroic deaths of Merlin and Arthur, and Sir Lancelot's vision of the Holy Grail—were barely observable with the naked eye,
offering only the most elliptical glimpses of washed-out color and faded images. This was a great exhibition that nobody—neither Philip Rosedale, nor
I, nor anyone else—could see.

"There must've been a technical glitch," Rosedale joked. "What operating system are they using on the walls here?"

Social Art

But it was no laughing matter. There really had been a technical problem
with the walls. Painted by Dante Gabriel Rossetti and a group of Pre-
Raphaelite Brotherhood friends[9] including William Morris and Edward
Burne Jones, just as Oxford itself was being radically transformed by what
Peter Drucker called the "first great industrial revolution of the 1830's and
1840's" (the railway, the most literal manifestation of the industrial network,
only reaching the university city in 1844), these romantically revolutionary
artists had brought King Arthur's mythological court back to life in seven
frescoes painted between 1857 and 1859.[10]

From the beginning, it had been a self-consciously amateurish enterprise
by a group of brilliantly talented yet disorganized Oxford undergraduates.

In keeping with its identity as what the historian Paul Johnson calls the "first avant-garde movement in art,"[11] the Pre-Raphaelite Brotherhood project to paint the Union library was a social art experiment. Having observed that the walls of Woodward's decagonal room were "hungry for pictures,"[12] Rossetti called on a group of his undergraduate friends to paint the walls with scenes from Alfred Tennyson's 1845 *Idylls of the King*—an epic poem that idealized the chivalrous age of King Arthur and his court.

Yes, I should have liked to have lived there then—color, excitement, power, freedom, Tennyson's 1845 poem about the preindustrial world says. And in a mid-nineteenth-century society where the new industrial network was savagely transforming all the certainties of traditional communal life, it was no wonder that *Idylls of the King* had such an impact on romantics like Rossetti and his Oxford friends.

Despite their yearning for the past, the Pre-Raphaelite Brotherhood's attitude toward modern technology was curiously ambivalent. On the one hand, influenced by the gothic romanticism of mid-nineteenth-century poets and writers like Tennyson, Thomas Carlyle and William Wordsworth, the Pre-Raphaelites were critical of the heartlessly individualistic nature of the industrial revolution and nostalgic for what the art historian E. H. Gombrich calls the "spirit of the Middle Ages."[13] As the historian of Victorian England, A. N. Wilson notes, "these young painters set out to criticize the spirit of the age" and to "revivify society" with their gothic art.[14] But their nostalgia for the simple community of the Middle Ages—not unlike Marshall McLuhan's idealization of the oral culture of primitive man, or Clay Shirky's and Robert Putnam's romanticized versions of participatory democracy in pre-twentieth-century communal life—was an invention that bore little, if any, actual truth to the past. This retreat into an idealized picture of the past that was, as Laurence des Cars notes in his study of the Pre-Raphaelites, "a way of replacing the realities of modern life with romance and chivalry."[15]

But the Pre-Raphaelite Brotherhood also had a certain sort of belief, perhaps even a McLuhanite religious faith in the power of technology to help them accurately represent the world and make their creative work accessible to their audience. According to Robert Hughes, the "bywords" of their revolutionary art were to *"purge, simplify, archaize"*[16] the decay of western art and return to a time before the sixteenth-century Renaissance artist Raphael to rediscover the purity of representative painting. For the Pre-Raphaelites, "God was in the details" of their art and thus they found what Hughes called the "technical fiction" of "painting with transparent colors on a wet white ground"[17] and to mix pigments with resinous varnish to keep their colors fresh"[18]—techniques which enabled them to exaggerate the impact of light and color and "to reproduce the dazzle of direct sunlight"[19] in their paintings. The Pre-Raphaelites thus relied on the most innovative modern technology to paint pictures which romanticized a past that could never and has never existed. Perhaps it wasn't coincidental, then, that the most brilliant of the frescoes was Rossetti's version of Sir Lancelot's Vision of the Holy Grail, that perennial symbol in western iconography—from Sir Thomas More to Sir Thomas Mallory to Alfred Tennyson to Philip Rosedale—of the perfectly impossible and the impossibly perfect thing.

At first, the Pre-Raphaelite social art project on the walls of Woodward's Union building was seen as a triumph, a magnificent representation of Tennyson's poem. "Never in the long history of Oxford had such groupings and individualities, forgathered to concentrate devotion on a common task," wrote one historian of the Oxford Union.[20] As Jan Morris notes, it is the "most famous Pre-Raphaelite project in Oxford."[21] John Ruskin, the most influential art critic of the Victorian era, considered Rossetti's own picture of Sir Lancelot's Vision of the Holy Grail to have been "the finest piece of colour in the world," while one contemporary described the colors as "so brilliant as to make the walls look like the margin of an illuminated manuscript."[22]

And yet open-source art, like open-source books, movies or revolutions, doesn't work—not now, not in the future and certainly not in the middle of the industrial nineteenth century. You see, for all Rossetti and his young friends' enthusiasm for their collective art project, it was an underfinanced and disorganized initiative lacking any coherent leadership or overall plan. Their greatest mistake—particularly ironic given the Pre-Raphaelite reliance on technology to exaggerate the visibility of their pictures—was failing to provide the necessary technical preparation to protect the paint from degeneration.

By 1858, it was clear that the frescoes were quickly fading from the walls and were on the verge of disappearing. "The only remedy for all is now whitewash, and I shall be happy to hear of its application," Dante Gabriel Rossetti said that year, having lost all interest in the project. [23] Thus, for the last century and a half, these Pre-Raphaelite frescoes have haunted the walls of the Union library, gradually becoming less and less decipherable (in spite of various expensive restoration projects), [24] their fame resting upon their illegibility.

But Second Life's Philip Rosedale knew none of this. All he could see were illegible pictures and walls that had forgotten their art. In the mind of this pioneer of transparency, the walls had suffered a technical glitch. They had failed to back up their information. Their operating system was faulty.

"So this proves my case," he said. "While the Internet remembers everything that we enter into it, this old library only knows how to forget."

"But what's the value of remembering everything?" I asked, smiling weakly.

Rosedale smiled, too. But his was a blinding smile, overflowing with Pre-Raphaelite color. "Remembering everything brings us all together," he told me. "It enables the unity of mankind."

"*The unity of man?*" I raised my champagne flute in mock tribute. "I've heard that one before. History repeats itself, eh?"

Rosedale raised his champagne flute, too. "Oh no, not this time," he said, clinking my flute with his. "This time it will be different."

But Rosedale was wrong. This time it won't be any different. You see, a holy grail is a holy grail, whether it's a Pre-Raphaelite social art project, a transparent three-dimensional world inhabited by avatars, or a global social network that brings humanity together. The unity of man is as much a delusion now, in our age of great exhibitionism, as it was in the mid-nineteenth-century during the age of the great exhibition.

No, this time it *won't* be different. And to explain why, let me tell you the sad story of a good prince from a fairy-tale kingdom whose noble ambition was to establish this unity of man.

The Unity of Mankind

In the early spring of 1850, three years before the Irish architect Benjamin Woodward began work on his gothic Oxford Union with its opaque windows onto an imaginary world, a good German prince from the fairy-tale kingdom of Saxe-Coberg and Gotha named Francis Albert Augustus Charles Emmanuel gave a speech about a much more transparent building. On March 21, 1850, this richly networked aristocrat—best known today as Prince Albert, the husband of Queen Victoria, and the father of Bertie, the Oxford undergraduate who would later become King Edward VII—spoke in London to two hundred of England's most powerful *aristocrazia*, the architects of the country's industrial revolution. His Royal Highness Prince Albert had a big idea. Like Philip Rosedale, he wanted to enable the unity of man by bringing everyone in the world together. And, like the Second Life founder, he planned to do this by creating something of crystalline transparency.

The speech was given in the Egypt Room of Mansion House, the formal residence of London's mayor, an eighteenth-century neoclassical building situated in the City of London, then the wealthiest square mile in the most richest and most populous city on earth.[25] Amongst the audience were the British prime minister Lord John Russell, the foreign minister Lord Palmerston, the former president of the Oxford Union William Gladstone, the

Archbishop of Canterbury, the French ambassador, masters of city guilds, and local politicians such as Henry Forbes, the mayor of Bradford, the center of the new global woolen industry.

With its massive neoclassical columns, painted shields and imposing statue of Britannia at one end of the hall, the Mansion House's palatial Egyptian room, designed by the eighteenth-century Palladian architect George Dance the Elder, was a suitably imposing stage for Prince Albert's grand message. After a banquet of turtle soup, eel, lobster, mutton, pigeon, fruit, cakes and ices, Prince Albert, who looked "resplendent"[26] in his uniform as Master of Trinity House Corporation, Britain's lighthouse authority, rose to speak.

"Nobody, however, who has paid any attention to the peculiar features of our present era, will doubt for a moment that we are living at a period of most wonderful transition, which tends rapidly to accomplish that great end, to which, indeed, all history points—the realisation of the unity of mankind," he began.

The prince was, in a sense, correct about this great historical "transition"—although, as he himself knew, it certainly wasn't "wonderful" for everyone who happened to be living through it. He was describing the epochal shift between the old fragmented agricultural communities idealized by romantics like Alfred Tennyson and the Pre-Raphaelite Brotherhood and the new networked industrial architecture of railways, telegraph and electric lines, roads and factories. To requote the fictionalized Sean Parker from *The Social Network* movie, "first we lived on farms, then we lived in cities." And as Peter Drucker has already reminded us, this technological transformation from agricultural to industrial life is one of the most momentous social and economic events in all of human history. "In two centuries," explains the economic historian Joel Mokr, "daily life changed more than it had in the 7,000 years before."[27]

Francis Albert Augustus Charles Emmanuel of Saxe-Coberg and Gotha, a scion of one of the most networked of ancient European dynasties, was an internationalist—somebody who believed that the technology of the industrial revolution was transforming us from enemies into friends and uniting us as a human race through mutual respect, love, friendship and trust. Like the technological upheaval itself, not only was this goal of uniting humans through technology a new idea, but even the word "international" was a relatively recent neologism, having been invented by our old friend, Jeremy Bentham, in his 1789 *Introduction to the Principles of Morals and Legislation.*[28]

Albert's internationalism was, so to speak, manufactured by his faith in industrial technology. With its mechanical railways, steamships, mass newspapers and telegraph lines, the industrial revolution had reinvented the idea of physical distance, transforming a once geographically splintered world into a nascent McLuhanite global village. What Albert called the "realisation of the unity of mankind" could already be seen a year before his Mansion House speech, in the 1849 San Francisco gold rush, that disastrous expedition to foreign shores, an industrial[29] event that not only transported a quarter of a million argonauts from all over the world to California in under three years, but also injected the gold necessary to provide liquidity into the new global economic system.[30]

"The distances which separated the different nations and parts of the globe are rapidly vanishing before the achievements of modern invention, and we can traverse them with incredible ease; the languages of all nations are known, and their acquirement placed within the reach of everybody; thought is communicated with the rapidity, and even by the power, of lightning," Prince Albert continued with his Mansion House speech. *"On the other hand, the great principle of division of labour, which may be called the moving power of civilization, is being extended to all branches of science, industry, and art."*

But in spite of the death of distance, Prince Albert knew there was something else holding up the realization of mankind's unity. The new technology of the industrial network, for all its miraculous destruction of distance and its dramatic increase in the capacity to produce goods, hadn't necessarily brought people together. Indeed, even though Britain was the most advanced industrial nation on earth in 1850,[31] it was also, in many other ways, the most divided. What Prince Albert called the "great principle of division of labour" had, in fact, resulted in an economic chasm not only between Britain and the rest of the world but also between the new rich, the capitalist architects of the industrial production, and the new poor, the new industrial working class that comprised a large proportion of London's one-and-half-million inhabitants in 1850 as well as the growing population of inmates locked inside Victorian Britain's industrially designed, Benthamite prisons.

In the mid nineteenth century, the industrial prison and the industrial factory were often indistinguishable. "Modern industry has converted the little workshop of the patriarchal master into the great factory of the industrial capitalist. Masses of labourers, crowded into the factory, are organized like soldiers," wrote Karl Marx and Friedrich Engels in their 1848 pamphlet *The Communist Manifesto*, along with John Stuart Mill's *On Liberty*, the most influential political treatise of the nineteenth century. "Not only are they slaves of the bourgeois class, and of the Bourgeois State; they are daily and hourly enslaved by the machine, by the overlooker, and, above all, by the individual bourgeois manufacturer himself."[32]

While there is no record that Prince Albert read the *Communist Manifesto*, he certainly was well aware of the dreadful lives of the English industrial proletariat, whom he described as "that class of our community which has most of the toil and least of the enjoyments, of this world."[33] Throughout 1848, for example, the year of acute political tension in England, and of revolutions throughout most of Europe, he pestered Lord John Russell about the suffering of the workers, telling the British prime minister that the government was "bound to do what it can to help the working classes over the present moment of distress." The Irish potato famine and Chartist violence of 1848 only made a bad situation even worse. "It is dreadful to see the sufferings at this moment," Prince Albert—who was also the president of The Society for Improving the Condition of the Labouring Classes—wrote that year after visiting a particularly grim London slum.[34]

The situation was seen as being so bad during the Chartist demonstrations of April 1848 that the Duke of Wellington, the popular general who defeated Napoleon at Waterloo in 1815, transformed London into a gigantic Inspection-House, teeming with police spies and controlled by a massive garrison of troops. Wellington, who was enlisted by the prime minister, Lord John Russell, as a popular symbol of law and order, barricaded Bloomsbury's British Museum, sandbagged the Bank of England, reinforced all of London's penitentiaries with heavily armed guards and mobilized a small army of prying security staff, including what A. N. Wilson describes as an "astonishing" 85,000 special constables.[35] Visibility had, already, become a trap. Indeed, it is likely that one of these special constables took the first-ever photographs of a major historical event, the earliest origins of contemporary photography social networks like Instagram, capturing daguerreotypes of what Wilson describes as "drizzly pathos" that were later used by police spies to identify and imprison troublemakers.

There were three ways of trying to heal the international discord and splintering of society during the mid-nineteenth-century industrial revolution. The first was, like Marx and Engels, to become a revolutionary communist and try to destroy capitalism in order to reassemble humanity via the holy grail of a universally classless, high-tech society in which we'd be free to "hunt in the morning, fish in the afternoon and rear cattle in the evening."[36] The second was to retreat, like the Pre-Raphaelite Brotherhood or the anti-industrial Luddite movement, into a reactionary medieval world, an ur-past of organic community and heroically unselfish knights—a strategy that transformed history into fairy tale pictures. And the third option was to try to reform the system from within, healing over social divisions and pursuing policies that seemed to unite rather than divide people.

Prince Albert was a reformer rather than a utopian revolutionary or reactionary. And that is what had brought him to the neoclassical Egyptian Room in the early Spring of 1850. He was there to describe his strategy for realizing the unity of mankind. "He [Prince Albert] believed that the world had reached a stage where all knowledge and innovation were recognized as being the property of the international community as a whole, not something that needed to be protected by secrecy from the gaze of outsiders," one historian observed.[37] Albert had, therefore, come to Mansion House to promote a transparent event that would openly celebrate science, technology and the laws of motion. This festival of innovation, with its faith in openness and transparency, would bring the world together. It was to be called the Great Exhibition.

"Science discovers these laws of power, motion, and transformation; industry applies them to raw matter, which the earth yields us in abundance, but which becomes valuable only by knowledge. Art teaches us the immutable laws of beauty and symmetry, and gives to our productions forms in accordance with them," Prince Albert explained to his audience in the Egypt room. *"Gentlemen—the Exhibition of 1851 is to give us a true test and a living picture of the point of development at which the whole of mankind has arrived in this great task, and a new starting point from which all nations will be able to direct their further exertions."*

London's 1851 "Great Exhibition of the Works of Industry of all Nations," as it officially became known, would indeed be a "true test" to transform warring social classes and nations into friends and realize the unity of mankind. But this was to be no ordinary exhibition. You see, Prince Albert, himself a gifted amateur portrait painter, had found a revolutionary architect to construct a temple of transparency for his Great Exhibition.

He had found a gardener with a genius for building glass houses.

The Crystal Palace

Prince Albert first came across the work of this gardener in December 1843. The Prince Consort and Queen Victoria had been visiting the Derbyshire estate of the Duke of Devonshire, today best known for Chatsworth House, a palatial seventeenth-century neoclassical country house with a panoramic view of the surrounding parks and gardens.

But at Chatsworth, the view that captivated Queen Victoria and Prince Albert was of a revolutionary iron-and-glass conservatory built by Chatsworth's head gardener, a landscape architect from humble roots named Joseph Paxton. Queen Victoria described it as "the finest thing imaginable of its kind," while Prince Albert called it "magnificent and beautiful."[38]

Prince Albert never forgot Joseph Paxton's great iron-and-glass building and, after other architectural projects were deemed too expensive, he called on Paxton—by then a minister of Parliament—to build an industrial glass and steel palace to house the works of industry of all nations. Thus, as Bill Bryson notes, "In the autumn of 1850, in Hyde Park in London, there arose a most extraordinary structure: a giant iron-and-glass greenhouse covering nineteen acres of ground and containing within its airy vastness enough room for four St. Paul's Cathedrals."[39]

What Paxton built in Hyde Park in just five months in 1850 was, according to Prince Albert, "truly a piece of marvelous art,"[40] Bill Bryson describes it as "the century's most daring and iconic building,"[41] and Eric Hobsbawm calls it a "brilliant monument"[42] for the achievements of the industrial revolution. Its architecture was the opposite of Benjamin Woodward's dark Oxford library. The building was comprised of 293,655 panes of glass, more than 4,500 tons of iron and, most amazingly, twenty-four miles of guttering. The satirical magazine *Punch* dubbed it "The Crystal Palace" and the name stuck. For his festival of innovation with its goal of eliminating the secrecy of the preindustrial world, Prince Albert had commissioned a transparent glass palace that would be impossible to protect from the gaze of outsiders.

"After breakfast we drove with the 5 children to look at the Crystal Palace, which was not finished when we last went, and really now is one of the wonders of the world, which we English can be proud . . ." Queen Victoria wrote in her journal in February 1850. "The galleries are finished, and from the top of them the effect is quite wonderful. The sun shining in through the transept gave a fairy-like appearance. The building is so light and graceful, in spite of its immense size. Many of the exhibits have arrived. . . . It made me feel proud and happy."[43]

Not everyone, of course, admired Paxton's industrial miracle of iron and glass with either Queen Victoria's enthusiasm or pride. The gothic skeptics of technology and progress were, to say the least, underwhelmed. The patron saint of the Pre-Raphaelite Brotherhood, the critic John Ruskin, described the Crystal Palace as "a cucumber frame between two chimneys," while Edward Burne-Jones, one of the Pre-Raphaelite artists who painted the walls of the Oxford Union, found Paxton's architectural design to be "cheerless and monotonous."[44]

But while the symbol of the Great Exhibition of 1851 was Paxton's transparent glass and iron palace, its social significance was Prince Albert's attempt to unify the human race through a universal celebration of technology and science. The exhibition showed off 100,000 items of 14,000 firms from Britain and around the world. It was a cornucopia of industrial design, mechanical technology and steam powered machines. There were machines for saving human labor, printing presses and steam engines, mechanical globes, exhibits of the recently invented science of photography, prototypes of submarines and industrial printing presses, even machines for tipping people out of bed. Ironically, the only exhibit missing was Charles Babbage's proto-computer, his Difference Engine, which, perhaps because of its or his unimaginable foreignness,[45] was rejected by the organizers of the exhibition.

The engineering achievements exhibited in the Crystal Palace were matched by the Great Exhibition's social engineering achievements. As the historian Benjamin Friedman notes, "the Great Exhibition was an exuberant celebration of the idea not just of scientific and therefore material progress but . . . of progress in social, civic and moral affairs too."[46] Prince Albert's grand goal—to bring people together and break down the social boundaries of nineteenth-century life—had, in many ways, been successful. So, in spite of the fears of socialist insurrection that resulted in the opening ceremony being a private rather than public event, the Great Exhibition was the first genuinely open, inclusive event of the nineteenth century in which the English working classes and the aristocracy physically mingled together as citizens of the same nation.

As Michael Leapman describes in *The World for a Shilling: How the Great Exhibition of 1851 Shaped a Nation*, his vivid narrative of how the exhibition affected the lives of ordinary people, Prince Albert's Great Exhibition really did contribute to the creation of a collective British identity. Indeed, after its move from Hyde Park to the South London suburb of Sydenham (today known as Crystal Palace) in 1854, Paxton's building was popularly known as the "Palace of the People"[47] and attracted 60 million visitors over the next thirty years.[48]

In many ways then, the Great Exhibition was a triumph of Prince Albert's faith in nineteenth-century industrial technology to realize the unity of mankind. But the internationalist Prince Consort, who died in 1861 at the young age of forty-two, departed from the historical stage at the very moment when all his precious optimism about the industrial revolution's "great transition" was beginning to shatter into many pieces. Rather than the unifier of mankind, industrial technology, it turned out, was helping to disunite us into distrustful social classes, tribes and nation-states at perpetual war with one another.

The Shattering of the Glass

On the night of November 30, 1936, the sky over London was bloodred with 500-foot flames fanned from a high northwesterly wind. Joseph Paxton's Crystal Palace, that mid-nineteenth-century hope for a more transparent and inclusive industrial world, was ablaze. In spite of the efforts of hundreds of fire engines, firemen, and policemen, Paxton's palace, all 293,655 panes of glass, quickly dissolved into a heap of melted glass and buckled metal, the victim of what fire experts called the "funnel effect" of the high winds and the building's combustible wooden floorboards. A *Daily Mail* reporter, watching the fire from a plane, described it as being "like a blazing crater of a volcano."[49] The fire was visible from Hampstead Heath in North London to the coastal cities of Brighton and Margate in the south. A half-million spectators watched the burning Crystal Palace in South London. And at nine P.M. that evening, even ministers of Parliament left a Commons debate to watch the fire from their Westminster committee rooms and terraces.

They were watching the burning down of Prince Albert's internationalist dream. But, in truth, this death was little more than symbolic, the burial of a corpse that had already been dead for half a century. "Haughty with hope of endless progress and irresistible power" had been John Ruskin's observation about the Crystal Palace when it moved from Hyde Park to Sydenham in 1854. Ruskin's warning about the hubris of Albert's faith in technology and science to bring us together had been right. As the nineteenth century drew to a close, the Crystal Palace struggled to establish what, in Silicon Valley, would be called a viable business model. Paxton's building fell into disrepair and debt. By 1911 it had declared bankruptcy and during World War I this glass and iron building was renamed HMS Crystal Palace and, with a savage irony, was used as a naval training station for the Great War against Germany.

By 1936, Prince Albert's dream had not only died in South London, but also throughout most of the world. His faith in industrialization and the belief that technology and science would unite us had proven to be tragically misguided. Yes, Prince Albert was right that the analog networks of the mechanized age would create new identities and social organization, but his dream of history's "wonderful transition" turned out, in much of the world, to be closer to a nightmare.

As the sociologist Ernest Gellner argues in *Nations and Nationalism*, the industrial revolution resulted in an explosion of nationalism rather than internationalism. "Work, in industrial society, does not mean moving matter. The paradigm of work is no longer ploughing, reaping, thrashing," Gellner argued. "Work, in the main, is no longer the manipulation of things, but of meanings. It generally involves exchanging communications with other people, or manipulating the controls of a machine."[50]

This new network of roads, railways, telegraph wires and the mechanized printing press did indeed provide the necessary architecture for this distribution of meaning, thereby replacing the old fragmented agricultural worlds with a much more physically connected society. But rather than Esperanto or a universal computer code, the dominant languages of this late-nineteenth- and early-twentieth-century industrial world were exclusive national discourses like Italian or German. These languages and their supposedly eternal cultural traditions and histories imprisoned us within narrow linguistic groups. Rather than creating the unity of man, they led to an age of the nation-state, a new kind of imaginary community in which we defined ourselves in unique terms that not only excluded neighboring nations but also cultural minorities within our own society.

Take, for example, the modern history of Germany. When the good internationalist Prince Albert died in 1861 his fairy-tale principality, Saxe-Coberg and Gotha, was a part of the South German confederation of Bavaria. In 1870, Bavaria joined Bismarck's Prussia in a war against France that culminated in the establishment of a united Germany in 1871. The history of Germany between 1871 and 1914 is dominated, on the one hand, by a remarkably successful industrial revolution and, on the other, by the rise of an increasingly assertive nationalism. Germany's defeat in World War I led to the rise of National Socialism and the emergence of an even more eschatological communal identity, fused with a cult of medieval valor, mostly directed against the Jews, those symbols of the very modernity and internationalism that Prince Albert had once idealized.

In 1936, the fateful year that the Crystal Palace burnt to the ground, the German National Socialists had seized power and were aggressively deploying the latest technology and science to rearm the country. In Germany, however, the bloody night of broken glass took place a couple of years later, in November 1938. The National Socialists organized Kristallnacht (literally: "the night of broken glass"), a modern, state-sponsored pogrom in which mobs destroyed the property of German Jews, smashing the windows of their homes and stores and carrying off a quarter of all German Jewish men to primitive high-tech prisons we now call concentration camps. So much glass was destroyed in forty-eight hours of rioting that it took two full years' production of the entire plate-glass production of Belgium to replace it all. But *Kristallnacht* was only the beginning of the violence and hatred against outsiders. After that came another world war and the industrial death camps of Auschwitz and Belsen, which deployed the latest technology and science in ways that Prince Albert, in his very worst nightmares, could never have imagined.

What is most shocking about the organization of the death camps was their corruption of those two great pillars of Benthamite utilitarianism: social efficiency and central planning. "Belsen is said to have looked like an atomic research station or a well-designed motion picture studio," wrote *Brave New World* author Aldous Huxley in a savage swipe at Bentham's Inspection-House. "The Bentham brothers have been dead these hundred years and more;

but the spirit of the panopticon, the spirit of Sir Samuel's *mujik*-compelling workhouse, had gone marching along to strange and horrible destinations."[51]

Meanwhile, to the east of Nazi Germany, the Russian Empire had degenerated from the enlightened despotism of Samuel Bentham's eighteenth-century sponsor, Catherine the Great, into the twentieth-century oriental despotism of Joseph Stalin. Here, in the brave new collective world that had been Orwell's dark muse for the Ministry of Truth, facecrime, *Ownlife* and Big Brother, technology and science were being deployed in a nightmarish manner that transformed the country into an entirely transparent "*mujik*-compelling workhouse."

Having been articulated in the utopian language of the brotherhood of man and the universal friendship of the working classes, the Soviet revolution had been so corrupted by Stalin's terror that, as Hannah Arendt argues in *Origins of Totalitarianism*, its true impact was of individual isolation and weaker and weaker social ties. By November 1936, when the sky over London was bloodred with flames, Stalin's version of the great exhibition, his public show trials, conducted by his so-called "apparatchik," the functionaries of his brutal five-year plans, were reaching their bloodily exhibitionistic climax.

What the apparat created was a regime in which the camera was never switched off and the peephole never slammed shut. Even after Stalin's death, Big Brother remained in power. In East Germany, for example, tens of thousands of citizens were recruited by Stasi secret police as spies to watch their neighbors. By transforming society into a transparent prison that outlawed the liberty of independent thought, by turning East Germans into a vertiginous nation of Scottie Fergusons looking at the lives of others, the apparat killed individual privacy. As the Harvard University Law professor Charles Fried argues, privacy is intimately bound up with respect, love, friendship and trust, and is the "oxygen" by which individuals are capable of building social "relations of the most fundamental sort."[52] And it was exactly this *oxygen* that the apparatchik switched off—thereby destroying the respect, love, friendship and trust that traditionally existed between human beings. Thus, in the notorious Room 101 of Orwell's *Nineteen Eighty-four*, what the apparatchik finally smashed was Winston Smith's love for Julia, the very thing that made him human and gave him hope for the future.

That was the real tragedy of totalitarianism. Instead of love, there was hatred; in place of friendship, there was individual isolation and mutual disrespect, fear and distrust. Hope for the future had been extinguished in a society that had become the most hideous parody of Jeremy Bentham's hideously omniscient Inspection-House prison.

The Return of the Future

You'll remember that Karl Marx wrote that history repeats itself—first as tragedy, then as farce—while Reid Hoffman, the co-owner of our future, predicted that this future is always sooner and stranger than we think. But today, when the dream of the unity of man has been resurrected by utopians like Philip Rosedale, what exactly is that collective future? Could the Internet really turn out to be a farcical gulag? Might Mark Zuckerberg's five-year plans to transform the Internet into a brightly lit dorm room incarcerate us all in an absurd global prison where we are all forced to live in public?

In today's digital age, we know that the Big Brother of industrial society has been replaced by Walter Kirn's "vast cohort of prankish Little Brothers" equipped with their BlackBerrys, iPhones and Android fame machines.[53] Thus it would be not only be wrong, but also rather silly to suggest that Mark Zuckerberg is Stalin 2.0, or—whatever Julian Assange might claim—that Facebook is the new Stasi.

In an April 2011 debate on TechcrunchTV, Tim O'Reilly, the publishing mogul who invented the term Web 2.0 and Reid Hoffman, the archangel behind today's Web 3.0 revolution, debated what we had most to fear in a digital world overflowing with more and more personalized data.[54] For

O'Reilly, the fear was all-powerful corporations, while @quixotic's greatest fear was government. But they both missed a third spectre (and the third rail in a democracy like the United States) that, in some ways, is more chilling than either snooping government or corporations. O'Reilly and Hoffman forgot about the billions of little brothers who will, by 2020, own 50 billion smart devices connected to the network. They thus failed to acknowledge that what we most have to fear in the twenty-first century might be ourselves.

"The seeing machine was once a sort of dark room into which individuals spied; it has become a transparent building in which the exercise of power may be supervised by society as a whole." Michel Foucault wrote about the way in which Bentham's Inspection-House "spread throughout the social body" in the industrial age.[55] But Foucault died in 1984, the fateful year that Apple told us to "think different," and thus was never able to see the resurrection of the Inspection-House as the great tribunal committee of our new digital world.

This shift in power from a single omniscient twentieth-century Big Brother to the vast cohort of twenty-first-century Little Brothers is what distinguishes our future from the age of the great exhibition. The failure of totalitarianism, the decline of the role and power of government in most democratic societies and today's general cynicism toward all forms of political authority is, as British filmmaker Adam Curtis argues, "the ideology of our times." Yet, while power has shifted from the analog center to the digital edge, away both from evil dictators like Stalin and well-intentioned reformers like Prince Albert, that doesn't mean that power has been eliminated or that we really are about to realize a new unity of man. What, in fact, we see when we gaze into the future is that all the glass once used by Joseph Paxton to build the Crystal Palace has, in our age of great exhibitionism, been transformed into billions of Auto-Icons.

What we see in this future are pictures so strange that they could have been created by the author of *Absurdistan*. We see the return of the apparat-chik as an omniscient wireless device. We see a society that is becoming its own electronic image, a (dis)unity of little brothers. We see human beings turned inside out, so that all their most intimate data is displayed in the full gaze of the public network. We see a reputation economy in which respect, love, friendship and trust are replacing cash as society's scarcest and thus its most valuable commodity. We see a *Super Sad True Love Story* featuring global super-nodes with millions of friends who don't know the names of their neighbors. We see digital vertigo. More and more digital vertigo.

Yes, these pictures from the future are as a weird as hell.

So imagine a world without either secrecy or privacy, where every-thing and everyone is transparent. Imagine the return of the apparatchik in a world where we all live in public. Imagine yesterday's crystal palace metamorphosing into tomorrow's crystal prison where we have incarcer-ated ourselves in an infinite hall of mirrors. And imagine, if you can, a nineteenth-century Benthamite Inspection-House that is simultaneously a twenty-first-century luxury hotel. Because that is exactly where we must go next to view these haunting pictures from the future.

7

THE AGE OF GREAT EXHIBITIONISM

@JetPacks: What kind of mother holds a press conference upon hearing of her little girl's death? Is THIS your shot at stardom that you can't pass up?

The Crystal Prison

It was the morning of my debate about the future with Reid Hoffman at Oxford. Later that day, we would discuss whether social media communities would replace the nation-state as the source of personal identity in the twenty-first century. But, for the moment, I was standing in the center of what appeared, at first glance at least, to be an industrial prison. The jail in which I found myself, to borrow some words from Michel Foucault, contained "so many cages, so many theatres in which each actor is alone."[1] Designed to maximize the visibility and solitariness of its inmates, this industrial prison was, in Foucault's language, the "reverse of the principle of the dungeon." Its goals were as simple as its architecture: surveillance and control.

From my perch on a second-floor metal staircase in the central atrium of the prison's "A" Wing, I had a panoramic view of the well-lit, airy building with its solitary cages and theaters spread out all around me. To my left and right stretched long corridors of symmetrically spaced cells, all with identical caste-iron doors and spy-holes crisscrossed with thin metal bars. Above and beneath me were more floors with more corridors lined with more cells, more metal doors and more peepholes. By swiveling around in a circle, I could see all the doors of all the cells on all the floors of "A" Wing. The view gave me a feeling of omniscient control. As if I was God, perhaps. Or Jeremy Bentham.

It isn't surprising that the original architect of this Oxford prison was William Blackburn (1750–1790), "the father of the radial plan for prisons"[2] and Britain's leading pioneer of Bentham's ideas. Begun in 1785, a couple of years before Bentham published his open letter from Russia about the Inspection-House, Blackburn's prison replaced what had popularly become known as the "dung-heap"[3] of Oxford castle's notoriously chaotic public dungeons with a brand-new semicircular building designed as a giant eye to watch over its inmates.

The prison's three-tiered "A" Wing had been added between 1848 and 1856—overlapping, as it happens, with the building of Prince Albert's equally light and airy Crystal Palace, and incarcerating many of the same impoverished men and women[4] that the enlightened Albert hoped would visit the Great Exhibition. It was a prison premised upon the principle of perpetual peeking, a very different kind of great exhibition from the festival of science and technology put on in the Crystal Palace. Cells were built with one-way spy-holes that destroyed the prisoner's privacy and enabled the authorities to watch them at will. Solitary confinement replaced physical beating as the dominant mode of punishment. Prisoners were given numbers that became their institutional identity. Beginning in the 1860s, the authorities developed a system of criminal record-keeping that took advantage of the then-revolutionary technology of photography to establish mug shots of the prisoners. Those incarcerated in Oxford prison, to borrow some words from Mark Zuckerberg, possessed only one identity. The point was to supervise the prisoners' every movement and manage their time down to the very minute so that they were transformed from complex human beings with their "own lives" into packaged time lines of processed information.

Not much changed in "A" Wing between the late nineteenth and twentieth centuries. "The present Oxford prison," notes Jan Morris in the mid-1960s, "in the grim purlieus of the castle . . . is a small but awful place, filled with the janglings of keys, the scraping of padlocks, the tramp of feet and the voices of warders echoing against old stone walls."[5] This is a picture with which many fans of classic sixties British movies will be familiar. The jail scenes of the 1969 movie *The Italian Job*—starring Michael Caine as the crooked Charlie Crocker and the inimitable Noel Coward as crime boss Mr. Bridger—were filmed in Oxford's "A" Wing and offer a blackly comic introduction to prison life during the late industrial age.[6]

By the early twenty-first century, however, "A" Wing jangled with the sound of a very different sort of key. In September 1996, Her Majesty's Prison (HMP) Oxford was, so to speak, unlocked and, in the language of its official guide, "redeveloped as a leisure and retail complex."[7] A British company called the Malmaison Group that creates hotels "that dare to be different"[8] acquired the prison and, maintaining the simple architecture of William Blackburn's Benthamite building, turned it into a boutique hotel.

It is now called The Oxford Mal and is a simulacrum of the nineteenth-century prison. The old cells have been transformed into luxury bedrooms distinguished by their original spyholes and caste iron doors. The "A" Block is now a bright, sunlit atrium, designed as a walkway between the hotel's private bedrooms and its public parts. And the old solitary confinement cells in the basement of the prison have been transformed into a tasteful restaurant, the Destination Brasserie, where I had just eaten a breakfast of grilled kippers and scrambled eggs with @quixotic.

In one memorable scene from *The Italian Job*, Charlie Crocker breaks into the high-security prison in order to pitch Mr. Bridger with the idea of stealing $4 million worth of Chinese gold. Today, however, the Oxford Mal has become such a desirable place that it's not just innovative criminals who would like to break into its luxurious rooms. *"This time we're taking no prisoners,"* the Oxford Mal's Web site playfully markets itself to guests like myself. *"Imagine a prison that's a hotel. . . . Now imagine a prison that's sud-denly a luxury boutique hotel in Oxford, destination brasserie and hang-out for high-life hoodlums. Pinch yourself. You're doing time at the Mal."*

And I wasn't alone *doing time* at the Oxford Mal. All the technology inno-vators who were speaking at the "Silicon Valley Comes to Oxford" event—from Reid Hoffman, Philip Rosedale and Biz Stone to Chris Sacca and Mike Malone—were also guests in this luxury boutique hotel. To imagine all these social media magnates—especially the geeky, cheeky Stone and the cherubic Hoffman—locked up inside the luxurious bedroom of a refurbished prison is, of course, deliciously ironic. But the hotel's significance extends beyond irony. It's a picture of where we may, one day, all be living.

As a British version of a Las Vegas theme hotel or a Hollywood set, some might see the Oxford Mal an example of what Umberto Eco and Jean Baud-rillard call hyperreality. "The *completely real* becomes identified with the completely fake. Absolute unreality is offered as real presence," Eco explains, while Baudrillard defines hyperreality as "the simulation of something which never really existed." History has repeated itself with the Oxford prison, Baudrillard and Eco might say, first as a tragedy and then as fake.

Rather than a simple fake like Madeleine Elster in Hitchcook's *Vertigo*, however, the Oxford Mal is both a historical fact and an artifact of the future. While the twenty-first-century hotel has the appearance of a nineteenth-century prison, its real identity is the exact reverse. Instead of giving the au-thorities the power to look into the cell, the Oxford Mal empowers its customers with the technology to gaze out into the public atrium. "The peephole is reversed, so that guests can look out," Fodor's travel guide ex-plains the revised technology on the Mal's doors.[9] With this reversal, Ben-tham's omnipresent master of the Inspection-House is replaced with Walter Kirn's atomized army of small brothers, the private peeps imprisoned in parallel electronic theaters, who can see out, but can neither be seen them-selves, nor know or observe their physical neighbor.

We are encouraged to *imagine a prison that's a hotel* by the Malmaison Web site. But a better way to think about the Oxford Mal is to *imagine a hotel that's a prison*—a place that incarcerates us without us knowing it. And that's exactly what I was imagining on the morning of my Oxford debate with @quixotic about whether digital man would be more socially connected than his industrial ancestor. As I gazed onto the Mal's spotlighted atrium, I imagined the hotel—with the reversed peepholes on its iron doors—to be a microcosm of our socially networked future. But, I realized, there was one key ingredient of the future missing from the "A" Block.

Hypervisibility.

My eyes rolled up and down the Mal's long corridors lined with cages in which each hotel guest is perfectly alone. What would happen, I wondered, if all the caste-iron doors in the hotel disappeared? What if everyone, all the peeps in their parallel cells, could see what everyone else was doing? What if we all lived in public?

I pinched myself. Then what?

We Live in Public

"The future is already here," William Gibson observed in 1993, "it's just unevenly distributed." One version of the future, at least our social future, may have arrived, a handful of years after Gibson first made this prescient remark, at the very end of the twentieth century. An entrepreneur named Josh Harris invented it. "The greatest Internet pioneer you've never heard of,"[10] Harris is one of the earliest dotcom millionaires who, in the Internet boom of the nineties, founded the New York City–based Jupiter Research consultancy firm and the video Web site Pseudo.com. But Harris is less well known as an innovative hotel proprietor. And yet if Josh Harris is remembered as any kind of pioneer, it will be as the founder of a real *malmaison*—a hotel that, quite literally, was a prison.

You'll remember that oversharing advocate Steven Johnson described today's Web 3.0 world as "a networked version of *The Truman Show*, where we are all playing Truman."[11] Josh Harris took this one crazy step further. Having seen *The Truman Show*, Peter Weir's 1998 movie about everyman Truman Burbank (played with Jimmy Stewart–style innocence by Jim Carrey) whose real life was broadcast to millions of rapt television viewers, Harris decided to transform Weir's fictional movie into a real-life experiment in uncensored, always-on broadcast media.

At the beginning of December 1999, as part of an art project entitled "Quiet: We Live in Public," Harris opened a basement hotel in New York City called Capsule. It comprised one hundred pod-style rooms that, in contrast with the Oxford Mal, had neither walls nor doors. Capsule was designed to eliminate loneliness. It was a boutique social hotel, containing architecture of such radical transparency that nothing, not even its guests' most intimate actions or thoughts, were kept private.

By turning his lens on his subjects so that they all became stars of their own twenty-four-hour-a-day broadcast show, Harris pioneered the social network business model a full decade before the birth of Hyperpublic, Airtime, BeKnown or LivingSocial. Everything in the Capsule hotel—from its food and alcohol served on its forty-foot dining table reminiscent of the communal tables in Sir Thomas More's *Utopia* to its pod-style accommodation to the use of its underground gun range—was free. Everything that is, except, the information that the Capsule hotel guests, the 100 Truman Burbanks, generated. Josh Harris *owned* that information, a Term of Service made unambiguously clear to all the participants in the Quiet project.

You see, the whole point of the Capsule hotel, its modus vivendi, was enabling real identities, blood-and-flesh people, to generate massive amounts of data. This Inspection-House envisioned @quixotic's idea of Web 3.0 before anyone had even imagined Web 2.0.[12] There were, therefore, cameras everywhere in the hotel—in the communal dining area, in the pods, in the showers, even in the bathrooms. Josh Harris's "business model," if that's the right term for this grossly exploitative project—was the collection of the most intimate personal data from the hotel's residents.

Fortunately, Harris's Capsule hotel experiment, this late-twentieth-century simulacrum of Bentham's Inspection-House, was itself captured on camera by the filmmaker Ondi Timoner in her 2009 documentary *We Live in Public*, which won the documentary Grand Jury Prize at the Sundance film festival. Timoner's uncompromisingly intimate work, which she described to me as a "hyperbolic version of reality," is sobering viewing in a social media age that Philip Rosedale insists will result in a unity of man. After a month of living in full view of the camera, the project broke down in collective paranoia, sexual jealousy, hatred and physical violence. In its portrayal of the anti-social nature of such radical social transparency, MIT Professor Sherry Turkle, the author of *Alone Together*, could have scripted *We Live in Public*. Rather than eliminating loneliness, Harris's experiment only compounded it. As one distraught participant in the Quiet project told Timoner, "The more you get to know each other, the more alone you become."

The most troubling thing of all about Josh Harris's Quiet project was the reappearance of the apparatchik. As one hotel guest told Ondi Timoner in *We Live in Public*, "It was an absolute surveillance police-state." Once volunteers checked into the Capsule Hotel, they weren't allowed to check out. With hyperreal bad taste, Harris and his minions even dressed themselves in the style of the apparat, cross-examining the citizens of Quiet in the sadistic style of the interrogators in Arthur Koestler's *Darkness at Noon* or Orwell's *Nineteen Eighty-Four*, digging for the most humiliating self-revelations about their mental breakdowns, drug addictions and attempted suicides.

Not satisfied with ruining other people's lives, Harris then destroyed his own life by transforming himself into Truman Burbank. After the Capsule Hotel was shut down by the New York police on New Year's Day 2000, he turned the prying, peeping cameras on himself and began to broadcast an entirely uncensored, twenty-four-hour version of his own life on WeLiveInPublic.com. This absurdly self-destructive experiment resulted not only in the death of Harris's most intimate friendship, his relationship with his girlfriend, but eventually in his own reputational and financial bankruptcy. Today, Harris lives in Ethiopia, in exile from his family, friends and creditors, the saddest Internet visionary you've never heard of, a corpse of a man who tried to own all of our images, but now owns nothing at all.

But, rather than signaling the end of the future, Josh Harris's failure is actually just its beginning. As Ondi Timoner told me, "The Internet is herding us along so that all of us are now trading our privacy." Instead, however, of WeLiveInPublic.com or the Capsule Hotel, the death of privacy will be authored by a little gadget that we tuck into our pockets or wear as a pendant.

The Return of the Apparatchik

The future might have once been unevenly distributed, but there will be a time when its distribution is universal. In this future, we will all have joined the apparat. Yes it will be as weird as hell.

This future is called a *Super Sad True Love Story*. It is imagined by satirist Gary Shteyngart, the author of a creepy 2010 novel[13] about a dystopian future in which we all own a chic little device called an Apparat that quantifies and ranks the massive amounts of personal data being generated by our real identities.

Shteyngart explains his data dystopia in which we all live in public: "Everyone has this device called the 'Apparat,' which they wear either tucked into their pocket or usually as a pendant. The moment you enter a room everyone judges you. So it has what's called 'Rate Me Plus' technology. So you're rated immediately. Everyone can chip in and rate everyone else, and everyone does."[14]

When he appeared on my TechcrunchTV show in July 2011, Shteyngart described this world as "William Gibson land."[15] It's a place where our personalities are quantified in universally accessible, real-time lists akin to

Internet reputation networks like Hashable or Kred. Mystery, privacy and secrecy will have all been eliminated in this transparent marketplace. Today's reputation stock market Empire Avenue will have replaced Wall Street as the key exchange of value. It will be a pure reputation economy, a marketplace of mirrors a perfect data market in how others see us.

This Apparat, Shteyngart explained to me, is a fully mature, all-knowing version of those contemporary gadgets like the iPhone and Google's Android smartphones that spy on us today. "My Apparat quickly zoomed in past the data outflows spilling out from the customers like polluted surf falling upon once pristine stores and focused on McKay Watson," *Super Sad True Love Story*'s narrator, Lenny Abramov, notes about a complete stranger he happens to meet in a retail store, but whose most intimate information he had immediately accessed on his Apparat. "I caressed McKay's data. . . . She had graduated from Tufts with a major in international affairs and a minor in Retail science. Her parents were retired professors in Charlottesville, Virginia where she grew up. She didn't have a boyfriend at present but enjoyed the "reverse cowgirl" position with the last one. . . ."[16]

In Shteyngart's world, we won't own the Apparat—it will own us. This all-knowing gadget is manufactured by a huge corporation called LandO'LakesGMFordCredit (today's "HyperPublicLivingSocialPeek-You," perhaps), which aggregates and stores all our personal information—our wealth, our worldliness, our dress sense, our sexuality—and broadcasts this to the entire world. In *Super Sad True Love Story*, we, the peeps, young women like McKay Watson, have been transformed, like Josh Harris and his pitiable girlfriend in WeLiveInPublic.com, into transparent data, that most desirable of information (for everyone except ourselves).

In this dystopia, we will all live in public in a permanent Capsule hotel, akin to contemporary social media networks like SnoopOn.me or Creepy. In this apparat-saturated world, everyone has a public profile with their income, their blood type, their cholesterol level, their sexual preferences, their spending power and, above all, their consumer habits. Nobody can escape the universal shadow of their apparat, which—with its Rate Me Plus technology—is the electronic realization of Bentham's Auto-Icon, an inescapable prison, a perpetual "A" Block in which we all live in our own image.

There is no doubt that Shteyngart's dark adventure in William Gibson land is a *super sad love* story. But is it realistic? Could it turn out to be *true*?

The Scoble Story

I have to confess that I made no reference to the Malmaison and Capsule hotels or the Apparat in my Oxford debate with Reid Hoffman. Nor did I mention Josh Harris, Gary Shteyngart or WeLiveInPublic.com. I suspect all these futuristic pictures of social media would have been dismissed by the rigorously analytical @quixotic as both excessively fantastic and pessimistic. Like Steven Johnson, Hoffman would probably have written off Josh Harris as a "holy fool" and "demented visionary"[17] who might be a compelling subject for a documentary movie, but who bore no relation to reality.

And so our debate was rather dull, full of polite, respectful disagreement about what Peter Drucker described as the "great transition" between industrial and knowledge society, rather than a serious exchange of views. We both acknowledged that social media communities would, in some ways, replace the nation-state as the source of personal identity in the twenty-first century. But what would this future look like? We didn't know because, in contrast with Gary Shetyngart, neither Reid Hoffman nor I had visited William Gibson land.

But a few weeks after my Oxford debate with @quixotic, after I had returned home to Northern California, I took a trip into the future to see how social media would replace the nation-state as a source of personal identity in the twenty-first century. My journey began in San Francisco, at the Golden Gate Bridge, the site of Madeleine Elster's iconic dive into the Bay in Hitchcock's *Vertigo*. I was driving south, down through San Francisco where Biz Stone's Twitter is headquartered, down through the Santa Clara Valley, once known as the "valley of heart's delight" but today the corporate location of Mark Zuckerberg's Facebook, Reid Hoffman's LinkedIn, Larry Page's Google and the hundreds of other Silicon Valley companies building the social architecture of our Web 3.0 world.

I drove south on Route 101, that notoriously clogged artery that links San Francisco with San Jose and, even farther south, passes close to San Juan Bautista, the eighteenth-century mission settlement where Hitchcock filmed Madeleine Elster's murder and Judy Barton's suicide. But I got off 101 before San Jose and headed west, winding my way through the Santa Cruz mountains where Hitchcock himself once had a house and arriving on the Pacific coast just north of Pescadero, the little fishing village where Gordon Moore, Intel's co-founder and the author of Moore's Law, grew up.

"One final thing I have to do and then I'll be free of the past," Scottie Ferguson tells Judy Barton in *Vertigo*'s final scene as they drive south from San Francisco down the Californian coast toward San Juan Bautista. But rather than freeing myself of the past, my business over the Santa Cruz mountains was visiting the future. I'd come to the Pacific coast to interview Robert Scoble, Silicon Valley's uber evangelist of social media and one of the earliest settlers in William Gibson land.

Unlike Josh Harris, Robert Scoble is neither a "holy fool" nor a "demented visionary." A former "chief Humanizing officer" at Microsoft, columnist at *Fast Company* magazine, and the co-author of a well-received book about the value of transparent conversation,[18] Scoble is a much admired evangelist of social media and among Silicon Valley's most influential cheerleaders of today's digital love-in. The *Economist* magazine described him as a "minor celebrity among geeks worldwide,"[19] and the *Financial Times* newspaper included Scoble—who tweets to his almost 200,000 followers as @scobleizer—in their March 2011 list of the five most influential tweeters in the world.[20]

If William Gibson is correct and the future has already arrived, then it has shown up in the shape of @scobleizer. He is among the most hypervisible figures in digital society, with a Klout ranking higher than that of Barack Obama.[21] In addition to his commitment to Twitter—where he has authored over 50,000 tweets in the five years since joining the service in 2006 and to Google+where he amassed 114,500 followers in just six weeks,[22] he has been a very vocal early champion of the geo-location service foursquare as well as the social planning network Plancast, the social driving network Waze, the social traveling network TripIt, the social photography network Instagram, the social food network My Fav Food, the social television network Into.now, and even Cyclometer, the social bicycling network where you can follow him as he rides around Silicon Valley.[23] Wherever he is, whatever he is doing or thinking, Scoble can be found by his network. He lives in William Gibson land—a place not unlike the town of Seahaven in *The Truman Show*, a giant electronic stage where all of his activities are broadcasted all of the time.

Above all, Scoble is a champion of what he calls an "open web" and of living in public. He frequently announces the death of privacy, confessing on my TechcrunchTV show in December 2010 that "even if we tried to have a conversation that was private, the likelihood that it would stay private isn't very high." Not that @scobleizer, who openly tweets about almost every aspect of his life, cares about the disappearance of the private realm. "I want to live my life in public. . . . Me, count me out of this whole privacy thing," he blogged in May 2010, confessing that "I wish Facebook had NO PRIVACY AT ALL!"[24]

This champion of publicness lives—physically resides, that is—with his wife and children in the exclusive Pacific coast town of Half Moon Bay, an idyllic seaside resort that, in its spotlessness, resembles *The Truman Show*'s Seahaven. Scoble's mock Mediterranean-style house is up the road from the luxury Ritz-Carlton Hotel, located inside a gated community made up

of identical mock Mediterranean-style houses. As I checked in with the security officer guarding Scoble's community from the outside world, I
couldn't help thinking about the not entirely unsurprising paradox of the
world's leading champion of openness living inside a gated community of an
exclusive Pacific coast town—an enclave within an enclave—that cut him
off from the rest of the world.

"What's the number of Robert Scoble's house?" I asked the uniformed
security guard who controlled the electronic gate to the housing complex.

But I must've misheard the number, because when I rang on the bell of
the house, the man in the baseball cap and shorts who opened the door had
never heard of the hypervisible Scoble. "Who?" he replied to me blankly about
a global celebrity who possesses one the most hypervisible brands on the
Internet. Obviously, the guy wasn't on Yatown, Nextdoor.com or Hey,
Neighbor!, the social networks that connected actual neighbors and neighborhoods.

As it happened, Scoble lived in the house over the street. He greeted me
with his signature "Hey, what's up!" and we went upstairs to the studio from
where he broadcasted himself. The personally very likeable social media
evangelist—whose cheerful manner, shiny face, and opaque eyes really do
bring to mind Truman Burbank—sat opposite me. Behind him was a thirty-
inch computer monitor broadcasting @scobleizer's page on Twitter. Every
few seconds, a new tweet from one of Scoble's Twitter friends appeared on
the screen. So, as I looked at the real Scoble, I was simultaneously looking at
his Twitter feed too. Here, I realized, was a digital Jeremy Bentham inside
his electronic Auto-Icon—a man who resembled his own *images*. He had,
quite literally, become information. Not only was it as weird as hell, but it
was super creepy, too.

"How long you have you been living opposite each other?" I asked Scoble
about his neighbor.

"A couple of years."

"And he doesn't know you!?"

The irony of one of the world's best known and most popular social media evangelists not being known by the man over the street only compounded the surreal experience of simultaneously staring at Scoble and his Twitter feed. I was looking for the human in Scoble, but couldn't see it. For a moment, I wondered if he really existed. Maybe Scoble really was @scobleizer. Perhaps, I imagined, this social media evangelist who has chosen to exist in public actually does live on the network.

In a sense, he does—on every network, that is, except Hey, Neighbor! or Nextdoor.com. As we sat that afternoon in his media-saturated room, the pixellated glow of his screen casting a flickering shadow over his Truman-like face, Scoble explained to me that he chose to make his friends through social networks rather than through his immediate physical community in Half Moon Bay. He confessed to me that he had more in common with Web programmers in Beijing and social media entrepreneurs in Berlin than he had with local people such as his unknown neighbor. Thus, he explained, he chose to make his friends on the Internet, using social networks to identify people around the world with whom he shared interests.

Scoble, I realized, represented a future that neither @quixotic nor I could clearly see in our Oxford debate. Scoble's individualized, personalized community—a peculiar synthesis of the cult of the individual and the cult of the social—offered the answer to how social media communities might eventually replace the nation-state as the source of identity in the twenty-first century. In the nineteenth and twentieth centuries, Ernest Gellner reminds us, individuals were united into physical communities by common languages and cultures; today, the community is becoming a reflection of that individual. Scoble's social media community was, therefore, an extension of his self, a never-ending hall of mirrors all reflecting the same opaque image of Scoble—which explained why, in spite of his self-styled openness and good cheer, he seemed so solitary and lost, so creepily childlike, so much like

Truman Burbank. Living within his enclave within an enclave, simultaneously connected with everybody and nobody, his story, *The Scoble Story,* so
to speak, is a sneak preview of how we will live alone together in the perpetually impermanent twenty-first century.

It was, I realized, the new (dis)unity of man—a crystal prison of the self.
As I stared at Scoble in his media room, crammed with the digital cameras,
screens and other self-broadcasting esoterica that he carried everywhere
with him, my mind went back to "A" Block in the Oxford Mal. His electronic peephole was precluding the social media evangelist from communicating with his neighbors. As Richard Sennett has put it, "electronic
communication is one means by which the very idea of public life has been
put to an end."[25] And Scoble, with his free agent identity and Truman Burbank existential confusion, is one of the first residents of a digital society in
which the social is simply an extension of what we, as individuals, want.

There is one important difference, though, between *The Scoble Story* and
The Truman Show. In Peter Weir's fictional movie, Truman Burbank had no
idea that his life had become a real-time reality television show. In contrast,
Robert Scoble not only stars in *The Scoble Story* but he is also the conscious
producer and the director of his nonfictional show. There is nothing inevitable about Scoble's hypervisible life. It's his choice to live so openly, to reveal his location to his foursquare followers, to author 51,000 tweets, to
photograph the Caesar salad on My Fav Food that he is eating at the Ritz-
Carlton hotel in Half Moon Bay[26] and to distribute the images on Instagram,
to be on Waze, TripIt, Into.Now, Cyclometer and all the other transparent
networks of the social Web.

"Are we all becoming Robert Scoble?" my TechcrunchTV show head-
lined in December 2010. "One day, for better or worse," I warned, "we may
all be Robert Scoble."[27]

The truth, however, is that the vast majority of us don't really want to
become Scoble. Most of us aren't comfortable living, like @scobleizer, in the

full glare of the electronic public spotlight. We aren't, as Reid Hoffman believes, primarily social beings. And thus, in spite of the social revolution, we don't want all of our information—our photographs, our location, our meals, our thoughts, our travel plans, our bicycling trips—published for everyone else to see.

So what to do? How can we make sure that our lives don't become versions of *The Scoble Show* and we become voyeuristic inmates of a luxury prison, entirely disconnected from our neighbors, yet possessing tens of thousands of "friends" that we have never and will never meet? How can we guarantee our right to privacy and secrecy in today's age of exhibitionism so that today's creepy doesn't become tomorrow's necessity? Above all, how can we be let alone so that we remain true to ourselves as human beings in a vertiginous Web 3.0 world that is already lurching into a weird synthesis of the eerily luxurious Oxford Mal and Josh Harris's radically transparent Capsule Hotel?

To begin our search for a cure to today's digital vertigo, we need to look at some pictures that were never intended to be displayed in public. And once again we must return to the middle of the nineteenth century, to a society grappling, like ours, with the consequences of technological innovation on an individual's right to protect their private lives from the public gaze.

THE BEST PICTURE OF 2011

@amgorder Andrea Michelle Yhor—6'2" black man w scruffy beard blue shirt tan shorts driving commercial truck call me. broke into wayne & raped me. Glad im alive. (27 May via HootSuite Favorite Retweet Reply)

@amgorder: The law has asked me to stop tweeting. Please contact their pr dept until I have clearance to discuss. Your support has been invaluable (5/27/11)

The Most Valuable Pictures of 1848

We begin with some pictures from an exhibition. This time, though, rather than a single painting, it is a series of copperplated etchings, made by two of the nineteenth-century's greatest paragons of private life, Prince Albert and Queen Victoria, in the first days of their marriage. There are sixty-three personal etchings, of domestic scenes and of their family and friends, including their two eldest children, Bertie—the heir to Victoria's throne who would, as an undergraduate, enjoy the debates at the Oxford Union—and Vicky. It is an unintended exhibition, private pictures created strictly for their own enjoyment and celebrating their intimate friendship.

Between October 1840 and November 1847, Victoria and Albert sent these pictures to a printer to make copies of the copperplates. But the printer's journeyman made his own copies of the etchings and sold them to London publisher William Strange, who released a printed exhibition of the works: *A Descriptive Catalogue of the Royal Victoria and Albert Gallery of Etchings.*[1] Strange even had the gall to promise purchasers of the catalogue a facsimile of either the queen's or the prince consort's autograph to go along with these private pictures.

In 1848, the dispute appeared in court as *Prince Albert v. Strange*, a "famous case" according to Samuel Warren and Louis Brandeis, the Boston lawyers who authored the iconic "Right to Privacy" *Harvard Law Review* article that, you'll remember, defined privacy as the legal right to be "let alone." In this 1890 article, written in reaction to the publication of an uninvited photograph in the *Washington Post* newspaper from the wedding of Samuel Warren's daughter,[2] the lawyers argued that the technology of the industrial revolution had compromised our right to privacy. "Instantaneous photographs and newspaper enterprise have invaded the sacred precincts of private and domestic life; and numerous mechanic devices threaten to make good the prediction that *what is whispered in the closet shall be proclaimed from the house-tops*," they wrote. "For years there has been a feeling that the law must afford some remedy for the unauthorized circulation of portraits of private persons."[3]

The English law came to the defense of Victoria and Albert's right to the privacy of their own pictures. The *Prince Albert v. Strange* case was ruled in favor of the plaintiff, the court holding that the common-law prohibited the reproduction of the etchings. And, as Warren and Brandeis argue, this ruling provided an important precedent in protecting the privacy of people's own images during the industrial age.

Today's Web 3.0 revolution offers similarly profound challenges to the traditional law protecting individual privacy. The Ryan Giggs case, for example, which pitted 75,000 people tweeting details of the footballer's extramarital sexual antics against a British High Court injunction banning public commentary about Giggs's private life, has resulted in what Lionel Barber, the editor of *The Financial Times*, described as the "freedom debate of our age."[4] On the one hand, the law obviously can't, of course, punish 75,000 people for tweeting about Giggs's sex life; on the other hand, however, that same law, which is supposed to protect individual rights against society, has to offer some defense against public ridicule in a digital age in which anyone, it seems, can publish anything about anybody else.

Lionel Barber is right to conclude that "the law is manifestly lagging" behind today's social media revolution. Unfortunately, the Giggs case is just the tip of today's legal iceberg. Everyone now—from the British plumber who tweeted about his supposedly adulterous wife[5] to Julian Assange, the self-appointed tsar of WikiLeaked transparency, to the myriad of free speech fundamentalists on Twitter—seems to think they have the right to publish whatever they want online, without any consequences at all. So how can the law catch up with our use of this networked technology? In our Web 3.0 world, should we be demanding more laws to protect the "sacred precincts of private and domestic life" against what nineteenth-century privacy advocates Warren and Brandeis called the "unseemly gossip" of public opinion?

Mark Zuckerberg and Eric Schmidt certainly don't think so. In late May 2011, in the week leading up to the G8 summit in Deauville, French President Nicolas Sarkozy invited Zuckerberg, Schmidt and several hundred super-nodes including myself to Paris to discuss the need for government to regulate the Internet. Responding to Sarkozy's call at the "e-G8" for the government to "civilize" the Internet and to protect the privacy of its users, Schmidt came out against what he called "stupid" governmental rules, arguing that "technology will move faster than governments, so don't legislate before you understand the consequences."[6] Zuckerberg was slightly more diplomatic, but nonetheless made it clear that government would be unwise to regulate the innovations of today's social media companies.

In some ways, Zuckerberg may be right. The most effective cure for today's destruction of privacy isn't an avalanche of new legislation. As I've already argued, I'm against calls from British and Mexican politicians to suspend social networks during times of civil unrest. Nor am I in favor of either calls from the US Congress to block the Taliban on Twitter[7] or to legally enable the US Justice Department to unilaterally search the Twitter accounts of elected politicians in other countries.[8] Like it or not, twenty-first-century democracy will be increasingly shaped by social media and so it's hard to argue that a democratic government should be able to shut down or control any network.

Besides, as Eric Schmidt has argued, social media is, in many ways, just a mirror. The problem is that nobody is forcing any of us to update our photos on Instagram, reveal our location on MeMap or broadcast what we've just eaten for lunch on My Fav Food. The most truthful picture in our age of great exhibitionism is The Scoble Story. So, in spite of my concern about the increasing publicness of life in the social media age, I'm ambivalent about calling on the government or the law courts to protect us from our own exhibitionism.

As John Stuart Mill argues in *On Liberty,* government exists to protect us from others rather than from ourselves and the reality, for better or worse, is that once a photo, an update or a tweet is publicly published on the network, it becomes de facto public property. So, without wishing to sound too much like the uber-glib Eric Schmidt, the only way to really protect one's own privacy is by not publishing anything in the first place.

That said, some governmental legislation in online privacy policy—such as the Federal Trade Commission's March 2011 settlement with Google over its egregiously "deceptive privacy practices" in the search engine's Buzz social network rollout[9]—is necessary. So is a government response to some of Facebook's more flagrant disregard for individual privacy, such as the company's June 2011 announcement that they were adding the "face recognition" to their service as well as the twenty-year privacy settlement that the government reached with Facebook in November 2011 which requires the social network to get permission from its users before altering how their personal information is given out.[10] But the problem, given the financial muscle, speed and virality of new networks like Twitter and Facebook compared with the slowness of government, is knowing where exactly to focus. As MSNBC's legal correspondent Bob Sullivan noted in March 2011, "there are no fewer than seven pieces of privacy-related legislation that have either been introduced in the U.S. House of Representatives, or soon will be."[11] That may be why the Obama adminstration called, in December 2010, for the creation of an Internet "privacy bill of rights." This eighty-eight-page Commerce Department report also called for the establishment of a Privacy Policy Office that would "serve as a center of commercial data privacy policy expertise."[12] The need for a more focused governmental response to the Web 3.0 revolution is also why, in May 2011, the White House announced its intention to offer up a National Data Breach Law intended to replace the patchwork of state laws with a single federal standard.[13]

Probably the most promising of this current U.S. legislation is West Virginian Senator John D. Rockefeller's May 2011 "Do Not Track" bill, which would require Web 3.0 data companies to provide their users with opt out data collection buttons. The Senate Commerce Committee chairman is correct to demand that "consumers have a right to decide whether their information can be collected and used online."[14] A number of companies, including Microsoft and Mozilla, have already complied with Rockefeller's bill and the American Federal Trade Commission (FTC) chairman, Jon Leibowitz, was right in April 2011 to call on the "laggard" Google to add a "Do Not Track" tool in its Chrome Internet browser.[15]

Other legislation is required to guarantee that the law doesn't continue to lag behind technology. The April 2011 brouhaha over Google and Apple smartphones that continually track their users is certainly worthy of the careful U.S. Congressional scrutiny being pursued by Minnesota Senator Al Franken.[16] The former *Saturday Night Live* TV star is right to demand that Google and Apple should have what he called, in May 2011, a "clear understandable privacy policy" for their smartphone mobile apps.[17] Given Google and Apple's pioneering role in the development of the cloud economy,

Franken would also be wise to call for a similarly transparent privacy policy with respect to massively powerful new services like iCloud.

The shift to the cloud opens up an entirely new front on the war to protect privacy. "A cloud gathers over our digital freedoms" warns Charles Leadbeater, a critic who sees, on the immediate horizon, a world of what he calls "Appbook" and "Facegoogle" corporations controlling our personal data.[18] Leadbeater is far from alone in fearing the cloud. "As the new new gadget I hold in my hand becomes increasingly personalized, easy to use, 'transparent' in its functioning, the more the entire set-up has to rely on work being done elsewhere, on the vast circuit of machines which coordinate the user's experience," notes the Slovenian cultural critic Slavoj Zizek about the symbiotic growth of personalized technology and corporate power.[19] Our data privacy, therefore, is particularly vulnerable to "Appbook" and "Facegoogle" on the cloud and will require the careful government scrutiny of responsible politicians like Al Franken.

Senators John Kerry and John McCain's 2011 proposal to establish a Commercial Privacy Bill of Right is promising—although, as the University of Chicago economist Richard Thaler argues[20]—it should also include the right for consumers to access their own data. And, as Senator Jay Rockefeller has consistently argued,[21] there is a strong need to update the Children's Online Privacy Protection Act (COPPA)—particularly given the phenomenal popularity of kids' social networks like Disney's Togetherville and Mark Zuckerberg's misguided belief that children under thirteen should be allowed on Facebook.

The European Union has been much more aggressive than the United States government in pushing for privacy rights over social networks. On the all-important issue of online tracking by social media companies, for example, European privacy regulators have been pushing to establish an arrangement in which consumers could only be tracked if they actively "opt in" and permit marketers to collect their personal data.[22] Europeans have also been more aggressive in pushing back against the leading Web 3.0 companies. In April 2011, for example, the Dutch government threatened Google with fines of up to $1.4 million if it continued to ignore data-protection demands associated with its Street View technology.[23] Apple and Google face much tighter regulation in Europe with the EU classifying the location information that they have been collecting from their smartphones as personal data.[24] European Union data protection regulators have aggressively scrutinized Facebook's May 2011 rollout of its facial recognition software that reveals people's identities without their permission.[25] Even European technology chieftans, like Vittorio Colao, the CEO of the wireless giant Vodaphone, has openly criticized Zuckerberg's antigovernment stance at the e-G8, arguing that laws which enhance online trust and guarantee privacy are critical if the web is to become a civilizing force in the world.[26] Certainly the privacy and data panel on which I spoke at the e-G8 was sharply divided between Europeans and Americans, with the chairperson of the Mozilla browser Mitchell Baker and *Public Parts* author Jeff Jarvis being much less sympathetic to government protection than European technology executives like Intel's Christian Morales.

EU justice commissioner Viviane Reding is even intending social networks to establish a "right to be forgotten" option that would allow users to destroy data already published on the network. "I want to explicitly clarify that people shall have the right—and not only the possibility—to withdraw their consent to data processing," Reding told the EU parliament in March 2011. "The burden of proof should be on data controllers— those who process your personal data. They must prove that they need the data, rather than individuals having to prove that collecting their data is not necessary."[27]

But, as much as legal or political action, we need more consumer literacy about the core nature of Web 3.0 businesses. What consumers have to understand is that "free" services on the Internet are never really free. As

Reputation.com's CEO Michael Fertik told me, the business models of supposedly free social networks like Facebook is the sale of our information to their advertisers. We, the producers of data on the free network, are its product rather than its friend or partner. In the Web 3.0 age, therefore, consumers should not only carefully read their social network's Terms of Service (TOS) which often need to be shortened and simplified so anyone can understand them (in contrast, for example, with LinkedIn's 6400 word novella of a Privacy Policy),[28] but also to recognize that Facebook, Twitter, Google, Zynga, Groupon, Apple, Skype and the other corporate pioneers of @quixotic's personal data revolution are all multi billion dollar for profit companies, no better and no worse than for-profit banks or oil or pharmaceutical companies.

Privacy: The Web's Hot New Commodity

The most effective solutions to protecting privacy may lie in the market and in technology rather than in an overreliance on the law. "Big oil. Big Food. Big Pharma. To the catalog of corporate bigs that worry a lot of us little people, add this: Big Data," you'll remember *The New York Times'* Natasha Singer arguing.[29] But, as we rightly worry more and more about "big data" in our reputation economy, so we are seeing an explosion of start-ups like Fertik's Reputation.com, Reppler.com, Personal Inc, Safety Web, Abine Inc, TRUSTe, IntelliProtect and Allow that all sell privacy services to consumers. *The Wall Street Journal* calls privacy the "web's hot new commodity" and argues that "as the surreptitious tracking of Internet users becomes more aggressive and widespread, tiny start-ups and technology giants alike are using a new product: privacy."[30]

The market is, of course, simply a reflection of our collective desires and actions. And it is to be hoped that we, as the market, will reject many of the more absurd or destructive social networks now being funded in today's social gold rush. The key issue here is trust. Facebook's chief technology officer

Bret Taylor, with whom I've publicly clashed in the past about online privacy,[31] framed it provocatively. "Trust is the foundation of the social web," Taylor explained to a highly skeptical Jay Rockefeller at a May 2011 Senate hearing about Facebook's policies toward children. "People will stop using Facebook if they don't trust in our services."[32] That trust may already be eroding. The *New York Times*' Jenna Wortham notes the growth of what she calls "Facebook Resisters," people, like myself (I shut my personal Facebook account in September 2011), who "steer clear of the site" because it makes "them feel more, not less, alienated."[33] Even Silicon Valley supernodes like Techcrunch founder Mike Arrington and the organizer of the popular Le Web conference Loic Le Meur seem to be losing trust in Facebook, with Arrington explaining that nobody goes to it anymore because "it's too crowded"[34] and Le Meur suggesting that the A-List now hang out with their friends on the supposedly more private Path network.[35]

But in spite of its resisters, research shows that today's Facebook users are more trusting than average Internet users,[36] which may be one reason why they are often so cavalier with the personal data that they reveal to their "friends." The challenge is to make users of networked Big Data services more, rather than less suspicious. Fortunately, there is some evidence that this is already happening in terms of our attitude toward some of the more radical social start-ups of today's Web 3.0 economy. Take, for example, Blippy, a much hyped 2009 social start-up co-founded by Philip Kaplan, the creator of Fucked Company, a notorious Web site founded during the 2000 dotcom crash that celebrated the bankruptcies of many online businesses. Blippy, which raised $13 million in venture capital funding, is a social media network that requires its users to publicly publish their credit card purchases. Fortunately, the market has said a resounding no to such a patently ludicrous idea. "So it turns out that almost nobody wants people to check out their new purchases," explained Techcrunch's Alexia Tsotsis in May 2011.[37] Apparently, Blippy's usage numbers were never "spectacular" and, not surprisingly, the site was mistrusted by most of its users. "Ouch," Tsotsis ex-claimed about the death of Blippy. Hallelujah, I say, about the demise of a social network that encouraged its users to publically publish all their credit card purchases. *Fucked Company,* indeed.

It's not just Blippy that the market has rejected. Back in chapter one, I warned about SocialEyes, a start-up founded in January 2010 that created a transparent wall of online video cubes in which we could all watch each other watching each other. But in spite of raising over $5 million, SocialEyes never attracted many users and, by January 2012, the service was no longer available. Hopefully, this shows that the vast majority of us don't want to be transparent cubes in somebody else's video wall. Perhaps our eyes aren't quite as social as the digital communitarians would have us believe.

The market may also be pushing the social networking companies to focus more on making privacy central to their service. As Vic Gundotra and Bradley Horowitz underlined when I interviewed them on my TechcrunchTV show, Google + is distinguished from other networks, particularly Facebook, by its networks of friends called "Circles," which operate from the default of privacy rather than openness. After the publicity fiascos and market failures of Buzz and Wave, Google seems to have learnt that the public actually doesn't want fully transparent networks that broadcast everybody's data to the world. "Rather than focus on new snazzy features . . . Google has chosen to learn from its own mistakes, and Facebook's. Google decided to make privacy the No. 1 feature of its new service," *The New York Times'* Nick Bilton notes about Google +.[38] This focus on privacy is certainly one reason why the service attracted 20 million users in just three weeks after its informal launch and doubled its membership in its first 100 days. And with new features like "Good to Know,"[39] which enables users to monitor what's happening with their Google data, one can only hope that Google will emerge as a corporate paragon of privacy in the Web 3.0 age.

The truth is that most of us don't want to share everything we read, watch and listen to online. Thus innovations in the marketplace may offer the most effective defense against invidious services like Facebook's Open Graph platform which, you'll remember, attempts to make all our media choices automatically public through Mark Zuckerberg's "Frictionless Sharing." After the updated launch of Open Graph at the f8 Conference in September 2011, for example, a number of third party developers began offering Facebook users a way of retracting sharing from the Open Graph, with news outlets like *The Washington Post, The Guardian, The Wall Street Journal* and *The Independent* also testing ways to enable their readers to mute Frictionless Sharing.[40] And the music subscription service Spotify has done the same thing, adding the much needed "private listening" mode after some of its Facebook users complained about Frictionless Sharing.[41]

In addition to the market, technology itself also offers the consumer a counter to what sometimes seems like the perfect memory of big data companies. According to *The New York Times'* Paul Sullivan and Nick Bilton, the Internet "is like an elephant"[42] that "never forgets"[43]—making it analogous to "S," the early twentieth-century Russian journalist described by Joshua Foer in *Moonwalking with Einstein,* as a man who, quite literally, remembered everything.[44] But Bilton and Sullivan are mistaken. The Internet doesn't have to be "S." Like the walls of the Oxford Union library, it is actually quite capable of forgetting. Not only is EU justice commissioner Viviane Reding trying to legislate forgetting into law, but a couple of recent technological innovations offer hope that the Internet can, indeed, learn how to forget. German researchers at Saarland University, for example, have developed software called X-Pire which, according to the BBC, "gives images an expiration date by tagging them with an encryption key." X-Pire is designed for those people who, in the words of Professor Michael Backes, of Saarland's Information Security and Crytography department, "join social networks because of social pressure . . . [and] tend to post everything on the first day and make themselves naked on the Internet."[45]

The BBC also reports that researchers at the University of Twente in the Netherlands are working on technology that will allow data to degrade over time. This work, carried out by the university's Center for Telematics and Information Technology, is designed to make data impermanent. Over time, for example, location data would become vaguer and vaguer, shifting from a street address to a neighborhood and to a town and then to a region. "You can slowly replace details with a more general value," explains the project director, Dr. Harold van Heerde, thus guaranteeing—at least in the long run—that one's data will remain private. I'm not arguing that the Internet should become like "EP," an eighty-four-year-old brain-damaged lab technician whom memory expert Joshua Foer describes as the "most forgetful man in the world."[46] But an architecture of absolute forgetting is no more human than one that remembers everything. So if the Internet really is to be our twenty-first-century home, then we need to humanize it so that it exists as a compromise between the perfect memory of "S" and "E. P." 's nonexistent one.

And if none of these cures work, there is always the Web 2.0 Suicide Machine, another technology of forgetting developed in the Netherlands. In contrast, however, with degrading data over time or giving it an expiration date, the Web 2.0 Suicide Machine kills all your social network data with a single software bomb. It's the nuclear option that enables you to totally "erase your virtual life."[47]

"Wanna meet your real neighbors again?" the Web 2.0 Suicide Machine asks[48] in a drastic version of Nextdoor.com. But the truth is that the nuclear option of the Web 2.0 Suicide Machine isn't a serious one in today's Web 3.0 world, even for super nodes like Robert Scoble who have never met their neighbors. Rather than erasing our virtual life, we need to manage it. Rather than killing our thousands of online friends with the click of a Web suicide button, we need to shrink them down to a manageable number so that they become genuinely intimate friends rather than just data points in our narcissistic hall of mirrors.

After all, how many complex relationships can one person really maintain?

A Pipe of Crystal Meth

According to the executive editor of *The New York Times*, friendship has become a kind of drug on the Internet, the crack cocaine of our digital age. "Last week, my wife and I told our 13-year-old daughter she could join Facebook," confessed *The New York Times'* Bill Keller in May 2011. "Within a few hours she had accumulated 171 friends, and I felt a little as if I had passed my child a pipe of crystal meth."[49]

A June 2011 Pew Research Center study of over two thousand Americans reported that electronically networked people like Keller's daughter saw themselves as having more "close friends" than those of us—those "weirdo outcasts" according to one particularly vapid social media commentator[50]— who aren't on Facebook or Twitter. The Pew report found that the typical Facebook user has 229 friends (including an average of 7 percent that they hadn't actually met[51]) on Mark Zuckerberg's network and has more "close relationships" than the average American.[52]

But this June 2011 Pew study made no attempt to define or calibrate the idea of "friendship," treating each one quantatively, like a notch on a bedpost, and presenting Facebook and Twitter as, quite literally, the architects of our intimacies. What this survey failed to acknowledge is that human beings aren't simply computers, silicon powered devices with infinitely expandable hard drives and memories, who can make more friends as a result of becoming more and more networked.

So how many real friends should we have? And is there a ceiling to the number of friendships that we actually *can* have?

A couple of miles north of the Oxford Mal hotel sits the gray-bricked

home of Oxford University's Institute of Cognitive and Evolutionary Anthology. It is here, in the nondescript academic setting of a north Oxford
suburb, that we find a man who has determined how many friends we really
need. Professor Robin Dunbar, the director of this institute, is an anthro-
pologist, evolutionary psychologist and authority on the behavior of
primates, the biological order that includes monkeys, apes and humans.
And he has become a social media theorist too, best known for formulating
a theory of friendship dubbed "Dunbar's Number."

"The big social revolution in the last few years has not been some great political event, but the way our social world has been redefined by social networking sites like Facebook, MySpace and Bebo," Dunbar explains his eponymous
number.[53] This social revolution, he says, attempts to break through "the
constraints of time and geography" to enable uber-connected primates like
@scobleizer to establish online friendships with tens of thousands of other
wired primates.

"So why do primates have such big brains?"[54] Dunbar asks, rhetorically. Their large brains, he says, borrowing from a theory known as the
"Machiavellian intelligence hypothesis," are the result of "the complex social world in which primates live." It's the "complexity of their social relations" defined by their "tangled" and "interdependent" personal intimacies,
Dunbar argues, that distinguishes primates from every other animal.[55] And
as the most successful and widely distributed member of the primate order,
he goes on, humans brains have evolved most fully of all because of the intricate complexity of our "intense social bonds."

Memory and forgetting are the keys to Dunbar's theory about human
sociability. You'll remember that *The New York Times*' Paul Sullivan suggested that the Internet is "like an elephant" because it never forgets. But
what really distinguishes animals like elephants from primates, Robin Dunbar explains, is that they "use their knowledge about the social world in
which they live to form more complex alliances with each other than other

animals."[56] Thus primates have a lot more to remember about our social intimacies than elephants—which may be one reason why humans forget things and elephants supposedly don't.

For better or worse, nature hasn't come up with a version of Moore's Law that could double the size and memory capacity of our brain every two years. Thus, while our big brains are the result of our complex social relationships, they are still confined by their limited memories. And it's our biological inability to remember the intricate social details of large communities, Robin Dunbar explains, that limits our ability to make intimate friendships.

"We can only remember 150 individuals," Dunbar says, "or only keep track of all the relationships involved in a community of 150." That is Dunbar's Number—our optimal social circle, for which we, as a species, are wired. From traditional academic and military communities to those "oral" villages romanticized by nostalgic McLuhanites, Dunbar's research reveals that the optimal number of complex relationships that our brains can effectively manage has stayed the same throughout human history. So much, then, for Philip Rosedale's chiliastic faith in the unity of man. Or for @quixotic's "liquid" individual able to build vast electronic networks of friends.

In *Cult of the Amateur,* my polemic against Web 2.0, I insulted some thin-skinned primates by comparing bloggers with monkeys. Rather than monkeys, however, Web 3.0 might be turning us into a small-brained species. Elephants perhaps, or sheep, or even swarms of insects. That's because, as Robin Dunbar argues, "there is a limit to the number of people we can hold a particular level of intimacy."[57] The 171 connections "accumulated" by Bill Keller's daughter within a few hours of her joining Facebook are, therefore, anything but "friends" in a truly primate sense and they do no justice to either her highly developed brain or her potential as a member of the human race to grasp the complexities of her community.

So how can we teach this social complexity to the Keller girl? What is the best picture we can show her of genuine human friendship and intimacy?

The Best Picture of 2011

Rather than government legislation or new laws, the best cure for digital
vertigo might be to watch a picture. Or two motion pictures, to be exact.

The ideal of friendship as the defining quality of the human condition,
rather than as a quantifiable asset to be aggregated, was demonstrated at the
eighty-third Academy Awards in 2011, the annual Hollywood awards for
the best movies of the year. Predictably enough, given the general hysteria
currently surrounding the Web 3.0 revolution, most of the news about the
2011 Oscars had been about social media. *The Wall Street Journal* described
the eighty-third annual Hollywood gala as "The socialized and appified Oscars" in which there were social media and mobile app tie-ins "up the wa-
zoo"[58] While on Twitter, there were 1.2 million tweets produced by 388,000
users during the three hours of the show's live television airing.[59] But social
media also starred in the 2011 Oscar content, with the semifactual story
about Mark Zuckerberg's controversial founding of Facebook—the David
Fincher produced and Aaron Sorkin written *The Social Network*, being one
of the two most popular and best received movies of the year.

The Social Network features many of the characters from this book as
semifictionalized characters in the story of Facebook's earliest history such
as the social media revolution's chief-rewiring-officer, Mark Zuckerberg and
Sean Parker, Facebook's one-time president and the co-founder of the social
video network Airtime. There are also minor roles for Adam D'Angelo, the
co-founder of the social knowledge network Quora, and for the original
angel investor in Facebook, Peter Thiel, who was introduced to Parker and
Zuckerberg by our old friend, @quixotic, the king of Silicon Valley connections.

Based on Ben Mezrich's controversially anecdotal 2009 book *Accidental
Billionaires*, Fincher and Sorkin's picture is a parable about friendship, identity and betrayal at Facebook's birth in the snowy New England winter of
2003/2004. As the big-brained son of a Jewish dentist from New Jersey,

Zuckerberg is presented as an outsider in Harvard's complex social world, with its ancient clubs, opaque customs and closed networks of American aristocrats. Professor Robin Dunbar, the director of Oxford University's Institute of Cognitive and Evolutionary Anthology, tells us our brains have been developed to grasp the complexity of Harvard's social arrangements, arguing "what keeps a community together is a sense of mutual obligation and reciprocity." But while it doesn't doubt the size of Mark Zuckerberg's brain, *The Social Network* presents Zuckerberg as a human being unable or, perhaps, unwilling to maintain the complex social obligations and reciprocity that enable us, in contrast with elephants, to develop intimate friendships with other primates.

This semifictionalized Zuckerberg in *The Social Network* could be seen as the model of what Georg Simmel, the turn of the twentieth century German sociologist, identified as the "individualism of difference" that defined modern democratic society.[60] Zuckerberg has no sense, none whatsoever, of social obligation or reciprocity, and he willfully chooses to ignore all the complexity and secrecy of social life at Harvard. In founding Facebook, a supposed "social network" of friends, Zuckerberg betrays his best friend and original partner who originally bankrolled the start-up, humiliates his girlfriend online, and steals the business idea from a couple of other undergraduates who had originally paid and trusted him to develop their Web site. For all his big-brained technical genius and business savvy, lonely Zuckerberg is portrayed as a friendless computer programmer incapable of real social relationships who betrayed what it is to be human. Perhaps, then, it isn't coincidental that this socially dysfunctional programmer founds the dominant social network of the early twenty-first century—the company at the heart of our Web 3.0 "like" economy, a "personalized community" of almost a billion discrete individuals all alone together in their luxury cells.

As it happens, the other illustrious picture of 2011 is also connected to some other characters from this book. You will remember Bertie, the oldest son of Albert and Victoria, whose childhood images had been amongst the private etchings at the source of the *Prince Albert v. Strange* lawsuit and who, as an eighteen-year-old undergraduate at Oxford in 1859, had frequented Benjamin Woodward's Union building every Thursday afternoon. After Queen Victoria's death in 1901, Bertie, the Prince of Wales, was crowned Edward VII. When Bertie died in 1910, his son, George V, became king. And therein lies the origins of 2011's other major picture, Tom Hooper's *The King's Speech*.

George V had two sons, Edward and Albert George (known to his loved ones also as Bertie). When George died in 1936, his eldest son became king, but by the end of the year had abdicated the throne to marry an American divorcee called Wallis Simpson. *The King's Speech* tells the story of Bertie, who would become King George VI on his brother's sensational abdication in November 1936.

Even compared with Mark Zuckerberg's Harvard in the winter of 2003/2004, the England in the winter of 1936/1937 was an intricately complex society, on the brink of war with Nazi Germany and confronted with one of the most serious constitutional crises in its history. *The King's Speech* is a movie about how Bertie—who, no doubt, had a smaller brain than Mark Zuckerberg—successfully navigated this complexity, both in his personal and his public life.

The heart of *The King's Speech* is the true story of an unlikely yet intimate friendship between the aristocratic Bertie and Lionel Logue, an unqualified and plebeian Australian voice therapist. Bertie's secret—which in today's Web 3.0 world would, no doubt, be tweeted into oblivion by the social media mob—was his stutter, which disabled him from making public speeches. The greatness of *The King's Speech* lies in its portrayal of the emotionally intense physical meetings between the future George VI and Logue, both the king and commoner taking care to remain themselves in a frighteningly complex social situation. The camera lingers on the two men as they build their mutual intimacy, establishing reciprocal trust, recognizing each other's social obligations, demonstrating loyalty to one another, arguing and joking, slowly getting to like and then love one another.

The 2011 Academy Awards offered us the choice, as best movie of the year, between one movie about betrayal and the breakdown of human relationships, and another about the beauty of human intimacy and friendship. *The Social Network* is about a friendless billionaire who invented the "like" economy, while *The King's Speech* is about a loving father, husband and friend who remained true to himself and united a country. And that's the choice we need to offer Bill Keller's daughter: The choice between liking and loving; the choice between being human and being an elephant or a sheep.

"There is no such thing as a person whose real self you like every particle of. This is why a world of liking is ultimately a lie," argues the novelist Jonathan Franzen in a passionate attack on the very social technology that enabled Bill Keller's daughter to accumulate 171 friends in a few hours. "But there is such a thing as a person whose real self you love every particle of. And this is why love is such an existential threat to the techno-consumerist order: it exposes the lie."[61]

Can you guess which movie won four Oscars at the eighty-third Academy Awards ceremony, a "coronation" that included awards for best director, best actor and best picture?[62]

CONCLUSION: THE WOMAN IN BLUE

*"'Take care to remain yourself' he had warned me so long ago. I wondered if
I had done so. It was not always easy to know."*
—TRACY CHEVALIER, *GIRL WITH A PEARL EARRING*

Exorcising Bentham

In conclusion, we need to return to the beginning of this story, back to my
vertiginous encounter in London with Jeremy Bentham's corpse. After that
giddy experience in front of the Auto-Icon, I needed a drink or two. Tum-
bling out of University College onto Gower Street—the Bloomsbury thor-
oughfare where Charles Darwin had once lived and where, in the winter of
1848–49, the Pre-Raphaelite Brotherhood had been founded[1]—I spied a
pub in an adjacent side street. Switching on my BlackBerry Bold to check
the time, I calculated that I had about another hour to myself in London—
one more hour of freedom in the soft city before I needed to leave for the
airport to catch my flight to Amsterdam where I was to speak at a social
media conference the next day.

It was getting dark as I crossed over Gower Street, darting between the
stream of black taxis and red double-decker buses heading south into central
London. Tucking my hands into my pockets, I walked briskly in the chill of
the November afternoon. The pub was on University Street, no more than a
few hundred yards from Bentham's Auto-Icon in the South Cloisters corridor of University College. As I got closer, I saw that, like most London

public houses, there was a sign hanging high above its door. Designed in the shape of a giant pendant, it contained an image of an old man with beady eyes and shoulder-length gray hair. In spite of the late afternoon gloom, I immediately recognized him. It was a picture of Jeremy Bentham, from whose corpse I had been fleeing.

Named The Jeremy Bentham, the pub was a living monument to the dead social reformer. There was even a historic black plaque on a wall outside the pub's front door boldly enscribed JEREMY BENTHAM that began with a description of his illustrious corpse on public show over the road in University College and ended in praise of his utilitarian philosophy:

> His "Auto-Icon" as he called it, is in fact his skeleton, dressed in his own clothes and topped with a wax model of his head. His actual head is mummified and kept in the college vaults. It is brought out for meetings of the college council and he is recorded as being present but not voting. Above the bar can be seen a copy of the wax head, made by students at the college. In renaming the pub after him, we are reminded of his greatest ideal, "the greatest happiness of the greatest numbers."

My heart sank. Just as Scottie Ferguson couldn't escape Madeleine Elster's corpse in Hitchcock's *Vertigo*, it seemed as if I couldn't get away from Jeremy Bentham's hypervisible dead body. Rather than having to sit at the bar and stare at a copy of Bentham's wax head while drinking my beer and eating my potato chips, I headed up a winding staircase to a small room that mercifully appeared to contain no mementos of the Inspection-House inventor. Nursing a pint of The Jeremy Bentham's best bitter in this Bentham-Free room, I contemplated my meeting with the illustrious corpse earlier that afternoon.

History really was repeating itself, I realized. The simple architecture of Bentham's Auto-Icon reflected, so to speak, the digital narcissism of our social media world. I recognized too that Bentham's Utilitarian ideals, particularly his greatest happiness of the greatest number principle, were little different from the ideals of contemporary digital visionaries like Mark Zuckerberg whose social network, you'll remember, is developing a Gross Happiness Index to quantify global sentiment. It occurred to me, therefore, that a critique of Bentham might also be the best strategy for critiquing to-day's social network revolution. So what was the most effective way, I mused, to demolish the principles of utilitarianism that are as corrosive today as they were in the nineteenth century?

And how, I wondered, taking a gulp of beer and glancing around the room to make sure there were no wax heads hanging on any of its walls, could I exor-cise the corpse of Jeremy Bentham from my mind?

On Digital Liberty

The solution came to me halfway through my second pint of bitter. As with any doctrinal system, I realized, the most effective critiques come from those who were once apostles of the creed. My mind settled on a man who had been born not far from The Jeremy Bentham—on Rodney Terrace in Pentonville,[2] no more than a mile or two east of Bloomsbury. That man was John Stuart Mill, the most influential British social and political thinker of the nineteenth century.

You'll remember that it was Mill, once "the apostle of the Benthamites,"[3] who, having experienced "a crisis" in his "mental history,"[4] turned against his legal guardian and accused him of being a "boy to the last." Mill rejected Bentham's interpretation of human beings as simply calculating machines. Instead, Mill saw our identities as being much more complex and unique, along the lines of the noble characters in *The King's Speech*, defined as much by our love and generosity of spirit, by our poetry and by our originality and independence of thought, as by the maximization of our pleasures and the minimalization of our pain.

Having been born in 1806 and died in 1873, Mill's life paralleled Britain's industrial revolution, the technological upheaval that replaced the traditional society of village life with the connected architecture of urban, mass society. Like today, it was a revolutionary world defined by the technology of connectivity—an "age of smoke and steam" in the words of the economic historian Eric Hobsbawn. Between 1821 and 1848 in the UK, for example, railway companies laid 5,000 miles of track, while John Loudon "tarmac" McAdam's innovative technology for road building, developed in 1823, had given Britain the best road system seen in the world since the Roman Empire. "This new world would need new thinkers," Mill's biographer, Richard Reeves explains, "and Mill was determined to be one of the foremost among them."[5]

There were two reasons why Mill became Britain's foremost thinker about this new connected world. The first was his realism. He recognized that, for better or worse, the industrial revolution was inevitable and thus regarded cultural conservatives such as the Pre-Raphaelites, who romanticized the preindustrial past, as "chaining themselves to the inanimate corpses of dead political and religious systems."[6] Nor, however, did he fall into the Marxist trap and glorify this new technology of connectivity, imagining that it would eventually enable an everlasting unity of man. So while he was concerned throughout his life with the suffering of the new industrial working class and recognized that government had an important role to play in society, Mill never was seduced by the utopianism that coerced many of his progressive contemporaries.

However, what most distinguishes Mill's thought and makes him Britain's most important nineteenth-century social and political thinker, lies in his understanding of how this new connected world impacted the autonomy of the individual. Utilitarians like Bentham were preoccupied with the rights of all individuals,[7] but Mill recognized that the new architecture of connected roads, railways and newspapers was creating a mass society that

endangered the most valuable thing of all in any society—the ability of individuals to think and act for themselves, independently of public opinion.
Mill laid out this critique of mass society in his 1859 classic *On Liberty*.
What Mill most feared in this connected industrial world was "the creative
mediocrity" of popular tastes, habits and opinions. "Men are not sheep,"[8] he
wrote, arguing that modern government has a responsibility to protect not
so much man from himself, but individuals from the tyranny of public opinion. We should be able to do what we like, he thus famously insisted, as long
as our actions didn't harm anyone else. If Bentham's creed was "the greatest
happiness of the greatest numbers," Mill's faith lay in individuals avoiding
being corrupted by the conformity of the newly networked masses and remaining true to themselves. To Mill, therefore, individual autonomy, privacy and self-development were all essential both to human progress and to
the development of a good life.

   As I sat upstairs in The Jeremy Bentham nursing my beer and thinking
about John Stuart Mill, what struck me is how acutely relevant *On Liberty* is
today, in an age also being revolutionized by a pervasive connective technology. This is a world, according to Mark Zuckerberg, in which education,
commerce, health and finance are all becoming social.[9] It's a connected world
defined by billions of "smart" devices, by real-time lynch mobs, by tens of
thousands of people broadcasting details of a stranger's sex life, by the bureaucratization of friendship, by the group-think of small brothers, by the
elimination of loneliness, and by the transformation of life itself into a voluntary Truman Show.

   Most of all, it's a world in which many of us have forgotten what it means
to be human. "But here I fear I am becoming nostalgic," writes the novelist
Zadie Smith, who along with Jonathan Franzen and Gary Shteyngart is
amongst the most articulate contemporary critics of social media. "I am
dreaming of a Web that caters to a person who no longer exists. A private
person, a person who is a mystery, to the world and—which is more

important—to herself. Person as mystery: This idea of personhood is certainly changing, perhaps has already changed."[10]

What Smith, as well as Franzen, Shteyngart and all the other critics of our increasingly transparent and social age are mourning is this loss of the private person, the disappearance of secrecy and mystery, the primacy of like over love, the victory of Bentham's utilitarianism over Mill's individual liberty and, most of all, the collective amnesia about what it really means to be human. It's a super-sad true love story in which we are forgetting who we really are.

As I thought about Zadie Smith's notion of what it means to be human, I felt a tingling in my groin. No, I wasn't giddy on the best Jeremy Bentham bitter. It was my BlackBerry Bold vibrating insistently in my pocket. My hour in London was up, the smartphone—which also acted as my watch, my alarm clock and my diary—was telling me. I needed to go to the airport. Amsterdam and the Rijksmuseum awaited me.

Social Pictures

Mark Zuckerberg once had a problem with pictures. As an undergraduate at Harvard, he enrolled in an Art History class. But he had no time to study or attend any of the lectures because he was building The Facebook (as it was then known). So a week before the final exam, he started to panic. Zuckerberg knew nothing about either the paintings or the artists in the course. So, inevitably, he came up with a social solution to his dilemma.

"Zuckerberg did what comes naturally to a native of the web. He went to the internet and downloaded images of all the pieces of art he knew would be covered in the exam," explains Jeff Jarvis, who got the story firsthand from the then twenty-two-year-old Zuckerberg when they met at the 2007 World Economic Forum in Davos. "He put them on a Web page and added blank boxes under each. Then he emailed the address of this page to his classmates, telling them he'd just put up a study guide.... The class dutifully came along and filled in the blanks with the essential knowledge about each piece of art, editing each other as they went, collaborating to get it just right."[11]

I've sometimes wondered which artists Zuckerberg was studying for his art history course. The Pre-Raphaelite Brotherhood, perhaps, with their nostalgia for a world that never existed. Or nineteenth-century landscape painters like Albert Bierstadt, with their dramatic western vistas of unlimited power. Or maybe Johannes Vermeer and Rembrandt Van Rijn, the two geniuses of seventeenth-century Dutch art who, in their different ways, were masters of reminding us who we really are. Perhaps the utilitarian Zuckerberg, the accidental billionaire who believes that the social can make us all more efficient and happy, downloaded paintings by Vermeer and Rembrandt. Maybe he even had these pictures up on his screen while he was hacking the Harvard university databases to launch The Facebook.

What particularly intrigues me are the blank boxes that Zuckerberg, in this social art experiment, put underneath the pictures. These boxes were for the "essential knowledge" about these paintings, suggesting that they, like programming, have right and wrong answers. I wonder what Zuckerberg would have written about Rembrandt's self-portraits, especially his self-portrait of himself as an old man, when he represented himself as the Apostle Paul. What is the truth, the "essential knowledge," about these pictures, that he would have entered into the blank box? You see, the essential knowledge about any pictures, particularly if they have anything *essential* about them, is that their mystery and secrecy are much more interesting than their answers. The truth about these pictures is that their meaning can't be socially fitted, like a Facebook update, into blank boxes on computer screens. The essential knowledge about any great picture—whether they have been created by Vermeer or Rembrandt or even by Hitchcock—is that they remind us who we, as human-beings, really are.

The Woman in Blue

Portraits—particularly self-portraits—happened to be on my mind. It was the morning after my social media speech in Amsterdam and I found myself in the Rijksmuseum, the museum that housed some of the most illustrious Dutch pictures from the seventeenth century. My BlackBerry Bold was switched off, buried deeply in my pocket. I was thus untethered from my Research in Motion gadget, disconnected from my followers, off the global network. I had no networked camera, no access to existential tweets, no Facebook or LinkedIn updates, no facial-recognition technology, no Tweetie asking for permission to reveal my location. The great exhibitionism of the early twenty-first century had, for a couple of hours, been replaced by a greater exhibition of seventeenth-century Dutch art.

Christine Rosen writes about the "painted anthropology" of pictures: "For centuries, the rich and the powerful documented their existence and their status through painted portraits. A marker of wealth and a bid for immortality, portraits offer intriguing hints about the daily life of their subjects—professions, ambitions, attitudes and most importantly, social standing," she notes.[12] Today, Rosen explains, with reference to social networking Web sites like Facebook, our portraits are "democratic and digital; they are crafted from pixels rather than paints."[13] But it hasn't always been this way, she reminds us. Once, portraits were universal statements rather than forms of narcissism; once they spoke to human beings collectively, rather than in the personalized language of today's social media.

At the Rijksmuseum, I had just finished gazing at two self-portraits by Rembrandt: one as a hubristic, red-haired youngster when the artist was no older than Mark Zuckerberg; the other as a weary old man distinguished by what the historian Simon Schama calls "Rembrandt's Eyes," when the artist, whose fortunes by then had dramatically declined, painted himself as a wizened Apostle Paul. In spite of their deeply personal nature, both pictures are universal statements, "essential knowledge," about the confidence of youth and the all-too-human exhaustion of old age. That's why, almost four hundred years later, I was standing in the Rijksmuseum gazing with wonder at pictures that were, to borrow some words from Christine Rosen, both a bid for immortality and a painted anthropology of seventeenth-century Dutch individualistic culture.

And then I saw her. I saw the woman who is anything but her own image. I saw a picture of who we really are.

Painted by Johannes Vermeer between 1663 and 1664, "Woman in Blue Reading a Letter" is a picture of a young Dutch woman, probably pregnant, raptly reading an unfolded letter that she is holding in both her hands. There is a map on the rear wall behind her, an open box in front of her and an empty chair in the foreground. These are all universal symbols of loss, opportunity and travel—Vermeer's clues, his time line, to making sense of the picture. The room is well lit, but we see no window, no source for what appears to be natural light. The young woman is so locked, so imprisoned in her own world, gripping the letter between her hands, that she is unaware of anyone else watching her.

Watching the "Woman in Blue" is, of course, an act of the purest voyeurism. I knew nothing and yet everything about her. Her concentration mesmerized me. The letter, I saw, could be full of news about a death or a birth, it could be from an old friend, a sick parent or a new love. But the longer I stared at her, the more secretive, the more private the picture became and the more relevant, the more pressing, the more eternal and the more mysterious the letter in her hands appeared.

There is a scene in Hitchcock's *Vertigo* when Scottie Ferguson first sees Madeleine Elster. They are in Ernie's, the plush old steakhouse in San Francisco's North Beach. Scottie is sitting at the bar drinking a martini and Madeleine is eating dinner. He notices her through a doorway as she walks toward him. She is dressed in a green shawl and a low-cut black dress. The violins in Bernard Herrmann's score crescendo. Scottie, the poor fool, is immediately hooked. And so are viewers like myself. I've even captured this image of Madeleine on my Twitter (@ajkeen) page.[14] It is now the wallpaper, the background to all my tweets.

It was a little like this at the Rijksmuseum that November morning when I saw Vermeer's "Woman in Blue." I sat in front of the picture in the same frozen pose that Madeleine sat in front of the painting of her nineteenth-century relative in the San Francisco Palace of Fine Arts. Unlike Madeleine, however, my infatuation with the picture was neither an act nor a ploy to mislead my audience. I really was staring into it raptly, with all my concentration focused on its unresolvable mysteries. The picture had become the architecture of all my intimacies. It had even exorcised the corpse of Jeremy Bentham from my mind.

It would be easy, of course, to make a conservative, comfortably nostalgic argument about how twenty-first-century technology, Christine Rosen's digital pixels, disables us from the production of such pictures today. "Yes, I should have liked to have lived there then, color, excitement, power, freedom," as that villainous Gavin Elster said, so disingenuously about the supposed idyll of mid-nineteenth-century San Francisco. But, as John Stuart Mill, who never enrolled in the "Jeremiah School"[15] reminds us, it is stupid to chain ourselves to dead political or social systems in order to denigrate the present. Besides as I've already argued, such a technocentric analysis is the Macguffin in this book. The truth is that Johannes Vermeer, who was as much a technophile as any twenty-first-century geek, focused on using all the most sophisticated technologies of his age to make his pictures more realistic. Indeed, as Philip Steadman argues in *Vermeer's Camera: Uncovering the Truth Behind the Masterpieces*, Vermeer's knowledge of seventeenth-century optical science enabled him to build a "camera obscura," a primitive version of the modern camera, which enabled him to capture the subjects of his pictures with more photographic accuracy.[16]

To borrow some words from Mark Zuckerberg, what "essential knowledge" does "Woman in Blue" teach us? What is the truth that we can uncover behind Vermeer's masterpiece? In Tracy Chevalier's novel *Girl with a Pearl Earring*, her brilliant reconstruction of the story behind another Vermeer masterpiece, there is a moment when the story's heroine, a young maid called Griet, is told by a local merchant to "take care to remain yourself."[17] And this was exactly what "The Woman in Blue" had remained. We know nothing about her except that she has taken care to *remain herself*, an entirely private being, *hyperinvisible*, a mystery to the world—the person that Zadie Smith fears we have lost. She may or may not be John Stuart Mill's "unique individual," but she does represent the condition for Mill's definition of the good life, somebody left to their own devices, autonomous, not a little lonely above all, private. Her authenticity lies in her mystery, not her nakedness. "Woman in Blue" is an image of herself without knowing it— the opposite of Jeremy Bentham's stuffed corpse gazing with such unreflexive self-satisfaction out of his Auto-Icon, the reverse of mad Josh Harris living in the fully public Quiet hotel or the shiny-faced Robert Scoble hypervisibly sitting in front of his flickering computer monitor watching his followers watching him.

I continued to sit for a while, mesmerized, staring at "Woman in Blue." I realized that this timeless picture is indeed what we are risking losing. In the great exhibitionism of our hypervisible Web 3.0 world, when we are always on public display, forever revealing ourselves to the camera, we are losing the ability to remain ourselves.

We are forgetting who we really are.

Remaining Ourselves

After a while, I got up to leave. I wandered through a couple of small rooms and found myself standing in front of perhaps the most famous picture in the world, Rembrandt van Rijn's 1642 painting "The Night Watch," his portrait of a group of Dutch burghers. First I looked at the almost 400-year-old huge painting that covered an entire wall of the museum and then at its description on an adjacent wall:

> *Rembrandt's best known and largest canvas was made for the club building of one of Amsterdam's militia companies—the arquebusiers. Every burgher was required to serve in the guard but those included in a group portrait had to pay for the privilege, it is the company's wealthiest members who are shown here. Rembrandt was the first to portray subjects in a portrait in motion.*

I blinked and read the final sentence on the wall again. "Rembrandt was the first to portray subjects in a portrait in motion." The very *first*! In the full span of human history, of course, 400 years isn't a long time. But the almost 400 years that have elapsed between Rembrandt's "NightWatch" now—shaped first by the industrial and now the digital revolutions—seem like an eternity. In our transparent age of global communications, when we are self-authoring mankind's collective portrait every minute of the day, where, for example, during the Osama Bin Laden assassination on May 1, 2011, there were 3,440 tweets about Bin Laden authored *per second*[18]—it is difficult to imagine a time when group portraits in motion didn't exist.

I tried to cast my mind forward not 400 years, but just forty—to the middle of the twenty-first century. How much quicker and more social, I wondered, could our group portrait in motion become? At Oxford, in an interview for a BBC show that I was making about the future of technology, I had asked Biz Stone if our communications would ever become faster than real-time. He had laughed, in his geeky cheeky way, at the absurdity of it. But in forty years' time, I wondered, when @quixotic's Web 3.0 world seems as archaic as Rembrandt's "The Night Watch" or Vermeer's "Woman in Blue

Reading a Letter," would we remain ourselves? Would we take on the identity of the walls of Benjamin Woodward's Oxford Union, which had lost everything that had been painted upon them? Could we really forget who we are?

I began this book with a lively corpse from the past, so let me end with a haunting corpse from the future. As an Oxford undergraduate, you'll remember, old Jeremy Bentham was scared of ghosts. Indeed, the inventor of the Inspection-House was so terrified of goblins throughout his life that he was scared to sleep alone at night and required his assistants to share his bedroom.[19] Unlike Bentham, I'm scared of neither ghosts nor goblins. But I have to confess that I am scared of the ghost of mankind, a ghost that would have forgotten what it is to be human. This ghost would be living hypervisibly with incalculable followers, associates and friends on every social network, past and future. The existence of this ghost, I confess, would make me scared to sleep alone at night too and would require my assistant to sleep closely beside me.

It was, I think, Alfred Hitchcock who once said that behind every good picture lay a great corpse. But mankind isn't a picture and there is nothing good about a species that has turned into a corpse because it has forgotten what it once was. John Stuart Mill, Bentham's greatest nineteenth-century critic, was right to argue that remaining human required us to sometimes disconnect from society, to remain private, autonomous and secretive. The alternative, Mill recognized, was the "tyranny of the majority" and the death of individual liberty. This isn't an unrealistic fear. As Michael Foucault, Bentham's most creative twentieth-century critic, warns "man is neither the oldest nor the most constant problem that has been posed for human knowledge" and thus he could easily be "erased, like a face drawn in at the edge of the sea.[20]

Today, more than 150 years after Mill published *On Liberty,* as a new, more virulent revolution of connectivity rages all around us and we are all dizzily broadcasting ourselves from our connected crystal palaces, we need to go back to the anti-Bentham, John Stuart Mill, for guidance. Men aren't sheep, Mill says. Nor are they armies of ants or herds of elephants. No, just as @quixotic is wrong to believe that we are primarily social beings and Biz Stone mistaken that the future must be social, so is Sean Parker wrong that today's creepy is inevitably tomorrow's necessity. Instead, as John Stuart Mill reminds us, our uniqueness as a species lies in our ability to stand apart from the crowd, to disentangle ourselves from society, to be let alone and to be able to think and act for ourselves.

The future, therefore, should be anything but social. That's what we need to remember as human beings at the dawn of the twenty-first century when, for better or worse, @quixotic's Web 3.0 world of pervasive personal data, this Internet of people, is becoming like home for all of us. And that's exactly the "essential knowledge" that I'd like you to take away from this picture of digital vertigo in our age of great exhibitionism.

ENDNOTES

EPIGRAPH

1. W. G. Sebald, *Vertigo* (New Directions, 2000) 94–95.

INTRODUCTION: HYPERVISIBILITY

1. Alexia Tsotsis, October 30, 2010.
2. For a full history of Bentham's corpse, see the James E. Crimmin's introduction to *Jeremy Bentham's Auto-Icon and Related Writings* (Bristol, 2002) (http://www.utilitarian.net/bentham/about/2002----.htm).
3. C.F.A. Marmoy, "The Auto-Icon of Jeremy Bentham at University College," *History of Medicine at UCL Journal*, April 1958 (http://www.ncbi.nlm.gov/pmc/articles/PMC1034365/).
4. Aldous Huxley, *Prisons* (Trianon & Grey Falcon Presses, 1949). See: http://www.john-coulthart.com/feuilleton/2006/08/25/aldous-huxley-on-piranesis-prisons/.
5. Bentham, John Dinwiddy, (Oxford, 1989), 18.
6. Manufactured by the appropriately named Research in Motion (RIM), Canada's largest technology company, globally headquartered in Waterlooville, Ontario. My model was the BlackBerry Bold.
7. A Canon Digital Rebel XSi 12.2 MP Digital SLR Camera with an EF-S 55–250mm f/4-5.6 IS zoom lens.
8. "Infographic: A Look at the Size and Shape of the Geosocial Universe in 2011," by Rip Empson, Techcrunch, May 20, 2011 (http://techcrunch.com/2011/05/20/infographic-a-look-at-the-size-and-shape-of-the-geosocial-universe-in-2011/).
9. See: "An Internet of People," by Chris Dixon, cdixon.org, December 19, 2011 (http://cdixon.org/2011/12/19/an-internet-of-people/). Dixon quotes the Sequoia venture capitalist Roelof Botha, who describes this internet of people as a "trust" and "reputation" economy.
10. "The Daily Dot Wants to be the Web's Hometown Paper," by Matthew Ingram, Gigaom,

April 1, 2011 (http://gigaom.com/2011/04/01/the-daily-dot-wants-to-be-the-webs-home-town-paper/).

11. For forty years of his adult life, Bentham lived in a Westminster house overlooking St. James Park that he called Queen's Square Place. Perhaps not uncoincidentally, given Bentham's keen interest in penal reform, this Westminster site, known today as 102 Petty France, is occupied by the British Ministry of Justice.

12. Bentham's "greatest happiness principle" was laid out in his 1831 pamphlet *Parliamentary Candidate's Proposed Declaration of Principles* in which he argued that the goal of government is to maximize the pleasure or happiness of the greatest number. (See: *Bentham*, John Dinwiddy, Oxford, Chapter 2, "The Greatest Happiness Principle.")

13. Richard Florida, *The Rise of the Creative Class*, (Basic, 2002), 74, John Hagel, John Seely Brown, *The Power of Pull* (Basic 2010), 90.

14. "The Metropolis and Mental Life," by Georg Simmel, from *The Sociology of Georg Simmel*, ed. Kurt H. Wolff (Free Press, 1950), 409.

15. Jonathan Raban, *Soft City*, (15). Raban is also the author of *Surveillance* (Pantheon 2006), an excellent novel about the growing ubiquity of electronic surveillance in our digital age.

16. "The Ministry of Truth—Minitrue, in Newspeak—was startlingly different from any other object in sight," Orwell described the Ministry of Truth in *Nineteen Eighty-four*. "It was an enormous pyramidal structure of glittering white concrete, soaring up, terrace after terrace three hundred metres into the air. From where Winston stood it was just possible to read, picked out on its white face in elegant lettering, the three slogans of the Party: WAR IS PEACE, FREEDOM IS SLAVERY, IGNORANCE IS STRENGTH.

17. Richard Cree, "Well Connected," *Director* magazine, July 2009.

18. See "Boom! Professional Social Network LinkedIn Passes 100 Million Members," by Leena Rao, Techcrunch, March 22, 2011 (http://techcrunch.com/2011/03/22/boom-professional-social-network-linkedin-passes-100-million-members/).

19. *Laptop Magazine*, February 2011, 71.

20. "LinkedIn Founder: "Web 3.0 Will Be About Data," by Ben Parr, Mashable, March 30, 2011. For a video of Hoffman's interview with Liz Gannes at the Web 20. Expo, see: http://www.web2expo.com/webexsf2011/public/schedule/detail/17716.

21. The other four are Netscape cofounder Marc Andreessen, legendary seed investor Ron Conway and Peter Thiel, Hoffman's colleague at Paypal and the founding angel investor in Facebook. See: "The 25 Tech Angels, 11 Good Angels and 18 Geeks Everyone Wants to Fly With," see *San Francisco Magazine*, December 2010. (http://www.sanfranmag.com/story/25-tech-angels-11-good-angels-and-18-geeks-everyone-wants-fly-with).

22. "The Midas List: Technology's Top 100 Investors," *Forbes*, April 6, 2011. (http://www.forbes.com/lists/midas/2011/midas-list-complete-list.html).

23. "Reid Hoffman," Soapbox, *The Wall Street Journal*, June 23, 2011. (http://online.wsj.com/article/SB10001424052702303657404576363452101709880.html).

24. "The King of Connections Is Tech's Go-To-Guy," by Evelyn M. Rusli, *The New York Times*, November 5, 2011 (http://www.nytimes.com/2011/11/06/business/reid-hoffman-of-linkedin-has-become-the-go-to-guy-of-tech.html?pagewanted=all).

25. For my own "Keen On" Techcrunch.tv interview with Reid Hoffman in August 2010, see: http://techcrunch.com/2010/08/30/keen-on-reid-hoffman-leadership/.

26. "Fail Fast Advises LinkedIn Founder and Tech Investor Reid Hoffman," BBC, January 11, 2001 (http://www.bbc.co.uk/news/business-12151752).

27. "LinkedIn Surpasses MySpace to Become No. 2 Social Network," by Leena Rao, Techcrunch, July 8, 2011 (http://techcrunch.com/2011/07/08/linkedin-surpasses-myspace -for-u-s-visitors-to-become-no-2-social-network-twitter-not-far-behind/).

28. The LinkedIn IPO took place on May 18, 2011. Beginning the day priced at $40, shares tripled in value at one point and finally ended the day at $94, valuing the company at almost $9 billion and giving Hoffman a more than two billion dollar stake in his start-up. See: "Linkedin's Top Backers Own $6.7 Billion Stake," by Ari Levy, Bloomberg News, May 18, 2011. (http://www.bloomberg.com/news/2011-05-19/linkedin-s-founder-biggest -backers-will-own-2-5-billion-stake-after-ipo.html). See, also: "Small Group Rode Linke- dIn to a Big Payday," by Nelson D. Schwartz, The New York Times, June 19, 2011. (http:// www.nytimes.com/2011/06/20/business/20bonanza.html?hp), for an analysis of the IPO and how "for Reid Hoffman, the chairman of LinkedIn, it took less than 30 minutes to earn himself an extra $200 million."

29. In conversation with Liz Gannes of All Things D, December 29, 2010. (http://network effect.allthingsd.com/20101229/video-greylocks-reid-hoffman-and-david-sze-on-the -future-of-social/).

30. Zygna—which includes the massively popular social game Farmville in its digital stable— has become so big so quickly that its value is about equal to that of Electronic Games (EA), the world's second largest game publisher. According to research published by SharesPost in October 2010, the privately held Zygna was worth $5.1 billion while the publicly traded EA was worth $5.16 on the Nasdaq Stock Market. For more, see Bloomberg Businessweek of 10/26/2010: http://www.businessweek.com/news/2010-10-26/zygna-s -value-tops-electronic-arts-on-virtual-goods.html.

31. Samuel Warren and Louis Brandeis, "The Right to Privacy," Harvard Law Review, Vol. IV, December 15, 1890, No.5. This article has been described as "legendary" and "the most influential law review article of all" and is considered by many privacy scholars to be the foundation of privacy law in the United States. For more, see: Daniel J. Solove, Under- standing Privacy (Harvard University Press, 2008), 13–10.

32. "One time prison becoming daring escape," is how the Malmaison brands itself for the modern traveler bored with traditional luxury hotels. To follow the Malmaison on Twit- ter, go to: http://twitter.com/#!/TheOxfordMal.

33. Aristotle's argument from The Politics that "man is by nature a social animal: an individ- ual who is unsocial naturally and not accidentally is either beneath our notice or more than human. Society is something that precedes the individual . . ." is the opening salvo of a two-thousand-year-old communitarian argument that places the importance of the so- cial above the individual. Aristotle's position that "anyone who either cannot lead the common life or is so self-sufficient as not to need to, and therefore does not partake of society, is either a beast or a god" was entertainingly countered by Friedrich Nietzsche's maxim from Twilight of the Idols that "in order to live alone, one must be an animal or a God—says Aristotle. The third case is missing: one must be both—a philosopher . . ."

34. Sacca runs a billion-dollar social media investment fund. As of late February 2010, his Lowercase Capital billion dollar fund (that includes JP Morgan as a major investor) was

the largest institutional owner of Twitter stock with a roughly 9 percent stake in the real-time social network. See: "New Fund Provides Stake in Twitter for JP Morgan," Evelyn Rusli, *The New York Times Deal Book,* February 28, 2011 (http://dealbook.nytimes.com/2011/02/28/new-fund-gives-jpmorgan-a-stake-in-twitter/).

35. See: http://andrewkeen.independentminds.livejournal.com/3676.html for an account of my conversations with Stone at Oxford as well as a photograph of the tuxedoed Stone and Hoffman in the Oxford Union library.

36. Oxford Union Debate, Sunday, November 23, 2008.

37. The speed of Twitter's market value is astonishing. In October 2010, the privately held company—which still remains effectively revenue-free—had a secondary market valuation of $1.575 billion. By December 2010, the blue chip Silicon Valley venture firm of Kleiner Perkins led a $200 billion investment round in Twitter at a valuation of $3.7 billion. Then in February 2011, *The Wall Street Journal* announced rumors that Google and Facebook were interested in acquiring Twitter for between $8 and $10 billion. And by March, 2011, Twitter's valuation on the secondary market has risen to $7.7 billion. While in April 2011, *Fortune* magazine reported that Twitter had turned down a $10 billion acquisition offer from Google. But by July, Twitter had raised another $400 million of venture capital investment at a $8 billion valuation. And by August 2011, the *Financial Times* confirmed Twitter's $8 billion valuation and its investment led by the Russian internet investment firm DST.

38. "New Twitter Stats: 140M Tweets Sent Per Day, 460K Accounts Created Per Day," by Leena Rao, Techcrunch, March 14, 2011. (http://techcrunch.com/2011/03/14/new-twitter-stats-140m-tweets-sent-per-day-460k-accounts-created-per-day/).

39. Before Twitter, Stone was an executive at a number of technology companies including Google. His books include *Blogging: Genius Strategies for Instant Web Content* (2002) *Who Let The Blogs Out: A Hyperconnected Peek at the World of Weblogs* (2004).

40. In June 2011, Stone retired from his full-time position at Twitter as "part evangelist, part storyteller, and part futurist" to become a strategic advisor at Spark Capital. See: "Twitter Co-Founder Joins Venture Capital Firm, by Claire Cain Miller," *The New York Times,* July 7, 2011 (http://bits.blogs.nytimes.com/2011/07/07/twitter-co-founder-joins-venture-capital-firm/).

41. "Twitter Founder to Join Huffington Post," by Dominic Rushe, *The London Guardian,* March 15, 3011 (http://www.guardian.co.uk/media/2011/mar/15/twitter-founder-joins-huffington-post).

42. "The Auto-Icon of Jeremy Bentham at University College, London" by C.F.A. Marmoy, *The History of Medicine at UCL Journal,* April 1958.

43. Bentham become John Stuart Mill's legal guardian six years after John's birth when James Mill fell seriously ill. See: Richard Reeves, *John Stuart Mill: Victorian Firebrand* (Atlantic, 2007), 11.

44. "Bentham" by John Stuart Mill, in *John Stuart Mill and Jeremy Bentham: Utilitarianism and Other Essays* (Penguin, 1987), 149.

45. Mill popularized the term "Utilitarian" in the winter of 1822–23 when he set up the "Utilitarian Society" (see: J. S. Mill, *Autobiography,* 49) The word itself, however, unbeknown to Mill, had first been used by Bentham in some eighteenth-century correspon-

dence with the French political theorist Pierre Etienne Louis Dumont (see: Richard Reeves, *John Stuart Mill*), 37.

46. "Bentham," by J. S. Mill, 149.

47. Umberto Eco, *Travels in Hyperreality* (Harcourt, Brace, Jovanovich: 1983), 6–7.

48. Pierre Boileau and Thomas Narcejac, *The Living and the Dead* (Washburn, 1957).

49. "Tracking is an Assault on Liberty," by Nicholas Carr, *The Wall Street Journal*, August 7, 2010.

50. "Soapbox: Reid Hoffman," *The Wall Street Journal*, June 23, 2011 (http://online.wsj .com/article/SB10001424052702303657404576363452101709880.html).

51. "Fail fast" advises LinkedIn founder and tech investor Reid Hoffman," BBC Business News, January 11, 2011 (http://www.bbc.co.uk/news/business-12151752).

52. At the March 2011 South by Southwest conference, Hoffman laid out his definition of Web 3.0. If Web 1.0 meant "go search, get data", and Web 2.0 meant "real identities" and "real relationships," Hoffman said, then Web 3.0 involves "real identities generating massive amounts of data." See: "LinkedIn's Reid Hoffman explains the brave new world of data," by Anthony Ha, March 15, 2011, VentureBeat. (http://venturebeat.com/2011/03/15/ reid-hoffman-data-sxsw/)

53. Estimate by Cisco (http://www.electrictv.com/?p=4323). See also the remarks of Ericsson CEO and President Hans Vestberg at the Monaco Media Forum in November 2010 (http://www.youtube.com/watch?v=vTT-WvelWWo). But even in the very short term, it is inevitable that the number of connected people and devices will rise dramatically. At the Feburary 2011 Mobile World Congress in Barcelona, for example, Nokia CEO Stephen Elop promised to "connect the unconnected" and bring three million people around the world online via their cellphones. See: "Nokia Wants to Bring 3 Billion More Online," by Jenna Wortham, *The New York Times*, February 18, 2011 (http://bits.blogs.nytimes.com/2011/02/16/nokia-wants-to-bring-3-billion-more -online/).

1. A SIMPLE IDEA OF ARCHITECTURE

1. Jeremy Bentham, *The Panopticon Writings*, ed. Miran Bozovic (Verso), 31.

2. John Dinwiddy, *Bentham*, 38 (Oxford, 1989).

3. The Inspection-House plan had originally intended to be implemented by the government. In 1813, to compensate Bentham for its nonimplementation, he was awarded £23,000 by Parliament which enabled him to rent a "magnificent house" in the west country where he spent his summers and autumns (see: John Dinwiddy, *Bentham*, 16–17).

4. Aldous Huxley, *Prisons* (Trianon & Grey Falcon Presses, 1949). See: http://www.john coulthart.com/feuilleton/2006/08/25/aldous-huxley-on-piranesis-prisons/.

5. Jeremy Bentham, *Panopticon Letters*, 1787, unpublished manuscript, University College London Library.

6. Bentham, together with his brother Samuel, were helping Prince Grigory Potemkin, Catherine the Great's lover and the most powerful landowner in Tsarist Russia, to design an English village with modern industrial factories in the eastern Belorussian town of Krichev. Potemkin, of course, is best remembered now for his "Potemkin Villages"—

artificial communities purely created to impress Catherine the Great. For more, see: "The Bentham Brother, their Adventure in Russia," Simon Sebag Montefiore (*History Today*, August 2003).

7. Michel Foucault, *Discipline & Punish—The Birth of the Prison* (Vintage, 1979), 200.

8. Letter 1, "Idea of the Inspection Principle, The Panopticon Writings," Jeremy Bentham, ed Miran Bozovic (Versa, 1995).

9. Norman Johnson, *Forms of Constraint: A History of Prison Architecture*, 56.

10. "The Metropolis and Mental Life," Georg Simmel, *The Sociology of Georg Simmel*, ed Kurt H. Wolff (Free Press, 1950), 409.

11. Michel Foucault, *Discipline and Punishment: The Birth of the Prison* (Vintage, 1979), 200.

12. In 2010, smart televisions only made up 2% of global household penetration, according to research conducted in August 2010 by the market research firm iSuppli. But by 2014, iSuppli projects, this global household penetration will have risen to 33% (http://www.ft .com/cms/s/2/9be3d412-b783-11df-8ef6-00144feabdc0.html?ftcamp=rss).

13. Such as Microsoft's Kinect console, a product that connects motion-controlled gaming with video-conferencing and voice interactivity.

14. At Las Vegas's Consumer Electronics Show in January 2011, for example, there were 380 in-vehicle electronics exhibitors showing such networked technology as high-speed Internet access for cars. See: "At CES, Cars Take Center Stage," *The New York Times,* January 6, 2011. (http://wheels.blogs.nytimes.com/2010/01/06/at-ces-cars-move-center -stage/).

15. Jeremy Bentham's vision of the Panopticon was sketched out in a series of letters he wrote in 1789 from Crecheff in the Crimea to an unnamed friend in England. See *The Panopticon Writings*, Edited & Introduced by Miran Bozovic (Verso 1995). Bentham had gone to Russia in 1785 with his brother Samuel to help Prince Potemkin, Catherine the Great's lover and the most powerful landowner in Russia, design an English industrial village. See: "Prince Potemkin and the Benthams," by Simon Sebag Montefiore, *History Today*, August 2003.

16. Clay Shirky, *Cognitive Surplus: Creativity and Generosity in a Connected Age* (Penguin 2010), 54.

17. From Clinton's "Remarks on Internet Freedom" speech in Washington D.C., on January 21, 2010. This term has also been used by Microsoft social media guru Marc Davis in his keynote speech at the Privacy Identity Innovation (PII) conference in Seattle on August 18, 2010 (http://vimeo.com/14401407).

18. *Cognitive Surplus*, 196–197.

19. "Julian Assange Tells Students That the Web Is the Greatest Spying Machine Ever," Patrick Kingsley, *The London Guardian*, March 15, 2011 (http://www.guardian.co.uk/ media/2011/mar/15/web-spying-machine-julian-assange).

20. "Wikileaks Founder: Facebook Is the Most Appalling Spy Machine That Has Ever Been Invented," Matt Brian, The Next Web, May 2, 2012 (http://thenextweb.com/facebook/ 2011/05/02/wikileaks-founder-facebook-is-the-most-appalling-spy-machine-that-has -ever-been-invented/).

21. A November 2011 Pew Internet and American Life research study reported that already 4% of online Americans are using these location-based services (http://www.pewinternet

.org/Reports/2010/Location-based-services.aspx), suggesting—as Jay Yarow at Business Insider argued (http://www.businessinsider.com/location-based-services-2010-11)—that services like Gowalla are growing at the same viral rate as Twitter in its earliest stage of development.

22. Shirky's comments about the increased "legibility" of society were expressed—to excuse the pun—most transparently when he was interviewed by the BBC's Diplomatic Correspondent Bridget Kendall on the BBC World Service radio show, "The Forum," on September 19, 2010 (http://www.bbc.co.uk/programmes/p009q3m3).

23. Katie Roiphe, "The Language of Fakebook," *The New York Times*, August 13, 2010.

24. On YouCeleb.com, see: "YouCeleb Lets You Look Like a Star For Cheap," by Rip Empson, Techcrunch, February 28, 2011 (http://techcrunch.com/2011/02/28/youceleb-lets-you-look-like-a-star-for-cheap/).

25. The Forum, September 19, 2010.

26. Jean Twenger and W. Keith Campbell, *The Narcissism Epidemic: Living in the Age of Entitlement* (Free Press, 2009).

27. Elias Aboujaoude, *Virtually You* (Norton 2011), 72.

28. "The Elusive Big Idea," Neal Gabler, *The New York Times*, August 13, 2011.

29. "The Insidious Evils of 'Like' Culture," Neil Strauss, *The Wall Street Journal*, July 2, 2011. (http://online.wsj.com/article/SB10001424052702304584004576415940086842866.html).

30. "Liking Is for Cowards. Go for What Hurts," Jonathan Franzen, *The New York Times*, May 29, 2011 (http://www.nytimes.com/2011/05/29/opinion/29franzen.html).

31. "Liking Is for Cowards. Go for What Hurts," Jonathan Franzen, *The New York Times*, May 29, 2011 (http://www.nytimes.com/2011/05/29/opinion/29franzen.html).

32. "Virtual Friendship and the New Narcissism," Christine Rosen, *The New Atlantis: A Journal of Technology and Society*, Number 17, Summer 2007.

33. "The Online Looking Glass," Ross Douthat, *The New York Times*, June 12, 2011.

34. "The Saga of Sister Kiki," David Brooks, *The New York Times*, June 23, 2011 (http://www.nytimes.com/2011/06/24/opinion/24brooks.html).

35. "A Billionaire's Breakup Becomes China's Social-Media Event of the Year," Loretta Chao and Josh Chin, *The Wall Street Journal*, June 17, 2011 (http://online.wsj.com/article/SB10001424052702304563104576357271321894898.html).

36. "In Praise of Oversharing," Steven Johnson, *Time* magazine, May 20, 2010.

37. Jeff Jarvis, "What If There Are No Secrets," Buzzmachine.com, 07/26/10.

38. Given in Berlin. See: http://www.buzzmachine.com/2010/04/22/privacy-publicness-penises/.

39. Jarvis announced his prostrate cancer in a post entitled "The Small c and Me" on his BuzzMachine blog on August 10, 2009 (http://www.buzzmachine.com/2009/08/10/the-small-c-and-me/).

40. See the March 2011 issue of the UK *Wired* magazine in which Jeff Jarvis, Steven Johnson, and I each lay out our positions about privacy on the web (http://www.wired.co.uk/magazine/archive/2011/03/features/sharing-is-a-trap). See my debate with Jarvis on the BBC Today show on February 5, 2011. (http://news.bbc.co.uk/today/hi/today/newsid_9388000/9388379.stm?utm_source=twitterfeed&utm_medium=twitter). See also

my August 2010 "Keen On" Techcrunch.tv show interview with Jarvis: http://tech-crunch.com/2010/08/12/keen-on-publicness-jeff-jarvis-tctv/.

41. Jeff Jarvis, *Public Parts: How Sharing in the Digital Age Improves the Way We Work and Live* (Simon and Schuster, 2012).

42. "Public Parts," by Jeff Jarvis, May 20, 2010 (http://www.buzzmachine.com/2010/05/20/public-parts/).

43. The ideal of "publicness granting immortality" was one of Jarvis's ten theses of publicness which he introduced in a speech at the Seattle Public/Privacy conference in August 2010. The other nine theses were that publicness 1) Makes and improves relationships; 2) Enables collaboration; 3) Builds trust; 4) Frees us from the myth of perfection; 5) Kills taboos; 6) Enables wisdom of our crowd; 7) Organizes us; 8) Protects us; 9) Creates value. See also, *Public Parts*, 56–58, in which he argues the Arendtian position that "only by being public can we leave our mark on the world."

44. David Kirkpatrick, *The Facebook Effect* (Simon & Schuster 2010), 67.

45. Jarvis, *Public Parts*, 11.

46. Doerr, who has a net worth estimated by *Forbes* to be over a billion dollars, was an early investor in many of the greatest Silicon Valley companies including Sun Microsystems, Netscape, Amazon, and Google.

47. See: "John Doerr on 'The Great Third Wave' of Technology," *The Wall Street Journal*, May 24, 2010.

48. "Kleiner Plays Catch-Up," Pui-Wing Tam and Geoffrey A. Fowler, *The Wall Street Journal*, August 29, 2011 (http://online.wsj.com/article/SB100014240531119033665045764 86432620701722.html).

49. "Kleiner Perkins Invests In Facebook at $52 Billion," *The Wall Street Journal*, February 14, 2011. "Kleiner Perkins Caufield & Byers and Facebook are together at last," the piece begins—but what is striking is how little $38 million will buy you in today's exuberant social media economy (http://blogs.wsj.com/venturecapital/2011/02/14/kleiner-perkins-invests-in-facebook-at-52-billion-valuation/).

50. By February 25, 2011, just eleven days after the Kleiner investment was announced, this $52 billion valuation had ballooned to $70 billion on SecondMarket.com, a Web site where secondary stock of private companies is bought and sold by investors. (See: "Facebook Valuation Back at a Cool $70 Billion on SecondMarket, by MG Siegler, February25, 2011, http://techcrunch.com/2011/02/25/facebook-70-billion/). Facebook's expected IPO in 2012 should put an end to these sorts of wild disparities and changes in the value of the company.

51. See Bing Gordon's interview with Techcrunch.tv in October 2010 (http://techcrunch.tv/whats-hot/watch?id=ZpYXZyMTqZYQbxJZVMzVi8—IMqliDi3) when he argues that the social category will grow 10 to 25 times over the next five years.

52. *The Social Network* is loosely adapted from Ben Mezrich's best-selling book, *The Accidental Billionaires: The Founding of Facebook: A Tale of Sex, Money, Genius, and Betrayal* (Doubleday, 2009).

53. "Generation Why" Zadie Smith, *The New York Review of Books*, November 25, 2010 (http://www.nybooks.com/articles/archives/2010/nov/25/generation-why/?page=1).

54. Zuckerberg used this phrase at the e-G8 (http://www.eg8forum.com/en/), the May 2011 conference in Paris organized by French President Nicolas Sarkozy, which brought to-

gether many of the world's leading Internet thinkers, entrepreneurs, and managers. I also attended this event, participating in a workshop about data privacy.

55. "Facebook's Grand Plan for the Future," David Gelles, *London Financial Times*, December 3, 2010 (http://www.ft.com/cms/s/2/57933bb8-fcd9-11df-ae2d-00144feab49a.html#axzz18UHJchkb).

56. Zuckerberg said this to the Silicon Valley social media evangelist Robert Scoble. For the full conversation between Zuckerberg, Scoble, and a number of other journalists, see Robert Scoble's blogpost of November 3, 2010, "Great Interview: Candid Disruptive Zuckerberg": http://scobleizer.com/2010/11/03/great-interview-candid-disruptive-mark-zuckerberg/.

57. "Mark Zuckerberg" Lev Grossman, *Time* magazine, December 15, 2010.

58. "A Trillion Pageviews for Facebook," labnol.org, August 23, 2011 (http://www.labnol.org/internet/facebook-trillion-pageviews/20019/).

59. "Facebook Now as Big as the Entire Internet Was in 2004," Pingdom, October 5, 2011 (http://royal.pingdom.com/2011/10/05/facebook-now-as-big-as-the-entire-internet-was-in-2004/).

60. "CIA's Facebook Proram Dramatically Cut Agency's Costs," *The Onion*, March 21, 2011 (http://www.theonion.com/video/cias-facebook-program-dramatically-cut-agencys-cos, 19753/).

61. "CIA's 'vengeful librarians' stalk Twitter and Facebook," *The Daily Telegraph*, November 4, 2011 (http://www.telegraph.co.uk/technology/twitter/8869352/CIAs-vengeful-librarians-stalk-Twitter-and-Facebook.html).

62. See: M. G. Siegler, "Pincus: In Five Years, Connection Will Be to Each Other, Not The Web; We'll Be Dial Tones," Techcrunch, October 21, 2010 (http://techcrunch.com/2010/10/21/pincus-web-connections/).

63. According to a December 2010 projection by Horace Dedlu of the market intelligence service Asymco (see: http://www.asymco.com/2010/12/04/half-of-us-population-to-use-smartphones-by-end-of-2011/).

64. "Adult Use of Social Media Soars," by Sarah E. Needleman, *The Wall Street Journal*, August 30, 2011 (http://blogs.wsj.com/in-charge/2011/08/30/adult-use-of-social-media-soars/).

65. Between 2006 and 2009, the Internet and American Life Project at the Pew Research Center revealed that teenage blogging fell by half. See: "Blogs Wane as the Young Drift to Sites Like Twitter," by Verne G. Kopytoff, *The New York Times*, February 20, 2011. (http://www.nytimes.com/2011/02/21/technology/internet/21blog.html).

66. "Adult Use of Social Media Soars," by Sarah E. Needleman, *The Wall Street Journal*, August 30, 2011 (http://blogs.wsj.com/in-charge/2011/08/30/adult-use-of-social-media-soars/).

67. Between 2006 and 2009, The Internet and American Life Project at the Pew Research Center revealed that teenage blogging fell by half. See: "Blogs Wane as the Young Drift to Sites Like Twitter," by Verne G. Kopytoff, *The New York Times*, February 20, 2011. (http://www.nytimes.com/2011/02/21/technology/internet/21blog.html)

68. "Is the Era of Webmail Over?" Joe Nguyen, Comscore.com, January 12, 2011 (http://blog.comscore.com/2011/01/is_the_era_of_webmail_over.html).

69. Official Facebook numbers, July 2010.

70. According to the Internet metrics service Hitwise, with 8.93% of all the web traffic in America going to Facebook in 2010 (http://searchengineland.com/facebook-most -popular-search-term-website-in-2010-59875).

71. "Facebook Achieves Majority" according to an April 2011 report by Edison Research and Arbitron Inc. (http://www.edisonresearch.com/home/archives/2011/03/facebook_ achieves_majority.php).

72. "ShareThis Study: Facebook Accounts For 38 Percent of Sharing Traffic on the Web," Erick Schonfeld, Techcrunch, June 6, 2011 (http://techcrunch.com/2011/06/06/sharethis -facebook-38-percent-traffic/).

73. Zuckerberg: As Many As 500 Million People Have Been on Facebook In A Single Day," by Leena Rao, Techcrunch, September 22, 2011 (http://techcrunch.com/2011/09/22/ zuckerberg-on-peak-days-500-million-people-are-on-facebook/).

74. "Facebook now as big as the entire Internet was in 2004," Pingdom, Royal Pingdom (http://royal.pingdom.com/2011/10/05/facebook-now-as-big-as-the-entire-internet-was -in-2004/).

75. "Twitter Is At 250 Million Tweets Per Day, iOS5 Integration Made Sign-Ups Increate 3X," Alexis Tsotsis, Techcrunch, October 17, 2011 (http://techcrunch.com/2011/10/17/ twitter-is-at-250-million-tweets-per-day/). See also: "Meaningful Growth," The Twitter Blog December 15, 2010 (http://blog.twitter.com/2010/12/stocking-stuffer.html).

76. "Twitter Hits 100 million "Active" Users" Greg Finn, Searchengineland.com, Septmber 8, 2011 (http://searchengineland.com/twitter-hits-100-million-active-users-92243).

77. "Groupon Shares Rise Sharply After I.P.O.," by Evelyn M. Rusli, *The New York Times*, November 4, 2011 (http://dealbook.nytimes.com/2011/11/04/groupon-shares-spike-40 -to-open-at-28/).

78. "LivingSocial Said to Weigh Funding at $6 Billion Instead of IPO", by Douglas MacMillian and Serena Saitto, Bloomberg, September 22, 2011 (http://www.bloomberg.com/ news/2011-09-22/livingsocial-said-to-weigh-funding-at-6-billion-rather-than-pursuing -ipo.html). See also, "LivingSocial's CEO Weathers Rapid Growth," Stu Woo, *The Wall Street Journal,* August 29, 2011 (http://blogs.wsj.com/venturecapital/2011/08/29/qa -with-livingsocial-ceo-tim-oshaughnessy/).

79. At the beginning of December 2010, Farmville was top of the Facebook app. leaderboard, with nearly 54 million users (see: http://www.appdata.com/). But by the end of December, Zynga's virtual reality social game CitiVille, which was only launched at beginning of the month, had eclipsed Farmville, racking up 61.7 million users (http://techcrunch .com/2010/12/28/zynga-cityville-farmville/).

80. See: "Zynga moves 1 Petabyte of Data Daily; Adds 1,000 Servers a Week," Leena Rao, Techcrunch, September 22, 2010. (http://techcrunch.com/2010/09/22/zynga-moves-1 -petabyte-of-data-daily-adds-1000-servers-a-week/).

81. "Zynga Raising $500 Million at $10 Billion Valuation," Kara Swisher, All Things Digital, February 17, 2010 (http://kara.allthingsd.com/20110217/zynga-raises-500-million-at-10 -billion-valuation/).

82. "Foursquare Gets 3 Million Check-Ins Per Day, Signed Up 500,000 Merchants," Pascal-Emmanuel Gobry, SAI Business Insider, August 2, 2011 (http://articles.businessinsider .com/2011-08-02/tech/30097137_1_foursquare-users-merchants-ins).

83. "Foursquare's Dennis Crowley talks check-ins," by Casey Newton, SFGate.com, De-

cember 25, 2011 (http://articles.sfgate.com/2011-12-25/business/30556083_1_check
-ins-location-based-service-social-service). For foursquare's business value, see my December 2011 TechcrunchTV interview with the author of *The Power of foursquare* (2011),
Carmine Gallo (http://techcrunch.com/2011/12/21/keen-on-carmine-gallo-the-power
-of-foursquare-tctv/).

84. "Tumblr Is Growing by a Quarter Billion Impression Every Week," Erick Schonfeld,
Techcrunch, January 28, 2011 (http://techcrunch.com/2011/01/28/karp-tumblr-quarter
-billion-impressions-week/).

85. "Tumblr Lands $85 Million in Funding," Jenna Wortham, *The New York Times*, Septem-
ber 26, 2011 (http://bits.blogs.nytimes.com/2011/09/26/tumblr-lands-85-million-in
-funding/).

86. See my TechcrunchTV interview with Cheever on May 27, 2011: http://techcrunch.com/
2011/05/27/quora-we-have-an-explicit-non-goal-of-not-selling-the-company/.

87. Q&A Site Quora Builds Buzz with A-List Answerers," by Lydia Dishman, *Fast Company*, January 4, 2011 (http://www.fastcompany.com/1713096/innovation-agents
-charlie-cheever-co-founder-quora).

88. "Quora Investor Scoffs at $1 Billion Offer Price," Nicholas Carson, Business Insider, Feb-
ruary 22, 2011 (http://www.sfgate.com/cgi-bin/article.cgi?f=/g/a/2011/02/22/busines
sinsider-quora-would-turn-down-a-1-billion-offer-says-investor-2011-2.DTL).

89. "Personal Data: The Emergence of a New Asset Class," World Economic Forum Report,
January 2011 (http://www.weforum.org/reports/personal-data-emergence-new-asset
-class).

90. Brin said this on the January 20th 2011 earning call with analysts where Eric Schmidt
announced his resignation as the company's CEO. See: "Sergey Brin: We've Touched 1
Percent Of What Social Search Can Be," Leena Rao.

91. "How to Use Facebook to Get Accepted to College," Dean Tsouvalas, StudentAdvisor
.com, February 22, 2011 (http://blog.studentadvisor.com/StudentAdvisor-Blog/bid/
53877/How-to-Use-Social-Media-to-Help-Get-Accepted-to-College-UPDATED).

92. "Are Social Networking Profiles the Resumes of the Future?" Kelsey Blair, SocialTimes
.com, 25 February 2011 (http://www.socialtimes.com/2011/02/are-social-networking
-profiles-the-resumes-of-the-future/).

93. "Social Media History Becomes a New Job Hurdle," Jennifer Preston, *The New York
Times*, July 20, 2011 (http://www.nytimes.com/2011/07/21/technology/social-media
-history-becomes-a-new-job-hurdle.html).

94. "Updating a Resume for 2011," *The Wall Street Journal*, Elizabeth Garone, June 3, 2011
(http://online.wsj.com/article/SB10001424052702303657404576363612674900024.
html?mod=WSJ_hp_us_mostpop_read).

95. "LinkedIn is About to Put Job Boards (and Resumes) Out of Business," Dan Schawbel,
Forbes, June 1, 2011 (http://blogs.forbes.com/danschawbel/2011/06/01/linkedin-is-about
-to-put-job-boards-and-resumes-out-of-business/). Schwabel is also the author of *Me 2.0: 4
Steps to Building Your Future* (2010).

96. In a November 2010 interview with Silicon Valley social media evangelist Robert Scoble.
See: "Great Interview—Candid, Disruptive Mark Zuckerberg", Scobleizer.com, November 3, 2010 (http://scobleizer.com/2010/11/03/great-interview-candid-disruptive-mark
-zuckerberg/).

97. "Zuckerberg: Kids under 13 Should Be Allowed On Facebook," Mical Lev-Ram, *Fortune*, May 20, 2011. (http://tech.fortune.cnn.com/2011/05/20/zuckerberg-kids-under-13 -should-be-allowed-on-facebook/).

98. Steven Levy, *In the Plex: How Google Thinks, Works and Shapes our Lives* (Simon & Schuster, 2011), 382.

99. "Prediction: Facebook Will Surpass Google in Advertising Revenue," Hussein Fazal, Techcrunch, June 6, 2011 (http://techcrunch.com/2011/06/05/facebook-will-surpass -google/).

100. "A Venture-Capital Newbie Shakes Up Silicon Valley," Pui-Wing Tam, Geoffrey A. Fowler and Amir Efrati, *The Wall Street Journal*, May 10, 2011. (http://online.wsj.com/ article/SB10001424052748703362904576218753889083940.html

101. "Sequoia Capital's Mike Moritz Added to LinkedIn's Board," David Cohen, Social Times, January 18, 2011 (http://socialtimes.com/sequoia-capital%E2%80%99s-michael -moritz-added-to-linkedin%E2%80%99s-board_b11438).

102. "New Fund Provides Stake in Twitter JP Morgan," Evelyn Rusli, *The New York Times*, February 28, 2011.

103. "With +1, Google Search Goes Truly Social – As Do Google Ads," MG Siegler, Techcrunch, March 31, 2011 (http://techcrunch.com/2011/03/30/google-plus-one/). See also, "Google Wants Search to Be More Social," Amir Efrati, *The Wall Street Journal*, March 31, 2011.

104. "Google Launches +1, a New Social Step," by Stephen Shankland, CNET, June 1, 2011 (http://news.cnet.com/8301-30685_3-20068073-264.html).

105. "Doing more with the +1 button, more than 4 billion times a day," Business Insider, August 24, 2011 (http://www.businessinsider.com/doing-more-with-the-1-button-more -than-4-billion-times-a-day-2011-8).

106. "Larry Page Just Tied ALL Employees' Bonuses to the Success of Google's Social Strategy," Nicholas Carlson, SAI Business Insider, April 7, 2011 (http://www.businessinsider .com/larry-page-just-tied-employee-bonuses-to-the-success-of-the-googles-social-strategy -2011-4).

107. "Keen On: Why Google Is Now a Social Company," TechcrunchTV, July 23, 2011 (http:// techcrunch.com/2011/07/22/keen-on-why-google-is-now-a-social-company-tctv/).

108. "Google + Pulls In 20 Million in 3 Weeks," Amir Efrati, *The Wall Street Journal*, July 22, 2011 (http://online.wsj.com/article/SB10001424053111904233404576460394032418 286.html).

109. "Google+ Added $20 Billion To Google's Market Cap," Erick Schonfeld, Techcrunch, July 10, 2011 (http://techcrunch.com/2011/07/10/google-plus-20-billion-market-cap/).

110. "Google Plus Users About to Get Google Apps, Share Photos Like Mad," Jerey Scott, reelseo.com, October 20, 2011 (http://www.reelseo.com/google-plus-google-apps/).

111. "Google+ Growth Accelerating. Passes 62 million users. Adding 625,000 new users per day. Prediction: 400 million users by end of 2012," by Paul Allen, Google +, December 27, 2011 (https://plus.google.com/117388252776312694644/posts/ZcPA5ztMZaj).

112. "Is Too Much Plus a Minus for Google," by Steven Levy, Wired.com, January 12, 2012 (http://www.wired.com/epicenter/2012/01/too-much-plus-a-minus/?utm_source=feed burner&utm_medium=feed&utm_campaign=Feed%3A+wiredbusinessblog+%28Blog +-+Epicenter | %28Business%29%29).

113. Microsoft's strategic anti-Google alliance with Facebook is likely to deepen over the next five years as the social economy matures. See, for example, "Bing Expands Facebook Liked Results, Bing.com, February 24, 2011 (http://www.bing.com/community/site_blogs/b/search/archive/2011/02/24/bing-expands-facebook-liked-results.aspx?wa=wsignin1.0). Once we get beyond the five year horizon, anything is possible including, perhaps, Facebook acquiring Microsoft.

114. "Does Gmail's People Widget Spell Trouble for Email Startups?" Anthony Ha, Social-Beat, May 26, 2011 (http://venturebeat.com/2011/05/26/gmail-people-widget/).

115. "Sean Parker: Agent of Disruption," Steven Bertoni, *Forbes,* September 21, 2011 (http://www.forbes.com/sites/stevenbertoni/2011/09/21/sean-parker-agent-of-disruption/).

116. Only founded in May 2010, GroupMe was already sending a million texts every day by February 2011. See: "GroupMe Is Now Sending One Million Texts Every Day," by Erick Schonfeld, Techcrunch, February 14, 2011 (http://techcrunch.com/2011/02/14/groupme-one-million-texts/). In August 2011, the year-old GroupMe was acquired for an undisclosed sum by Skye. See: "Skype To Acquire Year-old Group Messaging System GroupMe," Michael Arrington, August 21, 2011 (http://techcrunch.com/2011/08/21/skype-to-acquire-year-old-group-messaging-service-groupme/).

117. "Cliqset Founder Takes On Personal Publishing And Social Conversations With Stealthy Startup Glow," Leena Rao, Techcrunch, May 28, 2011 (http://techcrunch.com/2011/05/28/cliqset-founder-takes-on-personal-publishing-and-social-conversations-with-stealthy-startup glow/).

118. The Kleiner Perkins backed Path—which turned down a $100 million acquisition offer from Google in February 2011—is a good example of how complete privacy is no longer viable on the Internet. Founded in 2010 by former Facebook executive Dave Morin as a completely private social network for close friends and family, it switched to a more "open" model in January 2011 that enabled users to publically share their information. See: "Kleiner Perkins, Index Ventures lead $8.5 Million Round For Path," Michael Arrington, February 1, 2011 (http://techcrunch.com/2011/02/01/kleiner-perkins-leads-8-5-million-round-for-path/) For Path<#213>s meteoric growth, see: "Nearing 1 Million Users, Path Stays The Course," by Rip Empson, Techcrunch, October 20, 2011 (http://techcrunch.com/2011/10/19/nearing-1-million-users-path-stays-the-course/).

119. "Companies Are Erecting In-House Social Networks," Verne G. Kopytoff, *The New York Times,* June 26, 2011 (http://www.nytimes.com/2011/06/27/technology/27social.html?pagewanted=all).

120. See: "Social Power and the Coming Corporate Revolution", by David Kirkpatrick, *Forbes,* September 7, 2011 (http://www.forbes.com/sites/techonomy/2011/09/07/social-power-and-the-coming-corporate-revolution/). *Facebook Effect* author Kirkpatrick is much more sympathetic to Rypple than me, saying that it "taps social and peer pressure to make job evaluation more effective at driving future performance." In my mind, however, this is an unacceptable invasion of a worker's privacy and will add to the often already unbearable pressures of work in today's dismal economy.

121. "YouTube's New Homepage Goes Social With Algorithmic Feed, Emphasis On Google+ And Facebook," Eric Eldon, Techcrunch, December 1, 2011 (http://m.techcrunch.com/2011/12/01/newyoutube/?icid=tc_home_art&).

122. For my May 2011 TechcrunchTV "So What Exactly is Social Music?" interviews with

Alexander Ljung of Soundcloud and Steve Tang of Soundtracking see: http://techcrunch .com/2011/05/31/disrupt-backstage-pass-so-what-exactly-is-social-music-tctv/.

123. Reports in February editions of Entertainment Weekly and People indicated that both *The X Factor* and *American Idol* would reinvent themselves around social engagement and voting. See: "Facebook TV Invasion Looms Via American Idol Voting," Andrew Wallenstein, PaidContent.com, February 23, 2011 (http://paidcontent.org/article/419-facebook -tv-invasion-looms-via-american-idol-voting/).

124. "Miso Now Knows What You're Watching, No Check-In Required," Ryan Lawler, *The New York Times*, September 1, 2011 (http://www.nytimes.com/external/gigaom/2011/ 09/01/01gigaom-miso-now-knows-what-youre-watching-no-check-in-requ-109.html).

125. "Report: Netflix Swallowing Peak Net Traffic Fast," Erick Mack, CNET, May 17, 2011 (http://news.cnet.com/report-netflix-swallowing-peak-net-traffic-fast/8301-17938_105 -20063733-1.html).

126. "Reed Hastings: We Have a 'Five Year Plan' for Social Features and Facebook Integration," Leena Rao, Techcrunch, June 1, 2011 (http://techcrunch.com/2011/06/01/reed -hastings-netflix-is-a-complement-to-the-new-release-business/).

127. News.me was developed for *The New York Times* by Betaworks, the New York City based social media developer that has incubated a number of important startups including the URL shortener bit.ly and the Twitter app Tweetdeck. For my own "Keen On" Techcrunch interview with Betaworks CEO, John Borthwick see: http://techcrunch.com/ 2011/01/24/keen-on-john-borthwick-betaworks-tctv/.

128. "Flipboard Raises $50 Million, Inks Deal With Oprah's OWN," Mark Hefflinger, DigitalMediaWire, April 15, 2011 (http://www.dmwmedia.com/news/2011/04/15/flipboard -raises-50-million-inks-deal-oprah039s-own).

129. "First Look at ImageSocial, the Photo Sharing Start-Up That Just Raiseed $15 Million in Funding," Sarah Perez, Techcrunch, October 11, 2011 (http://techcrunch.com/2011/10/ 11/first-look-at-imagesocial-the-photo-sharing-network-that-just-scored-15-million-in -funding/).

130. "With $41 million in hand, Color Launches Implicit Proximity-Based Social Network," Liz Gannes, *All Things D*, March 23, 2011 (http://networkeffect.allthingsd.com/20110323/ with-41m-in-hand-color-deploys-new-proximity-based-social-network/). See also: "Money Rushes Into Social Start-Ups," Geoffrey A. Fowler, *The Wall Street Journal*, March 23, 2011. According to Fowler, Color's "view on privacy is that everything in the service is public—allowing users who don't yet know each other to peer into each other's lives." (http://online.wsj.com/article/SB10001424052748703362904576218970893843248 .html#ixzz1HTtSKXVl).

131. "MeMap App Lets You Track Facebook Friends on One Central Map," Riley McDermid, VentureBeat, March 24, 2011 (http://venturebeat.com/2011/03/24/memap-launches/).

132. "Focusing on the Social, Minus the Media," Jenna Wortham, *The New York Times*, June 4, 2011 (http://www.nytimes.com/2011/06/05/technology/05ping.html?_r=1&hpw).

133. "Finding a seatmate through Facebook," CNN, December 10, 2011 (http://articles.cnn .com/2011-12-14/travel/travel_social-media-seating_1_facebook-pals-seat-selection -klm-royal-dutch-airlines?_s=PM:TRAVEL).

134. In October 2011, the Waz raised $30 million in funding from Kleiner and from the Chinese

telecom billionaire and Facebook investor Li Ka-hing. See: "Social Navigation and Traffic App Waze Raises $30 Million From Kleiner and Li Ka-Shing, by Leena Rao, Techcrunch, October 18, 2011 (http://techcrunch.com/2011/10/18/social-navigation-and-traffic-app-waze-raises-30m-from-kleiner-perkins-and-li-ka-shing/).

135. "Is New Bump.com License Plate Fature A Privacy Car Wreck?" Katie Kindelan, March 18, 2011 (http://www.socialtimes.com/2011/03/is-new-bump-com-license-plate-feature-a-privacy-car-wreck/).

136. "Meet Proust, a social network that digs deeper," Colleen Taylor, GigaOm, July 19, 2011 (http://gigaom.com/2011/07/19/proust/).

137. The Ditto app allows us to use our social network to tell us what we should be doing. See: "Ditto: The Social App for What You Should Be Doing," M. G. Siegler, Techcrunch, March 3, 2011 (http://techcrunch.com/2011/03/03/ditto/).

138. "Microsoft in $8.5 billion Skype Gamble," Richard Waters, *Financial Times,* May 10, 2011 (http://www.ft.com/cms/s/2/9461dbb4-7ab8-11e0-8762-00144feabdc0.html#axzz1MP PBpiZb).

139. "Software from Big Tech Firms, Start-Ups Take Page From Facebook," Cari Tuna, *The Wall Street Journal,* March 29, 2011.

140. See again: "Social Power and the Coming Corporate Revolution," David Kirkpatrick, Forbes, September 7, 2011 (http://www.forbes.com/sites/techonomy/2011/09/07/social-power-and-the-coming-corporate-revolution/). Kirkpatrick's notion of "enlightened companies" here is rather like the "enlightenment" of Catherine the Great's Russia which embraced the Inspection House ideas of the Bentham brothers.

141. "Social Network Ad Revenues to Reach $10 Billion Worldwide in 2013," eMarketer, October 5, 2011 (http://www.emarketer.com/Article.aspx?R=1008625).

142. "RadiumOne About to Corner the Market on Social Data Before Competitors Even Know What's Happening," Michael Arrington, Techcrunch, May 20, 2011 (http://techcrunch.com/2011/05/20/radiumone-about-to-corner-the-market-on-social-data-before-competitors-even-know-whats-happening/).

143. See, for example, "SocialVibe Closes $20 Million Funding Round," Edmund Lee, *Ad Age,* March 22, 2011 (http://adage.com/article/digital/socialvibe-closes-20-million-funding-round/149506/).

144. CapLinked offers a collaborative platform for investors and startups. Launched in October 2010, with already more than two thousand companies and a thousand investors on its platform, CapLinked includes Peter Thiel, who Reid Hoffman introduced to Mark Zuckerberg as the original angel investor in Facebook, as an investor.

145. Cheapism, a social network for bargain diners, is already alerting privacy concerns. See, for example, "Do Tips on Nearby Bargains Outweigh Privacy Concerns?" Ann Carrns, *The New York Times,* May 20, 2011.

146. "Investors Cough up $1.6 Million to Dine with Grubwithus, the Brilliant Social Dining Service," by M. G. Siegler, Techcrunch, May 6, 2011 (http://techcrunch.com/2011/05/06/grubwithus-funding/).

147. For a confessional about social dieting, see: "Apps to Share Your Pride at the Gym," Owen Thomas, *The New York Times,* February 9, 2011 (http://www.nytimes.com/2011/02/10/technology/personaltech/10basics.html).

148. "Fitbit users are unwittingly sharing details of their sex lives with the world," The Next Web, July 3, 2011 (http://thenextweb.com/insider/2011/07/03/fitbit-users-are-inadvertently-sharing-details-of-their-sex-lives-with-the-world/).

149. "A Social Network for Neighbors—Former Googlers Launch Yatown," Kenna McHugh, *Social Times,* May 12, 2011 (http://socialtimes.com/a-social-network-for-neighbors-former-googlers-launch-yatown_b62012).

150. Zenergo is founded by Patrick Ferrell who co-founded SocialNet with Reid Hoffman in 1997. "Organizing Offline: Zenergo Launches Social Network for Real World Activities," by Rip Emerson, Techcrunch, May 5, 2011 (http://techcrunch.com/2011/05/06/organizing-offline-zenergo-launches-social-network-for-real-world-activities/).

151. Chime.in is backed by the well-respected Bill Gross and his Ubermedia incubator. See: "Bill Gross Explains What's Different About Chime.in: 'You Can Follow Part Of A Person,'" Leena Rao, Techcrunch, October 18, 2011 (http://techcrunch.com/2011/10/18/gross-chime-in-follow-part-person/).

152. "LAL People Is Now ShoutFlow, A "Magical" Social Discovery App," Liz Gannes, AllThingsD, September 15, 2011 (http://allthingsd.com/20110915/lal-people-is-now-shoutflow-a-magical-social-discovery-app/).

153. "Open Study Wants to Turn the World into 'One Big Study Group,'" Alexis Tsotsis, Techcrunch, June 8, 2011 (http://techcrunch.com/2011/06/08/openstudy-wants-to-turn-the-world-into-one-big-study-group/).

154. Asana is co-founded by Facebook co-founder Dustin Moskowitz, who was also Mark Zuckerberg's roommate at Harvard. Like Facebook, Asana has an obsession with becoming a "utility." See: "Finally: Facebook Co-Founder Opens the Curtain on Two-Year Old Asana," Sarah Lacy, Techcrunch, Feb 7, 2011 (http://techcrunch.com/2011/02/07/finally-facebook-co-founder-opens-the-curtain-on-two-year-old-asana/).

155. "Q&A: Joshua Schachter on How Jig Differs from Other Social Sites," Liz Gannes, AllThingsD, August 29, 2011 (http://allthingsd.com/20110829/qa-joshua-schachter-on-how-jig-is-different-from-other-social-sites/).

156. "Endomondo Raises $800,000 To Make Cardio Training Virtually Social," by Matthew Lynley, Mobile Beat, March 22, 2011 (http://venturebeat.com/2011/03/22/ctia-endomondo-app-launch/).

157. Disney buying Togetherville is an example of what Eco and Baudrillard meant by "hyper reality." As I tweeted in February 2011, *what is a satirist supposed to do when Disney really does buy kid's social network Togetherville? (http://bit.ly/fvPvPz).* For more on the Disney acquisition of Togetherville, see: "Disney Acquires Social Network for Kids Togetherville," Leena Rao, Techcrunch, 24 February 2011 (http://techcrunch.com/2011/02/23/disney-acquires-social-network-for-kids-togetherville/).

158. "Techcrunch Disrupt Champion Shaker Shakes Down Investors For $15 Million," Michael Arrington, Uncrunched, October 9, 2011 (http://uncrunched.com/2011/10/09/techcrunch-disrupt-champion-shaker-shakes-down-investors-for-15-million/). The idea of Shaker as a "social serendipity engine" was put forward by Silicon Valley venture capitalist Shervin Pishevar, whose company, Menlo Ventures, was a seed investor in Shaker.

159. "Amazon Brings Social Reading to Kindle—But Will You Use It?" Richard MacManus, ReadWriteWeb, August 8, 2011 (http://www.readwriteweb.com/archives/amazon_brings_social_reading_to_kindle.php).

160. Scribn mission statement. See: http://www.scribd.com/about.

161. "Scribn Raises Another $13 Million, Aims To Bring Social Reading To Every Device," by Jason Kincaid, January 18, 2011, Techcrunch (http://techcrunch.com/2011/01/18/scribd-raises-another-13-million-aims-to-bring-social-reading-to-every-device/).

162. "Rethinking the Bible as a Social Book," Erick Schonfeld, Techcrunch, January 24, 2011 (http://techcrunch.com/2011/01/24/rethinking-bible-social-book/?icid=maing|main5|dl13|sec1_lnk3|39393).

163. "A Social Networking Device for Smokers," Joshua Brustein, *The New York Times*, May 10, 2011 (http://www.nytimes.com/2011/05/11/technology/11smoke.html).

164. "RealNetworks founder in Online Video—Again," Russ Adams, *The Wall Street Journal*, March 1, 2011.

165. "The New Technology of Creepiness: Online Ways to Date, Stalk, Home-Wreck, and Cheat," by David Zax, *Fast Company*, February 28, 2011 (http://www.fastcompany.com/1732533/creepiness-innovation-new-ways-to-date-stalk-home-wreck-and-cheat).

166. "Creepy app uses Twitter and Flickr data to track anyone on a map," WSJ.com, 25 February 2011 (http://onespot.wsj.com/technology/2011/02/25/b2d19/creepy-app-uses-twitter-and-flickr-data).

2. LET'S GET NAKED

1. www.twitter.com/ericgrant.

2. George Orwell, *Nineteen Eighty-four*, (Penguin), 69.

3. Christopher Hitchens, *Why Orwell Matters* (Basic 2002). Hitchens ends his characteristically sparkling defense of Orwell's contemporary relevancy with an attack on the linguistic inexactitude of post-modernists like Michel Foucault. It seems to me, however, that if Foucault and Orwell were both still around today, they would form a united front, so to speak, against the prying eyes of social media.

4. Directed by Ridley Scott and produced by the New York advertising firm of Chiat/Day with a $900,000 budget, this one-minute commercial won TV Guide's 1999 "Great Commercial of All Time" award.

5. "Little Brother Is Watching," Walter Kirn, *The New York Times*, October 15, 2010 (http://www.nytimes.com/2010/10/17/magazine/17FOB-WWLN-t.html).

6. "Adam Curtis: Have computers taken away our power?" Katharine Viner, *The Guardian*, May 6, 2011 (http://www.guardian.co.uk/tv-and-radio/2011/may/06/adam-curtis-computers-documentary).

7. Ibid.

8. "Picture this, social media's next phase," by David Gelles, London *Financial Times*, December 28, 2010 (http://www.ft.com/cms/s/0/a9423996-11e2-11e0-92d0-00144feabdc0.html#axzz19UBncKAf).

9. "The Social Media Bubble," Umair Haque, HBR.org, March 23, 2010.

10. See: http://twitter.com/umairh.

11. "The Twitter 100", *London Independent Newspaper*, February 15, 2011. Fry and Brand were ranked fourth and sixth respectively. (http://www.independent.co.uk/news/people/news/the-twitter-100-2215529.html).

12. For my November 2010 "Keen On" Techcrunch.tv show interview with Don Tapscott, see: http://techcrunch.com/2010/11/02/keen-on-don-tapscott-macrowikinomics/.

13. Don Tapscott and Anthony D. Williams, *MacroWikinomics: Rebooting Business and the World* (Portfolio, 2010).

14. Ibid., ch 2.

15. "Upending Anonymity, These Days the Web Unmasks Everyone," by Brian Stelter, *The New York Times*, June 20, 2011 (http://www.nytimes.com/2011/06/21/us/21anonymity.html).

16. Rachel Botsford and Roo Rogers, *What's Mine Is Yours: How Collaborative Consumption Is Changing the Way We Live* (Harper Business 2010) See also: "The End of Consumerism," by Leo Hickman, *The Guardian*.

17. John Stuart Mill, *On Liberty* (Cambridge, 1989). 67.

18. "The Insidious Evils of 'Like' Culture," Neil Strauss, *The Wall Street Journal*, July 2, 2011.

19. "When We're Cowed by the Crowd," Jonas Lehrer, *The Wall Street Journal*, May 28, 2011.

20. "Why I Deleted My AngelList Account," Bryce Roberts, Bryce.VC, February 21, 2011.

21 "What's the Real Deal with AngelList?" Mark Suster, Techcrunch, February 26, 2011.

22. "United They Stand," by Clive Cookson and Daryl Ibury, *The Financial Times*, December 28, 2011 (http://www.ft.com/intl/cms/s/0/9eec57ac-2c8e-11e1-8cca-00144feabdc0.html #axzz1hyS6HQ3p).

23. "Let's Get Naked: Benefits of Publicness Versus Privacy," Scot Hacker, March 14, 2011 (http://birdhouse.org/blog/2011/03/14/publicness-v-privacy/).

24. "One Identity or More?" Jeff Jarvis, Buzzmachine, March 8, 2011.

25. "In Small Towns, Gossip Moves to the Web, and Turns Violent," by A. G. Sulzberger, September 16, 2011 (http://www.nytimes.com/2011/09/20/us/small-town-gossip-moves -to-the-web-anonymous-and-vicious.html?_r=1).

26. Ibid.

27. Ibid.

28. "How the Casey Anthony Murder Case Became the Social-Media Trial of the Century," by John Cloud, *Time* magazine, June 16, 2011 (http://www.time.com/time/nation/arti cle/0,8599,2077969,00.html).

29 "Little Brother Is Watching," Walter Kirn, *The New York Times*, October 20, 2010.

30. "Fake Identities Were Used on Twitter to Get Information on Weiner," by Jennifer Preston, *The New York Times*, June 17, 2011 (http://www.nytimes.com/2011/06/18/nyre gion/fake-identities-were-used-on-twitter-to-get-information-on-weiner.html?_r=2& partner=rss&emc=rss&pagewanted=all).

31. "Naked Hubris": "When it comes to scandal girls won't be boys . . ." Sheryl Gay Stolberg; ". . . while digital flux makes it easier for politicians to stray" Kate Zernike, *The New York Times*, June 12, 2011 (http://www.nytimes.com/2011/06/12/weekinreview/12women .html?partner=rss&emc=rss).

32. Dick Meyer, *Why We Hate Us: American Discontent in the New Millenium* (Crown, 2008), 6, 16.

33. See, for example, "Athlete-Fan Dialogue Becomes Shouting Match," George Vecsey, *The New York Times*, June 18, 2011. (http://www.nytimes.com/2011/06/19/sports/basket ball/george-vecsey-lebron-jamess-words-and-a-deeper-meaning.html).

34. "Birdbrained," James Poniewozik, *Time* magazine, Vol. 177 No. 25, June 20, 2011.

35. The August 2010 Facebook comment from the British Columbian dealership worker said: "Sometimes ya have good smooth days, when nobodys f***ing with your ability to earn a

living....and sometimes accidents DO happen, its unfortunate, but thats why [they're] called accidents right?"

36. "Teen Sacked for 'Boring' Job Facebook Comment," Lester Haines, *The Register*, February 26, 2009 (http://www.theregister.co.uk/2009/02/26/facebook_comment/).

37. "When Teachers Talk Out of School," Jonathan Zimmerman, *The New York Times*, June 3, 2011 (http://www.nytimes.com/2011/06/04/opinion/04zimmerman.html).

38. "Gilbert Gottfried Fired as Aflac Duck after Japanese Tsunami Tweets," Huffington Post, March 13, 2011 (http://www.huffingtonpost.com/2011/03/14/gilbert-gottfried-fired-aflac_n_835692.html).

39. "Man on Trial over Twitter 'Affair' Claims Says Case Has 'Big Legal Implications,'" Press Assocation, *The Guardian*, June 15, 2011 (http://www.guardian.co.uk/technology/2011/jun/15/twitter-affair-claims-legal-implications).

40. "Kent Girls Harass Friend, 10, Make Lewd Posts on Her Facebook Account," Tereance Corcoran, Lohud.com, September 24, 2011 (http://www.lohud.com/article/20110924/NEWS04/109240353/Kent-girls-harass-friend-10-make-lewd-posts-her-Facebook-account).

41. "Case of 8,000 Menacing Posts Tests Limits of Twitter Speech," Somini Sengupta, *The New York Times*, August 26, 2011 (http://www.nytimes.com/2011/08/27/technology/man-accused-of-stalking-via-twitter-claims-free-speech.html).

42. George Orwell, *Collected Works* (Secker & Warburg, 1980), "Inside the Whale," 494–518.

43. Jarvis, *Public Parts*, 11.

44. "Sean Parker: Yes, My New Start-Up Is Called Airtime," Matt Rosoff, *Business Insider*, October 17, 2011 (http://www.businessinsider.com/sean-parker-yes-my-new-startup-is-called-airtime-2011-10?op=1).

45. "Sharing to the power of 2012," by Sheryl Sandberg, *The Economist*, November 12, 2011 (http://www.economist.com/node/21537000).

46. "Google's Schmidt: I Screwed Up on Social Networking," Sam Gustin, Wired.com, June 1, 2011 (http://www.wired.com/epicenter/2011/06/googles-schmidt-social/).

47. http://www.theregister.co.uk/2009/12/07/schmidt_on_privacy/.

48. "Google and the Search of the Future," Holman W. Jenkins, *The Wall Street Journal*, August 14, 2010 (http://online.wsj.com/article/SB10001424052748704901104575423294099527212.html).

49. This is an internal Facebook initiative announced in late 2009 (see, *The Facebook Effect*, 332).

50. See, for example, Zuckerberg's interview with Techcrunch's Michael Arrington on January 8, 2010, at the Crunchies Award Ceremony (http://www.youtube.com/watch?v=LoWKGBloMsU).

51. Zuckerberg first stated this law at a Silicon Valley event in November 2008. See: "Zuckerberg's Law of Information Sharing," Saul Hansell, *The New York Times*, November 6, 2008 (http://bits.blogs.nytimes.com/2008/11/06/zuckerbergs-law-of-information-sharing/).

52. "Zuckerberg: 'We Are Building A Web Where The Default Is Social,'" Erick Schonfeld, Techcrunch, April 21, 2010 (http://techcrunch.com/2010/04/21/zuckerbergs-buildin-web-default-social/).

53. "The Big Picture of Facebook f8: Prepare for the Oversharing Explosion," Liz Gannes,

September 22, 2011 (http://allthingsd.com/20110922/the-big-picture-of-facebook-f8 -prepare-for-the-sharing-explosion/).

54. "Facebook Boldly Annexes the Web," Ben Elowitz, AllThingsD, September 22, 2011 (http://allthingsd.com/20110922/facebook-boldly-annexes-the-web/).

55. "With 'Frictionless Sharing,' Facebook and News Orgs Push Boundaries of Oline Privacy," Jeff Sonderman, September 29, 2011 (http://www.poynter.org/latest-news/media -lab/social-media/147638/with-frictionless-sharing-facebook-and-news-orgs-push -boundaries-of-reader-privacy/).

56. "Facebook Boldly Annexes the Web," Ben Elowitz, AllThingsD, September 22, 2011 (http://allthingsd.com/20110922/facebook-boldly-annexes-the-web/).

57. "Take care how you share," Chris Nutall, *Financial Times,* October 6, 2011 (http://www .ft.com/intl/cms/s/0/7409813c-ef48-11e0-918b-00144feab49a.html#axzz1avqVXfyt).

58. "The Big Picture of Facebook f8: Prepare for the Oversharing Explosion," Liz Gannes, September 22, 2011 (http://allthingsd.com/20110922/the-big-picture-of-facebook-f8 -prepare-for-the-sharing-explosion/).

59. "With 'Frictionless Sharing,' Facebook and News Orgs Push Boundaries of Oline Privacy," Jeff Sonderman, September 29, 2011 (http://www.poynter.org/latest-news/media -lab/social-media/147638/with-frictionless-sharing-facebook-and-news-orgs-push -boundaries-of-reader-privacy/).

60. "The Facebook Timeline Is the Nearest Thing I've Seen to a Digital Identity (And It's Creepy As Hell)," Benwerd.com, September 23, 2011 (http://benwerd.com/2011/09/ facebook-timeline-nearest-digital-identity-creepy-hell/).

61. "Your Life on Facebook, in Total Recall," by Jenna Wortham, *The New York Times,* December 15, 2011 (http://www.nytimes.com/2011/12/16/technology/facebook-brings -back-the-past-with-new-design.html?pagewanted=all).

62. "The World's Most Powerful People List", Forbes, 2 November, 2011 (http://www.forbes .com/powerful-people/).

63. "Facebook Boldly Annexes the Web," Ben Elowitz, AllThingsD, September 22, 2011 (http://allthingsd.com/20110922/facebook-boldly-annexes-the-web/).

64. According to Bloomberg, Facebook's valuation rose to over $41 billion in December 2010 (http://www.bloomberg.com/news/2010-12-17/facebook-groupon-lead-54-rise-in-value -of-private-companies-report-find.html). Then, on January 2, 2011, *The New York Times* announced that Goldman Sachs had lead a $500 million investment in Facebook at a valuation of $50 billion. (http://dealbook.nytimes.com/2011/01/02/goldman-invests-in -facebook-at-50-billion-valuation/).

65. Facebook's $45 billion valuation would put it ahead of the GDPs of forty African countries in 2009.

66. "Facebook's best friend" William D. Cohan, *The New York Times,* January 4, 2001(http:// opinionator.blogs.nytimes.com/category/william-d-cohan/).

67. See: "Why $50bn may not be that much between friends," Richard Waters, *Financial Times,* January 8/9, 2011(http://online.wsj.com/article/SB10001424052748703951704 576091993394718716.html) and "Why Facebook Looks Like a Bargain—Even at $50 Billion" by James B. Stewart, *Wall Street Journal,* January 22, 2011 (http://online.wsj .com/article/SB10001424052748703951704576091993394718716.html).

68. "Facebook Secondary Stock Just Surged to $34—That's an $85 Billion Valuation," by

M. G. Siegler, Techcrunch, March 21, 2011 (http://techcrunch.com/2011/03/21/facebook-85-billion-valuation/).

69. *The Facebook Effect*, 200.

70. Ibid.

71. It was H.L.A. Hart, the Professor of Jurisprudence at Oxford University, who described Bentham in these memorable terms. (*Bentham*, Dinwiddy), 109.

72. *The Facebook Effect*, 199.

73. MingleBird was introduced at San Francisco's Launch Conference on February 24, 2011, the annual start-up event produced by Jason Calacanis. See: "MingleBird wants to make event networking less awkward," Anthony Ha, VentureBeat, February 24, 2011 (http://venturebeat.com/2011/02/24/minglebird-launch/).

74. For an introduction to this reputation economy, see: "Wannable Cool Kids Aim to Game the Web's New Social Scorekeepers," Jessica E. Vascellaro, *The Wall Street Journal*, February 8, 2011 (http://online.wsj.com/article/SB1000142405274870463770457608238346641782.html).

75. AOL acquired About.me for "tens of millions of dollars" in December 2010, only four days after its official launch: "AOL acquires Personal Profile Start-Up About.Me", by Michael Arrington, Techcrunch, December 20, 2010 (http://techcrunch.com/2010/12/20/aol-acquires-personal-profile-startup-about-me/).

76. Virtual Friendship and the New Narcissism," Christine Rosen, *The New Atlantis: A Journal of Technology and Society*, Summer 2007.

77. "Politics and the English Language," George Orwell.

78. "The Rise of the Zuckerverb: The New Language of Facebook," Ben Zimmer, *The Atlantic*, September 30, 2011 (http://www.theatlantic.com/technology/archive/2011/09/the-rise-of-the-zuckerverb-the-new-language-of-facebook/245897/).

79. Ibid.

80. "Got Twitter? You've Been Scored," Stephanie Rosenbloom, *The New York Times*, June 26, 2011 (http://www.nytimes.com/2011/06/26/sunday-review/26rosenbloom.html).

81. Like MingleBird, eEvent was introduced at the February 2011 Launch event in San Francisco. See: "eEvent Helps Spread the Word," by Anthony Ha, VentureBeat, February 24, 2011 (http://venturebeat.com/2011.02/24.eevents-launch/).

82. John Dewey, *Experience and Nature*. For a fuller discussion of Dewey's ideas, see Daniel J. Solove's *The Future of Reputation*.

83. *Experience and Nature*, 166

84. "The Eyes Have It," Peggy Noonan, *The Wall Street Journal*, May 22–23, 2010.

85. *The Facebook Effect*, 200.

3. VISIBILITY IS A TRAP

1   This Facebook exchange took place on June 16, 2011, in the aftermath of riots in Vancouver after the local Canucks ice hockey team lost the final game of the Stanley Cup. See: "Vancouver Rioters Exposed on Crowdsourced Tumblr," by Brenna Ehrlich, Mashable, June 16, 2011 (http://mashable.com/2011/06/16/vancouver-2011-tumblr/).

2. *The Facebook Effect*, 200.

3. "Little Brother Is Watching," Walter Kirn, *The New York Times*, October 20, 2010 (http://www.nytimes.com/2010/10/17/magazine/17FOB-WWLN-t.html).

4. "Social Isolation and New Technology," Keith Hampton, Lauren Session, Eun Ja Her and Lee Rainie, November 2, 2009 (http://www.pewinternet.org/Reports/2009/18–Social -Isolation-and-New-Technology.aspx).

5. "My Space: Social Networking or Social Isolation?" Rob Nyland, Raquel Marvez and Jason Beck, Brigham Young University, Department of Communications. Paper presented at the AEJMC Midwinter Conferencer, Feb 23–24 2007.

6. "Empathy: College Students Don't Have as Much as They Used to, Study Finds," Science Daily, May 29, 2010 (http://www.sciencedaily.com/releases/2010/05/100528081434.htm).

7. "Science Proves Twitter Really Has Become More Sad Since 2009," by Graeme McMillan, Time, December 22, 2011 (http://techland.time.com/2011/12/22/science-proves-twitter -really-has-become-more-sad-since-2009/).

8. For my February 2011 "Keen On" Techcrunch.tv interview with Turkle, see: http:// techcrunch.com/2011/02/15/keen-on-sherry-turkle-alone-together-in-the-facebook -age-tctv/.

9. Sherry Turkle, Alone Together: Why We Expect More from Technology and Less from Each Other (Basic 2011).

10. Ibid., 17.

11. Ibid., 181.

12. Ibid., 280–281.

13. "Facebook Fuelling Divorce Research Claims," Daily Telegraph, December 21, 2009 (http://www.telegraph.co.uk/technology/facebook/6857918/Facebook-fuelling-divorce -research-claims.html).

14. "Serendipity Is No Algorithm on College Dating Site," Hannah Miet, February 25, 2011 (http://www.nytimes.com/2011/02/27/fashion/27DATEMYSCHOOL.html ?partner=rss&emc=rss).

15. Alone Together, 192.

16. Ibid., 160.

17. Ibid., 173.

18. Ibid., 192.

19. Elsewhere U.S.A, Dalton Conley (Pantheon, 2009), 7.

20. Guy Debord, Society of the Spectacle (Black and Red, 1983), #167.

21. "Social Websites Harm Children's Brains: Chilling Warning to Parents from Top Neuroscientist," David Derbyshire, London Mail, February 24, 2009 (http://www.dailymail.co .uk/news/article-1153583/Social-websites-harm-childrens-brains-Chilling-warning-parents -neuroscientist.html).

22. "Small Change: Why the revolution Will Not Be Tweeted," Malcolm Gladwell, The New Yorker, October 4, 2010 (http://www.newyorker.com/reporting/2010/10/04/101004fa_ fact_gladwell). See also the March 27, 2011, debate between Gladwell and Fareed Zakaria on Zakaria's CNN show "Fareed Zakaria GPS": (http://transcripts.cnn.com/TRAN SCRIPTS/1103/27/fzgps.01.html).

23. Schmidt made this defense of the internet when he spoke at the Media Guardian Edinburgh Interneational Television Festival at the end of August 2011. See: "Google's Eric Schmidt: don't blame the internet for the riots," The Daily Telegraph, 27 August (http:// www.telegraph.co.uk/technology/google/8727177/Googles-Eric-Schmidt-dont-blame -the-internet-for-the-riots.html).

24. The call for blackouts was led by the prominent Conservative MP, Louise Mensch, See: "Louise Mensch MP calls for Twitter and Facebook blackouts during riots," Martin Beckford, *The Daily Telegraph,* August 12, 2011 (http://www.telegraph.co.uk/news/uknews/crime/8697850/Louise-Mensch-MP-calls-for-Twitter-and-Facebook-blackout-during-riots.html).

25. Amongst the politicians calling for the baning of rioters from social media were British Prime Minister David Cameron. See: "David Cameron considers banning suspected rioters from social media," Josh Halliday, *The Guardian,* August 11, 2011 (http://www.guardian.co.uk/media/2011/aug/11/david-cameron-rioters-social-media).

26. Joshua Cooper Ramo, *The Age of the Unthinkable: Why the New World Disorder Constantly Suprises Us and What We Can Do About It* (Little Brown 2009). Although this stimulating book was published in 2009, it nonetheless predicted events like England's 2011 flash riots.

27. "Protests Spurs Online Dialogue on Inequity," Jennifer Preston, *The New York Times,* October 8, 2011 (http://www.nytimes.com/2011/10/09/nyregion/wall-street-protest-spurs-online-conversation.html).

28. "Occupy Wall Street? These protests Are Not Tahir Square, but Scenery," *The Guardian,* October 20, 2011 (http://www.guardian.co.uk/commentisfree/2011/oct/20/occupy-wall-street-tahrir-scenery).

29. "How Russia's Internet Hamsters Outfoxed Vladimir Putin," by Andrew Keen, CNN, December 13, 2011 (http://www.cnn.com/2011/12/13/opinion/andrew-keen-russia/index.html).

30. "The Protester," by Kurt Andersen, *Time* magazine, December 14, 2011 (http://www.time.com/time/specials/packages/article/0,28804,2101745_2102132_2102373,00.html).

31. "Keen On...Kurt Andersen: Why 2011 Has Only Just Begun," TechcrunchTV, December 29, 2011 (http://techcrunch.com/2011/12/29/keen-on-kurt-andersen-why-2011-has-only-just-begun/).

32. "People Power: A New Palestinian movement," Joe Klein, *Time* magazine, March 31, 2011 (http://www.time.com/time/magazine/article/0,9171,2062474,00.html).

33. "London, Egypt and the Nature of Social Media," Ramesh Srinivasan, *The Washington Post,* August 11, 2011 (http://www.washingtonpost.com/national/on-innovations/london-egypt-and-the-complex-role-of-social-media/2011/08/11/gIQAIoud8I_story.html).

34. George Friedman, *The Next Decade: Where We've Been ... and Where We're Going* (Doubleday, 2011).

35. "A Wake-up Call from a Fake Syrian Lesbian Blogger," Evgeny Morozov, *The Financial Times,* June 17, 2011.

36. Invented, as a pejorative terms, by the GigaOm columnist Matthew Ingram, to critique both Morozov and Malcolm Gladwell. See: "Malcolm Gladwell: Social Media Still Not a Big Deal", GigaOm, March 29, 2011.

37. Evgeny Morozov, *The Net Delusion: The Dark Side of Internet Freedom* (Public Affairs, 2011).

38. "Keen On Yevgeny Morozov: Why America Didn't Win The Cold War and Other Net Delusions," Techcrunch, January 11, 2011 (http://techcrunch.com/2011/01/11/keen-on-evgeny-morozov-why-america-didn%E2%80%99t-win-the-cold-war-and-other-net-delusions-tctv/).

39. "Thai Facebookers warned not to 'like' anti-monarchy groups," *The Guardian,* November

25, 2001 (http://www.guardian.co.uk/world/2011/nov/25/thai-facebookers-warned-like-button).

40. "Beijing Imposes New Rules on Social Networking Sites," by Edward Wong, *The New York Times,* December 16, 2011 (http://www.nytimes.com/2011/12/17/world/asia/beijing-imposes-new-rules-on-social-networking-sites.html).

41. "Iran Clamps Down on Internet Use," by Saeed Kamali Dehghan, *The Guardian,* January 5, 2011 (http://www.guardian.co.uk/world/2012/jan/05/iran-clamps-down-internet-use).

42. In Veracruz, for example, the State Assembly has actually made it a crime to use Twitter. See: "Mexico Turns to Social Media for Information and Survival," by Damien Cave, *The New York Times,* September 24, 2011 (http://www.nytimes.com/2011/09/25/world/americas/mexico-turns-to-twitter-and-facebook-for-information-and-survival.html).

43. "Bodies hanging from bridge in Mexico are warning to social media users", by Mariano Castillo, CNN.com, September 14, 2011 (http://articles.cnn.com/2011-09-14/world/mexico.violence_1_zetas-cartel-social-media-users-nuevo-laredo?_s=PM:WORLD).

44. In conversation with Liz Gannes of All Things D, December 29, 2010 (http://networkeffect.allthingsd.com/20101229/video-greylocks-reid-hoffman-and-david-sze-on-the-future-of-social/).

45. "All animals are equal, but some animals are *more equal than others.*" From Orwell's *Animal Farm.*

46. From "Twitter Statistics for 2010"—A December 2010 report by the social media monitoring group Sysomos which examined more than a billion tweets (http://www.sysomos.com/insidetwitter/twitter-stats-2010).

47. "The Web is Dead, Long Live the Internet," Chris Anderson, *Wired,* August 17, 2011 (http://www.wired.com/magazine/2010/08/ff_webrip/all/1).

48. "Got Twitter? You've Been Scored," Stephanie Rosenbloom, *The New York Times,* June 26, 2011 (http://www.nytimes.com/2011/06/26/sunday-review/26rosenbloom.html).

49. "To Tweet or Not to Tweet," Zachary Karabell, *Time* Magazine, April 11, 2011 (http://www.time.com/time/printout/0,8816,2062464,00.html#).

50. *The Rise and Fall of Elites,* Vilfredo Pareto (Bedminster Press, 2008), 36.

51. See *The Numerati* (2008, Houghton Miflin), Stephen Baker's excellent introduction to our new numerati ruling class.

52. Meglena Kuneva, Keynote Speech, "Roundtable on Online Data Collection, Targeting and Profiling," Brussels, March 31, 2009.

53. James Gleick, *The Information: A History, A Theory, A Flood* (Pantheon, 2011), 8.

54. "The Web's New Gold Mine: Your Secrets," Julia Angwin, July 30, 2010 (http://online.wsj.com/article/SB10001424052748703940904575395073512989404.html).

55. Ibid.

56. James Gleick, *The Information* (Pantheon, 2011), 8. See also my June TechcrunchTV interview with Gleick.

57. Eli Pariser, *The Filter Bubble: What the Internet is Hiding from You* (Penguin, 2011), 6. See, also, my TechcrunchTV.

58. "Does Facebook Really Care About You?" Douglass Rushkoff, CNN.com, September 23, 2011 (http://edition.cnn.com/2011/09/22/opinion/rushkoff-facebook-changes/index.html?hpt=hp_bn11).

59. "The Mobile Allure," by Barney Jopson, *The Financial Times*, December 21, 2011 (http://www.ft.com/intl/cms/s/0/8f992b56-2b0b-11e1-a9c4-00144feabdc0.html #axzz1i4QIU1rn).

60. "Less Web Tracking Means Less Effective Ads, Researcher Says," Somini Sengupta, *The New York Times*, September 15, 2011 (http://bits.blogs.nytimes.com/2011/09/15/less -web-tracking-means-less-effective-ads-researcher-says/).

61. "Online Trackers Rake in Funding," Scott Thurm, *The Wall Street Journal*, February 25, 2011.

62. "Generation Why," Zadie Smith.

63. See: "The Web's New Gold Mine: Your Secrets" (July 30, 2010), "Microsoft Quashed Effort to Boost Online Privacy" (August 2, 2010), "Stalkers Exploit Cellphone GPS" (August 3, 2010) "On the Web's Cutting Edge, Anonymity in Name Only (August 4, 2010), "Google Agonizes on Privacy as Ad World Vaults Ahead" (August 10, 2010).

64. "Your Apps Are Watching You" Scott Thurm and Yukari Iwantani Kane, *The Wall Street Journal*, December 18, 2010 (http://online.wsj.com/article/SB10001424052748704694 004576020083703574602.html).

65. "Like" Button Follows Web Users," Amir Efrati, *The Wall Street Journal*, May 18, 2011 (http://online.wsj.com/article/SB10001424052748704281504576329441432995616. html).

66. "Why Facebook's Facial Recognition Is Creepy," Sarah Jacobsson, PC World, June 8, 2011 (http://www.pcworld.com/article/229742/why_facebooks_facial_recognition_is_ creepy.html).

67. "How Facebook Is Making Friending Obsolete," Julia Angwin, *The Wall Street Journal*, December 15, 2009 (http://online.wsj.com/article/SB126084637203791583.html).

68. "How Facial Recognition Technology Can Be Used to Get Your Social Security Number," Kashmir Hill, *Forbes*, August 1, 2011 (http://www.forbes.com/sites/kashmirhill/ 2011/08/01/how-face-recognition-can-be-used-to-get-your-social-security-number/).

69. "Computers That See You and Keep Watch Over You," Steve Lohr, January 1, 2011 (http://www.nytimes.com/2011/01/02/science/02see.html).

70. Steven Johnson, *Where Good Ideas Come From*, Chapter IV (Riverhead, 2010)

71. "Computers That See You and Keep Watch Over You."

72. The two researchers are Pete Warden, a former Apple employee, and Alasdair Allan, a data visualisation scientist. See: "iPhone keeps record of everywhere you go," by Charles Arthur, London Guardian, April 20, 2011 (http://www.guardian.co.uk/technology/2011/ apr/20/iphone-tracking-prompts-privacy-fears).

73. "Apple, Google Collect User Data," Julia Angwin and Jennifer Valentino-Devries, *The Wall Street Journal*, April 22, 2011 (http://online.wsj.com/article/SB100014240527487 039837045762771017234536410.html).

74. "Is Google Making Us Stupid?" Nicholas Carr, *The Atlantic*, July/August 2008 (http://www .theatlantic.com/magazine/archive/2008/07/is-google-making-us-s tupid/6868/).

75. "Google Calls Location Data 'Valuable,'" Amir Efrati, *The Wall Street Journal*, May 1, 2011 (http://online.wsj.com/article/SB10001424052748703703304576297450030517830.html?mod=googlenews_wsj).

76. "Amazon Big Brother patent knows where you'll go," by Eric Sherman, CBS News,

December 14, 2011 (http://www.cbsnews.com/8301-505124_162-57342567/amazon-big
-brother-patent-knows-where-youll-go/), by knowing where we've been and where we will
go, promises to be a particularly intrusive algorithm of digital coercion and seduction.

77. "The Evolution of a New Trust Economy," Brian Solis, BrianSolis.com, December 9,
2009.

78. Dan Gilmor, Google +. September 28, 2011. (https://plus.google.com/11321043100
6401244170/posts/YYwcR5Ua5JN).

79. Robert Vamosi, When Gadgets Betray Us: The Dark Side of our Infatuation with New
Technologies (Basic, 2011). Also see my April 28, 2011 TechcrunchTV interview with Vamosi (http://techcrunch.com/2011/04/28/keen-on-robert-vamosi-when-gadgets-betray-us
-book-giveaway/).

80. "Internet Probe Can Track You Down to Within 690 Metres," Jacob Aron, New Scientist,
April 5, 2011 (http://www.newscientist.com/article/dn20336-internet-probe-can-track
-you-down-to-within-690-metres.html).

81. "Data Privacy, Put to the Test," Natasha Singer, The New York Times, April 30, 2011.

82. "Who's Watching You? Data Privacy Day Survey Reveals Your Fears Online," PRNews-
wire, January 28, 2011 (http://techcrunch.com/2011/01/28/karp-tumblr-quarter-billion
-impressions-week/).

83. "Report finds Internet users worry more about snooping companies than spying Big
Brother," Associated Press, June 2, 2011 (http://www.washingtonpost.com/business/
technology/report-finds-internet-users-worry-more-about-snooping-companies-than
-spying-big-brother/2011/06/03/AG7CyeHH_story.html).

4. DIGITAL VERTIGO

1. Dan Auiler, Vertigo, The Making of a Hitchcock Classic (St Martin's 2000), xiii (from introduction by Scorcese).

2. Filmed in the second half of October 1957 in Stage 5 of Paramount Studios in Bel Air.

3. The screenplay written by Alec Coppell, Samuel Taylor and Hitchcock himself, and
adapted from the 1954 French novel The Living and The Dead (D'Entre Les Morts) by
Pierre Boileau and Thomas Narcejac.

4. The spiral is the central motif of the movie. See, for example, Vertigo's mesmerizingly
twisted opening titles, designed by Hitchcock's long-time collaborator, Saul Bass, or Madeleine's hair style, or the twisted streets of San Francisco.

5. Fitzgerald quote (Tender Is the Night).

6. Kevin Starr, Americans and the California Dream 1850–1915 (Oxford University Press
1973), 58.

7. Gray Brechin, Imperial San Francisco (University of California Press, 2006), 32.

8. Both played by Kim Novak. It is universally acknowledged that this was Novak's greatest
role, in spite—or perhaps because of—her distaste for the bullying Alfred Hitchcock.

9. All the clothing in the movie was designed by Edith Head, another member of Hitchcock's team of longtime collaborators.

10. Francois Truffaut, Hitchcock Truffaut: The Definitive Study of Alfred Hitchcock, (Touchstone, 1983), 111.

11. In the 2002 British Film Institute/Sight and Sound magazine list of the greatest movie of
all time, a poll determined by a leading group of international movie critics, Hitchcock's

Vertigo was voted the second best movie of all time, behind Orson Welles' *Citizen Kane*. http://www.bfi.org.uk/sightandsound/topten/poll/critics.html.

12. In the Universal DVD, chapter 31 at 1:58:27.

13. See, in particular, the 1937 essay "The Nature of the Firm" by the University of Chicago economist Ronald Coase which lays out the necessity of the firm and explains its central role in the twentieth-century economy.

14. *The Power of Pull: How Small Moves, Smartly Made, Can Set Big Things in Motion*, John Hagel III, John Seely Brown & Lang Davidson, (Basic 2010), 36.

15. *The Organization Man*, William H. Whyte (University of Pennsylvania Press, 2000), 51.

16. *The Fifties*, David Halberstam (Villiard Books, 1993), 526–527.

17. The term "Silicon Valley" was coined by a Californian entrepreneur called Ralph Vaerst and popularized in 1971 by the *Electronic News* journalist Don Hoefler.

18. There are many excellent histories of the computer and the Internet including David Kaplan's *Silicon Boys And Their Valley of Dreams* (1999, Perennial); Tracy Kidder's *Soul of the New Machine* (Back Bay 2000); John Naughton's *A Brief History of the Future* (Overlook, 2000); and Robert Cringley, *Accidental Empires* (Harper, 1996).

19. David Kaplan, *Silicon Boys and Their Valley of Dreams* (1999, Perennial) 40.

20. Ibid., 49.

21. Mike Malone called them "the greatest collection of electronics genius ever assembled. In addition to Moore and Noyce, they included Julius Blank, Victor Grinich, Eugene Kleiner, Jean Hoerni, Jay Last and Sheldon Roberts. (*The Big Score*), 68–69.

22. Mike Malone, *The Big Score*, Doubleday 1985, 40.

23. Joseph Schumpeter, *Capitalism, Socialism and Democracy* (New York: Harper, 1975) [orig. pub. 1942], 82–85.

24. John Markoff, "Searching for Silicon Valley," *The New York Times*, April 16, 2009.

25. Kelly's *What Technology Wants* (Viking, 2008) and Carr's *The Shallows* (2008) represent different sides of the same coin. Kelly presents technology as our brain; Carr says that technology is destroying our brain. I confess that I have sometimes fallen into this trap too, especially in my 2007 book *Cult of the Amateur*, which oversimplified the causal relationship between the Internet and our culture.

26. Richard Florida, *The Rise of Creative Class*, 17.

27. Available on DVD: The Complete Monterey Pop Festival—Criterion Collection, (Blu-Ray) (2009).

28. *San Francisco Oracle*, Vol.1, Issue 5, 2.

29. Todd Gitlin, *The Sixties: Years of Hope, Days of Rage* (Bantam, 1993), 203.

30. Published by Malcolm Cowley at Viking Press. See David Halberstram, *The Fifties* (Villiard Books, 1993) ch 21, 306.

31. Theodore Roszak, *The Making of the Counter Culture* (Doubleday 1968) 184.

32. Mark Andrejevic, *Reality TV: The Work of Being Watched* (Rowman & Littlefield, 2004), 26.

33. *A History of Private Life*, Volume III, "Passions of the Renaissance" (Harvard, 1989), 376.

34. Ibid.

35. Karl Marx, "The 18th Brumaire of Louis Bonaparte," from *Karl Marx, Selected Writings*, edited by David McLellan (Oxford University Press, 1977), 300.

36. Theodore Roszak, *The Making of a Counter Culture*, (Doubleday 1968), chapter 1. "By

technocracy, Rosznak meant: 'that social form in which an industrial society reaches the peak of its organizational integration. It is the ideal men usually have in mind when they speak of modernizing, up-dating, rationalizing, planning.'"

37. For an incisive cultural critique of our contemporary cult of authenticity, see Andrew Potter's *The Authenticity Hoax: How We Get Lost Finding Ourselves* (Harper Collins, 2010). See also "Public and Private," my essay on J. S. Salinger in The Barnes & Noble Review of March 22, 2010 (http://bnreview.barnesandnoble.com/t5/Reviews-Essays/Public-and-Private/ba-p/2322).

38. Sennett, *The Fall of Public Man*, 220.

39. Christopher Lasch, *The Culture of Narcissism: American Life in an Age of Diminishing Expectations*, (Norton, 1991), 10.

40. Alvin Toffler, *Future Shock* (Random House, 1970), 284.

41. "Adam Curtis: Have Computers Taken Away our Power?" Katharine Viner, *The Guardian*, May 6, 2011 (http://www.guardian.co.uk/tv-and-radio/2011/may/06/adam-curtis-computers-documentary).

5. THE CULT OF THE SOCIAL

1. Patrick McGilligan, *Alfred Hitchcock: A Life in Darkness and Light* (ReganBooks, 2003), 159.

2. *The Power of Pull*, 42. For more on Hagel and Seely Brown's theory of the "big shift" from an industrial to a digital economy, see my "Keen On" Techcrunch.tv interview with them from September 2010 (http://techcrunch.com/2010/09/08/keen-on-power-of-pull-tctv/).

3. "The Online Looking Glass," Ross Douthat, *The New York Times,* June 12, 2011.

4. John Markoff, *What the Dormouse Said: How the 60s Counterculture Shaped the Personal Computer Industry,* (Viking, 2005).

5. Fred Turner, *From Counterculture to Cyberculture: Stewart Brand, The Whole Earth Network, and the Rise of Digital Utopianism* (Chicago University Press, 2006).

6. James Harkin, *Cyburbia, The Dangerous Idea That's Changing How We Live and Who We Are* (Little Brown, 2009).

7. Tim Wu, *The Master Switch: The Life and Death of Information Empires*, (Knopf, 2010).

8. Ibid., 169.

9. Tim Berners-Lee, *Weaving The Web: The Original Design and Ultimate Destiny of the World Wide Web* (Harper Business, 2000).

10. Ibid., 201.

11. Ibid., 172.

12. Turner, *From Counterculture to Cyberspace*, 14.

13. David Brooks, *Bobos in Paradise: The New Upper Class and How They Got There* (Touchstone, 2000).

14. Thomas Frank, *The Conquest of Cool: Business Culture, Counterculture, and the Rise of Hip Consumerism* (University of Chicago, 1997).

15. Apple's iconic marketing campaign around "Think Different" was produced by the Madison Avenue firm of TBWA/Chiat/Day, who produced the equally iconic 1984 Super Bowl advertisement for the Apple Macintosh personal computer.

16. "Social Power and the Coming Corporate Revolution," David Kirkpatrick, *Forbes,* Sep-

tember 7, 2011 (http://www.forbes.com/sites/techonomy/2011/09/07/social-power-and
-the-coming-corporate-revolution/).

17. "The Challenge Ahead," Peter Drucker. From *The Essential Drucker, (Harper Business, 2001),* 347.

18. Ibid., 348.

19. Ibid., 348.

20. Daniel Pink, *Free Agent Nation: The Future of Working for Yourself* (Warner Business Books, 2001).

21. "While We Weren't Paying Attention the Industrial Age Just Ended," Techcrunch.tv, 7 February 2011 (http://techcrunch.com/2011/02/07/keen-on-seth-godin-while-we-werent -paying-attention-the-industrial-age-just-ended-tctv/).

22. Seth Godin, *Linchpin: Are You Indispensable?"* (Portfolio, 2010).

23. Hugh McLeod, *Ignore Everybody: and 39 Other Keys to Creativity* (Portfolio, 2009).

24. Gary Vaynerchuck, *Crush It: Why Now Is the Time to Cash In On Your Passion* (Harper Studio, 2009).

25. Reid Hoffman and Ben Casnocha, *The Start-Up of You: An Entrepreneurial Approach to Building a Killer Career* (Crown, 2012).

26. "The Start-Up of You," Thomas L. Friedman, *The New York Times,* July 12, 2011 (http:// www.nytimes.com/2011/07/13/opinion/13friedman.html).

27. Kevin Kelly, *Out of Control: The Biology of Machines, Social Systems, & the World* (Perseus, 1994).

28. For more on Kelly's vision of the connected future, see my January 18, 2011 "Keen On" Techcrunch.tv interview with him (http://techcrunch.com/2011/01/18/keen-on-kevin -kelly-what-does-kevin-kelly-want-tctv/).

29. Turner, 174.

30. Harkin, 1930.

31. Kirkpatrick, 332.

32. James Gleick, *The Information: A History, A Theory, A Flood* (Pantheon 2011) 48.

33. Michael Malone, *Valley of the Heart's Delight: A Silicon Valley Notebook 1963–2001* (Wiley, 2002).

34. Robert Puttnam, *Bowling Alone,* 2000 (Simon & Schuster), 410.

35. Charles Leadbeater, *We-Think: Mass Innovation, Not Mass Production* (Profile, 2008).

36. Yochai Benkler, *The Wealth of Networks: How Social Production Transforms Markets and Freedom,* (Yale, 2006), Yochai Benkler (Yale, 2006).

37. Erik Qualman, *Socialnomics: How Social Media Transforms the Way We Live and Do Business* (Wiley, 2009).

38. Clay Shirky, Here Comes Everyone: The Power of Organizing Without Organizations (Penguin, 2008).

39. Charlene Li, *Open Leadership: How Social Technology Can Transform the Way You Lead.* See also my July 2010 "Keen On" Techcrunch.tv interview with Li and Shirky (http:// techcrunch.com/2010/07/07/techcrunch-tv-keen-on-connectivit/).

40. Mitch Joel, *Six Pixels of Separation: Everyone Is Connected, Connect Your Business to Everyone* (Business Plus, 2009).

41. Simon Mainwaring, *We First: How Brands and Consumers Use Social Media to Build a Better World* (Palgrave Macmillan, 2011).

42. Eric Greenberg and Karl Weber, *Generation We: How Millennial Youth Are Taking Over America and Changing Our World Forever* (Puchatusan, 2008).

43. Nicholas A. Christakis and James H. Fowler, *Connected: The Surprsing Power of Uur Social Networks and How They Shape Our Lives* (Little Brown, 2009).

44. Jane McGonigal, *Reality Is Broken: Why Games Make Us Better and How They Can Change the World* (Penguin, 2011). See, in particular, chapter 4: "Stronger Social Connectivity." See also my March "Keen On" Techcrunch.tv interview with McGonigal in which she argues that "social is everything."

45. Lisa Gansky, *The Mesh: Why The Future of Business Is Sharing (*Portfolio, 2010*)*. See also my September 2010 "Keen On" Techcrunch.tv interview with Gansky (http://techcrunch .com/2010/09/22/keen-on-lisa-gansk/).

46. Francois Gossieaux, *The Hyper-Social Organization: Eclipse Your Competition by Leveraging Social Media* (McGraw-Hill, 2010).

47. Gleick, *The Information*, 322. See "Into the Meme Pool" (ch 11), Gleick's lucid and informative chapter on the history of meme, both as a scientific and cultural idea.

48. "Social Networking Affects Brains Like Falling in Love," Adam Penenberg, *Fast Company*, July 1, 2010.

49. BBC News, August 10, 2010 (http://www.bbc.co.uk/news/science-environment -10925841).

50. Harold, the fictional hero (Brooks's self-styled Emile of this twenty-first Rousseauan guide to happiness) of *The Social Animal* and the apotheosis of sociability is known to his school friends as "the mayor"—perhaps not uncoincidentally giving him the same status as the most popular networkers on the geo-location service. David Brooks, *The Social Animal: The Hidden Sources of Love, Character and Achievement* (Random House, 2011).

51. "It's Not About You," David Brooks, *The New York Times*, May 30, 2011.

52. Steven Johnson, *Where Good Ideas Come From: The Natural History of Innovation* (Riverhead, 2010).

53. Ibid., 44.

54. Ibid., 206.

55. Jaron Lanier, "Digital Maoism: The Hazards of the New Online Collectivism," Edge.org 5/3/06 (http://www.edge.org/3rd_culture/lanier06/lanier06_index.html).

56. Power of Pull, 247.

57. Jeff Jarvis, Public Parts, (Simon & Schuster, 2011), 70–71.

58. Clay Shirky, *Cognitive Surplus,* (Penguin, 2010). For more on Shirky's vision of a collaborative future, see my July 2010 "Keen on" Techcrunch.tv interview with him (http:// techcrunch.com/2010/07/07/techcrunch-tv-keen-on-connectivit/)

59. Cognitive Surplus, 19.

60. See "Ringside at the Web Fight" by Michael Wolff, *Vanity Fair,* March 2010. As Wolff argues, "Clay Shirky . . . is a man whose name is now uttered in technology circles with the kind of reverence with which left-wingers used to say, "Herbert Marcuse."

61. *Connected*, Christakis & Fowler, chapter 2.

62. *Cognitive Surplus*, 60.

63. "Gilgamesh to Gaga," by John Tresch, Lapham's Quarterly, Winter 2011 (http://www .laphamsquarterly.org/essays/gilgamesh-to-gaga.php?page=7).

6. THE AGE OF THE GREAT EXHIBITION

1. Jean Baudrillard, *The Conspiracy of Art* (Semiotext, 2005), 26.

2. The Oxford Union, Christopher Hollis (Evans Brothers, 1965), 96.

3. Jan Morris, *Oxford* (Oxford, 1979).

4. Ibid., 21.

5. Ibid., 3.

6. http://secondlife.com/whatis/?lang=en-US.

7. "Fun in Following the Money," Daniel Terdiman, *Wired* magazine, May 8, 2004 (http://www.wired.com/gaming/gamingreviews/news/2004/05/63363).

8. Christopher Hollis, *The Oxford Union* (Evans Brothers, 1965), 106.

9. In addition to Rossetti, the other artists who painted the murals were Valentine Prinsep, John Hungerford Pollen, William Morris, Edward Burne-Jones, Rodham Spencer Stanhope, Arthur Huges and William and Briton Riviere.

10. For the best introduction to the Pre-Raphaelite project, see: John D. Renton, *The Oxford Union Murals*.

11. Paul Johnson, *Art: A New History* (Harper Collins, 2003), 533.

12. Hollis, *The Oxford Union*, 209.

13. E. H. Gombrich, *The Story of Art* (Phaidon, 1995) 384.

14. A.N. Wilson, The Victorians (Norton, 2003).

15. Laurence Des Cars, *The Pre-Raphaelites: Romance and Realism* (Discoveries), 69.

16. *Nothing If Not Critical*, 115.

17. Ibid., 116.

18. Paul Johnson, *Art: A New History* (Harper Collins, 2003), 534.

19. Robert Hughes, *Nothing If Not Critical* (Knopf, 1990), 116.

20. *The Oxford Union 1823–1923*, Herbert Arthur Morrah (Cassell & Co, 1923), 175.

21. *Oxford*, Jan Morris, 219.

22. The Oxford Union, Christopher Hollis (Evans Brothers, 1965).

23. Ibid., 101.

24. In the 1980s, for example, over £125,000 was raised by the Landmark Trust to help restore the building. See the Union booklet: *The Oxford Union Murals*, John D. Renton, 15–16.

25. Eric Hobsbawn, *The Age of Revolution 1989–1848* (Vintage, 1996), 168.

26. Michael Leapman, *The World for a Shilling: How the Great Exhibition of 1951 Shaped a Nation* (Headline, 2001).

27. Joel Mokyr, *The Level of Riches: Technological Creativity and Economic Progress* (Oxford University Press, 1990), 81.

28. As Bentham notes in *Introduction to the Principles of Morals and Legislation first published in 1798*: "The word international, it must be acknowledged, is a new one; though, it is hoped, sufficiently analogous and intelligible. It is calculated to express, in a more significant way, the branch of law which goes commonly under the name of the law of nations: an appellation so uncharacteristic, that, were it not for the force of custom, it would seem rather to refer to internal jurisprudence." Bentham other neologisms include the words "maximize" and "minimalize," as well as "codify" and "codification" (see: John Dinwiddy, *Bentham*, 47).

29. The industrial nature of the 1949 gold rush is reflected in the emergence of the mining engineer as San Francisco's new *aristocrazia* (see: Brechlin, *Imperial San Francisco*, 53).

30. Eric Hobsbawn, *The Age of Capital: 1848–1875* (Vintage 1996), 34, 63.

31. Eric Hobsbawn, *The Age of Revolution: 1789–1848* (Vintage), 168.

32. Karl Marx and Friedrich Engels, *The Communist Manifesto* (Oxford University Press).

33. Robert Rhodes James, *Prince Albert: A Biography* (Knopf, 1984), 190.

34. Ibid.

35. A. N. Wilson, *The Victorians* (Norton, 2003).

36. *German Ideology*

37. Michael Leapman, *The World for a Shilling: How the Great Exhibition of 1851 Shaped a Nation* (Headline, 2011), 24.

38. Robert Rhodes James, *Prince Albert: A Biography* (Knopf, 1984), 147.

39. Bill Bryson, At Home: A Short History of Private Life (Doubleday, 2010), 7.

40. James, *Prince Albert*, 199.

41. Bryson, *At Home*, 11.

42. Hobsbawn, *Age of Revolution*, 186.

43. James, *Prince Albert*, 200.

44. Michael Leapman, *The World for a Shilling*, 59.

45. The eccentric Babbage and his even more eccentric ideas were a thorn in the side of many prominent Victorians. "What shall we do to get rid of Mr. Babbage and his calculating machine" British Prime Minister Robert Peel wrote in 1842 (Gleick, *The Information*, 104–105).

46. George Friedman, *The Moral Consequences of Economic Growth* (Knopf, 2005), 20.

47. J. R. Piggott, *The Palace of the People: The Crystal Palace at Sydenham, 1854–1936* (Hurst, 2004).

48. Ibid., 61.

49. Ibid., 207.

50. Ernest Gellner, *Nations and Nationalism* (Cornell, 1983), 32–33.

51. Aldous Huxley, *Prisons* (Trianon & Grey Falcon Presses, 1949). See: http://www.john coulthart.com/feuilleton/2006/08/25/aldous-huxley-on-piranesis-prisons/.

52. Charles Fried, "Privacy," 77 *Yale Law Journal* (1968), 475, 477–478.

53. "Little Brother Is Watching," Walter Kirn, *The New York Times,* October 15, 2010 (http://www.nytimes.com/2010/10/17/magazine/17FOB-WWLN-t.html).

54. "So Is Web 3.0 Already Here?" Sarah Lacy, Techrunch, April 18, 2011 (http://techcrunch .com/2011/04/18/so-is-web-3-0-already-here-tctv/).

55. *Discipline & Punish: The Birth of the Prison*, 207.

7. THE AGE OF GREAT EXHIBITIONISM

1. *Discipline & Punish*, 200.

2. Norman Johnson, *Forms of Constraint: A History of Prison Architecture* (University of Illinois Press, 2000), 56.

3. William Blackburn's building of the modern Oxford prison was triggered by the posting of a inmate's crude caricature showing the gaoler of Oxford Castle standing on a mound of dung. Then, in 1786, the prison governors dismissed the gaoler and appointed a prison reformer called Daniel Harris in his place.

4. A separate women's prison was built in 1851, the same year as the Great Exhibition.

5. Jan Morris, *Oxford*, 35.

6. In its representation of Mr Bridger's life of luxury inside the jail, *The Italian Job* inadvertently predicted the future of the Oxford prison with its cells offering all the finest conveniences of life.

7. "Oxford Castle Unlocked", Official Guide (www.oxfordcastleunlocked.co.uk).

8. MALMAISON/TAGLINE

9. "Sentenced to Luxury: Malmaison Oxford Castle Hotel," Fodors.com, February 16, 2007.

10. *We Live in Public*.

11. "Web Privacy: In Praise of Oversharing," Steven Johnson, May 20, 2010.

12. The term Web 2.0 was invented and marketed by the Tim O'Reilly, the founder and CEO of O'Reilly Media in 2004.

13. Gary Shteyngart, *Super Sad True Love Story* (Random House, 2010).

14. "Apparat Chic: Talking with Gary Shteyngart, Shelfari, August 11, 2010 (http://blog.shelfari.com/my_weblog/2010/08/apparat-chic-talking-with-gary-shteyngart.html).

15. Keen On . . . Gary Shteyngart, Techcrunch, July 15, 2011 (http://techcrunch.com/2011/07/15/keen-on-a-super-sad-true-love-story-tctv/).

16. *Super Sad True Love Story*, 209–210.

17. Johnson is convinced that Harris's vision failed to come true. "It is far easier to set up web cameras and share video online today – thanks to YouTube and ubiquitous high-speed bandwidth—and yet almost no one chooses to display themselves in such an extreme way," he argues in his May 20, 2010 *Time* magazine essay "Web Privacy: In Praise of Oversharing." One wonders, however, which Internet Johnson is watching and whether he simply chooses to ignore the manifold self-revelationary networks that are shaping the Web 3.0 world.

18. Robert Scoble and Shell Israel, *Naked Conversations: How Blogs Are Changing the Way Businesses Talk with Customers* (Wiley, 2006).

19. "The Chief Humanizing Officer," *The Economist*, Feb 10, 2005 (http://www.economist.com/node/3644293?story_id=3644293).

20. The List: Five Most Influential Tweeters," Tim Bradshaw, *The Financial Times*, March 18, 2011 (http://www.ft.com/cms/s/2/01a1dc56-50e3-11e0-8931-00144feab49a.html#axzz1LK2XdH9T). In addition to Scoble, the other four leading tweeters were the American actor Ashton Kutcher (@aplusk), the British comedian Stephen Fry (@stephenfry), the student blogger James Buck (@jamesbuck) and Sarah Brown (@SarahBrownuk), the wife of former British Prime Minister Gordon Brown.

21. "Klout Finally Explains Why Obama Is Ranked Lower Than Robert Scoble," by Alyson Shontell, Business Insider, December 2, 2011 (http://articles.businessinsider.com/2011-12-02/tech/30466703_1_social-media-klout-president-obama).

22. "Help, I've fallen into a pit of steaming Google+ (what that means for tech blogging)," Robert Scoble, Scobleizer, August 18, 2011 (http://scobleizer.com/2011/08/18/help-ive-fallen-into-a-pit-of-steaminggoogle/).

23. For an up-to-date summary of Scoble's use of social media, see his speech in Amsterdam to The Next Web conference on 29 April, 2011 (http://thenextweb.com/eu/2011/04/29/robert-scoble-the-next-web-human-reality-virtual-video-tnw2011/).

24. "Much ado about privacy on Facebook (I wish Facebook were MORE OPEN!!!)", Scobleizer .com, May 8, 2010.

25. Richard Sennett, *The Fall of Public Man* (Norton, 1974), 282.

26. "Caesar Salad @ The Ritz-Carlton, Half Moon Bay" (http://www.foodspotting.com/ reviews/556332).

27. "Keen On . . . . Are We All Becoming Robert Scoble?" Techcrunch, December 1, 2010.

8. THE BEST PICTURE OF 2011

1. Stanley Weintraub, *Uncrowned King: The Life of Prince Albert* (Free Press, 1997), 209.

2. Larry Downes, *The Laws of Disruption*, (Basic, 2009), 73.

3. "The Right to Privacy," Earl Warren and Louis Brandeis, *Harvard Law Review*, Vol. IV, December 15, 1890.

4. "How a soccer star sparked the freedom debate of our age," by Lionel Barber, *The Financial Times,* May 28/29, 2011.

5. "Man on Trail over Twitter 'Affair' Claims Says Case Has 'Big Legal Implications,'" Press Association, June 15, 2011 (http://www.guardian.co.uk/technology/2011/jun/15/twitter -affair-claims-legal-implications).

6. "Zuckerberg, Schmidt Counter Sarkozy's Calls for Internet Regulation at 'EG8,'" by Rebecca Kaplan, NationalJournal, May 28, 2011 (http://www.nationaljournal.com/ tech/zuckerberg-schmidt-counter-sarkozy-s-calls-for-internet-regulation-at-eg8 –20110526).

7. "Congress Calls on Twitter to Block Taliban," by Ben Farmer, *Daily Telegraph*, December 25, 2011 (http://www.telegraph.co.uk/technology/twitter/8972884/Congress-calls-on -Twitter-to-block-Taliban.html).

8. "US Court Verdict 'Huge Blow' to Privacy, Says former WikiLeaks Aide," by Dominic Rushe, *The Guardian*, November 11, 2011 (http://www.guardian.co.uk/world/2011/nov/ 11/us-verdict-privacy-wikileaks-twitter).

9. "Google Reaches Agreement on FTC's Accusations of "Deceptive Privacy Practices" in Buzz Rollout," Lenna Rao, Techcrunch, March 30, 2011 (http://techcrunch.com/2011/ 03/30/google-reaches-agreement-on-ftcs-accusations-of-deceptive-privacy-practices-in -buzz-rollout/).

10. "Facebook 'Unfair' on Privacy", by Shayndi Raice and Julia Angwin, *The Wall Street Journal*, November 30, 2011 (http://online.wsj.com/article/SB10001424052970203441704 577068400622644374.html).

11. "Why should I care about digital privacy?" Bob Sullivan, MSNBC, March 10, 2011 (http://www.msnbc.msn.com/id/41995926/ns/technology_and_science/).

12. "US Urges Web Privacy Bill of Rights," Julia Angwin, *The Wall Street Journal*, Deceber 18, 2010 (http://online.wsj.com/article/SB1000142405274870339520457602352165966 72058.html).

13. "The White House Offers Up a National Data Breach Law," Kashmir Hill, *Forbes*, May 12, 2011 (http://blogs.forbes.com/kashmirhill/2011/05/12/the-white-house-offers-up-a -national-data-breach-law/).

14. "Sen. Rockefeller Introduces 'Do Not Track' Bill for Internet," Cecilia Kang, *Washington Post*, May 9, 2011 (http://www.washingtonpost.com/blogs/post-tech/post/sen-rockefeller -introduces-do-not-track-bill-for-internet/2011/05/09/AF0ymjaG_blog.html).

15. "Leibowitz pushes Google on privacy," Mike Zapler, April 19, 2011 (http://www.politico
.com/news/stories/0411/53440.html).

16. In late April 2011, Senator Al Franken announced his intention to hold Congressional
hearings about this data spill. See: "Franken sets hearings on Apple Google tracking," *The
Wall Street Journal*, Marketwatch, May 4, 2011 (http://www.marketwatch.com/story/
franken-sets-hearing-on-apple-google-tracking-2011-04-26).

17. "Sen. Franken wants Apple and Google to require privacy policies for all smartphone
apps," Gautham Nagesh, The Hill, May 25, 2011 (http://thehill.com/blogs/hillicon-valley/
technology/163293-sen-franken-wants-apple-and-google-to-require-privacy-policies-for
-all-smartphone-apps).

18. "A cloud gathers over our digital freedoms," Charles Leadbeater, *The Financial Times*,
June 6, 2011 (http://www.ft.com/cms/s/0/e7253a6e-9073-11e0-9227-00144feab49a.
html#axzz1Pdrwd8fs).

19. "Corporate Rule of Cyberspace," Slavoj Zizek, Inside Higher Ed, May 2, 2011 (http://
www.insidehighered.com/views/2011/05/02/slavoj_zizek_essay_on_cloud_computing_
and_privacy).

20. "Show Us the Data. (It's Ours, After All.), Richard H. Thaler, *The New York Times*, April
23, 2011.

21. "Senators: Net Privacy Law for Children in Need of Overhaul," Matthew Lasar, Ars
Technica, April 30, 2010 (http://arstechnica.com/tech-policy/news/2010/04/senators
-net-privacy-law-for-children-in-need-of-overhaul.ars).

22. "Setting Boundaries for Internet Privacy," Kevin J. O'Brien, *The New York Times* September 18, 2011.

23. "Google Faces New Demands in Netherlands Over Street View Data," Archibald Preus-
chat, Wall Street Journal, April 20, 2011 (http://online.wsj.com/article/SB10001424052
748703922504576273151673266520.html).

24. "Apple and Android phones Face Tighter Laws in Europe," Tim Bradshaw and Maija
Palmer, *The Financial Times*, May 18, 2011.

25. "Facebook to Be Probed in EU for Facial Recognition in Photos," Stephanie Bodoni,
Bloomberg Businessweek, June 8, 2011 (http://www.businessweek.com/news/2011-06
-08/facebook-to-be-probed-in-eu-for-facial-recognition-in-photos.html).

26. "Facebook is wrong to back a light touch for the web," Vittorio Colao, June 5, 2011
(http://www.ft.com/cms/s/0/e78517f6-8fa9-11e0-954d-00144feab49a.html#axzz
1PLSGwcH9).

27. "EU to Force Social Network Sites to Enhance Privacy," Leigh Phillips, *London Guardian*, March 16, 2011.

28. "LinkedIn 'Does a Facebook'—Your Name and Photo Used in Ads by Default," Paul
Duckin, NakedSecurity.com, August 11, 2011 (http://nakedsecurity.sophos.com/2011/
08/11/linkedin-copies-facebook-does-a-privacy-bait-and-switch/).

29. "Data Privacy, Put to the Test," Natasha Singer, *The New York Times*, April 30, 2011
(http://www.nytimes.com/2011/05/01/business/01stream.html).

30. "Web's Hot New Commodity: Privacy," *The Wall Street Journal*, Julia Angwin and Emily
Steel, February 28, 2011. See also: "How to Fix (or Kill) Web Data about You," Riva Rich-
mond, *The New York Times*, April 13, 2011 (http://www.nytimes.com/2011/04/14/
technology/personaltech/14basics.html?_r=1).

31. See in particular my conversation with Bret Taylor on online technology show, The Gillmor Gang, on April 22 2010 (http://gillmorgang.techcrunch.com/2010/05/15/gillmor-gang-04-22-10/) when I turn the tables on the social media executive and interrogate him about his identity.

32. "Facebook Executive Takes Heat on Hearing About Privacy," Jim Puzzanghera, *The Los Angeles Times,* May 20, 2011 (http://articles.latimes.com/2011/may/20/business/la-fi-facebook-privacy-20110520).

33. "The Facebook Resisters," by Jenna Wortham, *The New York Times*, December 13, 2011 (http://www.nytimes.com/2011/12/14/technology/shunning-facebook-and-living-to-tell-about-it.html).

34. "Nobody Goes To Facebook Anymore, It's Too Crowded," Mike Arrington, *Uncrunched*, January 2, 2012 (http://uncrunched.com/2012/01/03/nobody-goes-to-facebook-anymore-its-too-crowded/).

35. "Path Is Where the A List Hangs Out, Don't Tell Anyone," by Loic Le Meur, Loiclemeur.com, January 2, 2012 (http://loiclemeur.com/english/2012/01/path-is-where-the-a-list-hangs-out-dont-tell-anyone.html).

36. See the June 18, 2011 "Social Networking Sites and our Lives" report by the Pew Internet and American Life Project (http://www.pewinternet.org/Reports/2011/Technology-and-social-networks.aspx). While this report appears to celebrate the fact that Facebook users are more trusting than average, my conclusion is less optimistic. Given Facebook's history on privacy and their record on other deeply controversial issues like facial recognition technology, it's hard to avoid being cynical about the intelligence of these "trusting" Facebook users.

37. "The end of Blippy as we know it," Alexia Tsotsis, Techcrunch, May 19, 2011 (http://www.google.com/search?client=safari&rls=en&q="The+end+of+Blippy+as+we+know+it", &ie=UTF-8&oe=UTF-8).

38. "Privacy Isn't Dead. Just Ask Google+," Nick Bilton, *The New York Times*, July 18, 2011 (http://bits.blogs.nytimes.com/2011/07/18/privacy-isnt-dead-just-ask-google/).

39. "Google Steps Up its Privacy Game, Launches Good to Know," Violet Blue, ZDNet, October 18, 2011 (http://www.zdnet.com/blog/violetblue/google-steps-up-its-privacy-game-launches-good-to-know/746).

40. "News Outlets Preserve Privacy by Giving Users Ways to mute Facebook's Frictionless Sharing," Josh Constine, Inside Facebook, October 7, 2011 (http://www.insidefacebook.com/2011/10/07/news-frictionless-sharing/).

41. "Spotify Adds 'Private Listening' Mode After Complaints from Facebook Users," Ellis Hamburger, Business Insider, September 29, 2011 (http://articles.businessinsider.com/2011-09-29/tech/30216833_1_spotify-ceo-facebook-friends-founder-daniel-ek).

42. "Negative Online Data Can Be Challenged, at a Price," Paul Sullivan, *The New York Times,* June 10, 2011 (http://www.nytimes.com/2011/06/11/your-money/11wealth.html).

43. "Erasing the Digital Past," Nick Bilton, *The New York Times,* April 1, 2011 (http://www.nytimes.com/2011/04/03/fashion/03reputation.html).

44. Joshua Foer, *Moonwalking with Einstein: The Art and Science of Remembering Everything,* (Penguin, 2011), 21–24.

45. "Web Images to Get Expiration Date," BBC Technology News, January 20, 011 (http://www.bbc.co.uk/news/technology-12215921).

46. *Moonwalking with Einstein,* ch 4.

47. "Web 2.0 Suicide Machine: Erase Your Virtual Life," January 9, 2010 (http://www.npr
    .org/templates/story/story.php?storyId=122379695).

48. http://suicidemachine.org/.

49. "The Twitter Trap," Bill Keller, *The New York Times,* May 18, 2011. Keller, whose tenure
    as executive editor of *The New York Times* was marked by a number of public spats with
    Arianna Huffington about the real value of social media, announced his retirement in
    June 2011.

50. "Internet Users Now Have More and Closer Friends Than Those Offline," Casey Johnson,
    Ars Technica, June 16, 2011.

51. "Study: You've Never Met 7% Of Your Facebook 'Friends,'" Alexia Tsotsis, Techcrunch,
    June 16, 2011.

52. Pew Internet & American Life Project, "Social Networking Sites and our Lives: How
    people's trust, personal relationships, and civic and political involvement are connected to
    their use of social networking sites and other technologies", by Keith N. Hampton, Lau-
    ren Sessions Goulet, Lee Rainie and Kristen Purcell, June 16, 2011.

53. Robin Dunbar, *How Many Friends Does One Person Need? Dunbar's Number and Other
    Evolutionary Quirks* (Harvard University Press, 2010), 21.

54. Ibid., 22.

55. Ibid.

56. Ibid., 23.

57. Ibid., 34.

58. "The Socialized and Appified Oscars," Liz Gannes, *The Wall Street Journal's All Things D,*
    February 25, 2011 (http://networkeffect.allthingsd.com/20110225/the-socialized-and
    -appified-oscars/).

59. "The Oscars on Twitter: Over 1.2 Million Tweets, 388K Users Tweeting," by Alexia Tsotsis,
    Techcrunch, February 28, 2011 (http://techcrunch.com/2011/02/28/the-oscars-twitter/).

60. Steven Lukes, *Individualism* (Blackwell 1973), 21.

61. "Liking Is for Cowards. Go for What Hurts," Jonathan Franzen, *The New York Times,*
    May 28, 2011.

62. "Oscar Coronation for 'The King's Speech,'" Brooks Barnes and Michael Cieply, *The
    New York Times,* February 27, 2011 (http://www.nytimes.com/2011/02/28/movies/
    awardsseason/28oscars.html?adxnnl=1&pagewanted=print&adxnnlx=1308428523
    -T2YIxoWp8UZNaTcv/la1PA).

CONCLUSION: THE WOMAN IN BLUE

1. The movement had been founded at the Gower Street home of the parents of John Everett
   Millais, one of the most influential of Pre Raphaelite Brotherhood artists. Millais didn't
   participate in Rossetti's Oxford Union project.

2. Richard Reeves, *John Stuart Mill,* 11.

3. This term was coined by a fellow Benthamite, Henry Taylor. See: Reeves, *John Stuart
   Mill,* 52.

4. John Stuart Mill, *Autobiography,* ch 5 (Riverside, 1969).

5. Ibid.

6. Ibid.

7. John Dinwiddy, Bentham.

8. J. S. Mill, *On Liberty and Other Writings* (Cambridge, 1989), 86.

9. "Zuckerberg: Kids Under 13 Should Be Allowed on Facebook," Michael Lev-Ram, CNNMoney.com, May 20, 2011.

10. *New Yorker* review of *The Social Network*.

11. Jeff Jarvis, *What Would Google Do?* (Collins Business, 2009), 48.

12. "Virtual Friendship and the New Narcissism," Christine Rosen, *The New Atlantis*, Number 17, 15.

13. Ibid.

14. www.twitter.com/ajkeen.

15. Richard Reeves, *John Stuart Mill,* 126.

16. Philip Steadman, *Vermeer's Camera: Uncovering the Truth Behind the Masterpieces* (Oxford, 2001).

17. Tracy Chevalier, *Girl with a Pearl Earring* (Harper Collins, 2000), 247.

18. "Bin Laden Announcment Has Highest Sustained Tweet Rate Ever, at 3440 Tweets Per Second," by Alexia Tsotsis, Techcrunch, May 2, 2011 (http://techcrunch.com/2011/05/02/bin-laden-announcement-twitter-traffic-spikes-higher-than-the-super-bowl/).

19. Richard Reeves, *John Stuart Mill,* 15.

20. Michel Foucault, *The Order of Things: An Archeology of the Human Sciences* (Vintage, 1973), 386–387.

INDEX

DATE DUE